Ken Poolman served through the war in
destroyers, minesweepers and aircraft carriers,
both in the Royal Navy and the Fleet Air Arm.
After the war and Cambridge he joined the BBC
as a writer and radio producer and TV script
editor. He is the author of many books on the
Second World War, notably KELLY, the story of
the late Earl Mountbatten's destroyer command,
FAITH HOPE AND CHARITY, about the
famous air defence of Malta by Gloster Gladiator
biplanes, and the recent NIGHT STRIKE FROM
MALTA. Ken Poolman now lives and works as a
freelance author in Surrey.

P.20-03

The Sea Hunters

Escort Carriers v. U-Boats, 1941–1945

KENNETH POOLMAN

*There's a lot of waffle in
this; just as there was in
'HMS Kelly'
and to read further requires a translator
from USAish into English
(cannot believe Poolman is a Britisher —
expect he lived somewhere in the USA
USA's hoping to get the film rights
it's certainly not a book
for the historian / unless
he's interested in the genealogy
of the participants!!!)*

ARMS AND ARMOUR PRESS
London — Melbourne

Published in 1982 by Arms and Armour Press, Lionel
Leventhal Limited.
Great Britain: 2–6 Hampstead High Street, London NW3
1QQ.
Australasia: 4–12 Tattersalls Lane, Melbourne, Victoria
3000.

First published simultaneously in Great Britain by
Sphere Books Ltd and Arms & Armour Press Ltd 1982

1 2 3 4 5 6 7 8 9 0

British Library Cataloguing in Publication Data:
Poolman, Kenneth
The sea hunters.
1. World War, 1939–1945 – Atlantic Ocean
2. World War, 1939–1945 – Naval operations
3. World War, 1939–1945 – Aerial operations
4. Aircraft carriers
I. Title
940.54′21   D770
ISBN 0-85368-544-4

Cartography by A. A. Evans.
Maps © Lionel Leventhal Limited.

Printed in Great Britain.

Contents

Acknowledgements

I wish to thank Mr Dean Allard, Head of Operational Archives Branch of the United States Navy's Naval Historical Centre, Washington DC, for his generous and expert help in guiding me through U.S. Navy records, and Mr David Brown and his staff at the Ministry of Defence Historical Branch (Navy) in London for their kind and valuable co-operation.

I am also grateful to Mr Irving Paley, Director, Public Relations, Museum of Science and Industry, Chicago, Illinois, U.S.A., for his kindness in providing me with information and photographs of U-505, on permanent exhibition at the museum.

In the course of research I gained particularly useful information from: Professor/Rear-Admiral Samuel Morison's *History of United States Naval Operations in World War II*, in particular Volume X, *The Atlantic Battle Won; Clear The Decks* and *We Captured A U-boat*, books by the late Rear-Admiral Daniel V. Gallery, U.S. Navy.

Mr Robert Golling, Mr Jack Malloy and Mr Walter Skeldon gave me useful information from their recollections of life in the C.V.E.s.

Kenneth Poolman

Introduction

In World War One, the submarine and the aeroplane both made their marks as new weapons of war, especially the German U-boats, which forced the Allies to use convoys to protect merchant shipping, and very nearly won the war. Aircraft, with their limited range and reliability, made less impact on sea warfare than on land, though some of their potentialities were realized. A seaplane, crane-lifted into the water, scouted for the British Grand Fleet at Jutland, and elsewhere the one revolutionary weapon was used to counter the other. Flying-boats met Allied incoming convoys a hundred miles from Ireland and searched ahead of them. Their tiny bombs needed a direct hit to damage a U-boat, but British submarines in the shallower Baltic were sighted and bombed quite heavily by enemy aircraft. Towards the end of the war the first genuine aircraft carrier, HMS *Furious,* operated Sopwith Camel fighter-bombers beyond the range of land aircraft to drive off enemy bombers and destroy Zeppelins, also used for maritime scouting.

After World War One, the great naval powers, Great Britain, Japan and the USA, all experimented with carriers but, because of limited size, their aircraft did not score the successes that land-based bombers achieved against static targets, usually old battleships. However, the Royal Navy, while concentrating on the use of aircraft as scouts and target spotters for big guns, developed the attack by torpedo-bomber. The US Navy put much emphasis on dive-bombing, and the Japanese perfected an all-purpose naval air arm.

Soon after World War Two began in September 1939, the British Admiralty was forced, by the renewed threat from U-boats, to use the convoy system again. They were desperately short of escort vessels of all kinds, and had only six ageing aircraft carriers and the new *Ark Royal* in commission. Only a fortnight after war was declared, HMS *Courageous* was grudgingly diverted from use with the

Home Fleet to search for U-boats, and, with only a light destroyer screen, was torpedoed and sunk by one of her quarries. No more of the large Fleet carriers could be spared for commerce protection. Search and strike capability by aircraft from Canada, Iceland and Britain improved, but bad weather and navigational difficulties hampered them, and even with a maximum effort a gap some 300 miles wide was left in mid-Atlantic.

When France fell in 1940, the U-boats used French bases to increase their time on station in the Atlantic, and Luftwaffe bombers, particularly the long-range Focke Wulf Condors, flew from Biscay airfields not only to sink ships themselves but to scout for the U-boats. The need for aircraft to accompany the convoys was clear. As stop-gaps the Admiralty used catapult ships, each equipped with from one to three Hurricane or Fulmar fighters, which could not return to their ships once launched. These ships scored 'kills', but kept U-boats down and Condors at a distance.

Meanwhile, the Royal Navy commissioned the first 'escort carrier', the converted German banana boat HMS *Audacity*, a primitive little vessel with no hangar and six American Martlet fighters. She sailed with Gibraltar convoys and fought off the Condors, as well as directing surface escorts to U-boats, in late 1941, until torpedoed and sunk by a U-boat just after the Japanese naval air arm attacked the US Fleet at Pearl Harbor.

More escort carriers were desperately needed, particularly to counter the ever-growing U-boat menace. The British Ministry of War Transport was unwilling to release merchant ships for conversion, but the US Navy had begun an ambitious programme of escort carrier construction, and promised the first batch to Britain. The first of these CVEs, as they were later called, were plagued by engine trouble, and there were other delays in starting operations against the U-boats, partly caused by the time taken to extend flight decks to operate the obsolete, but often effective, British Swordfish, partly, after HMS *Dasher* had blown up, to allow for the replacement of the American petrol system by a British one in all RN-manned escort carriers. The US

Navy, impatient at these delays, put their own USS *Bogue* on the North Atlantic convoy run, and on 22 May 1943 her modern Avenger bombers became the first aircraft from an escort carrier to sink a U-boat *(U569).* Next day, a Swordfish from HMS *Archer,* first of the Lease-Lend escort carriers, was the first to score with the new rocket projectiles, which sank *U752.*

CVEs began to operate in the North and Central Atlantic in increasing numbers, with the British at first favouring their deployment with the convoy close escorts, the Americans preferring independent hunting groups, each with several anti-submarine destroyer-escorts based round an escort carrier. USS *Bogue, Card, Core* and *Santee* all led hunter-killer groups. Helped sometimes by 'Ultra' information from decoded U-boat signals, in June and August 1943, just after the U-boat 'wolf packs' had made their biggest score of the war, these vessels helped to break the back of the U-boat offensive by sinking fourteen submarines. In October, *Card* sank four. The CVE groups had their losses: USS *Block Island* was sunk by a U-boat; and *Card's* faithful, old 'four-piper' destroyer-escort *Borie* was damaged and fought bravely but vainly for her life.

The Royal Navy's escort carriers, with their anti-submarine capability based on the slow, poorly protected Swordfish, had less spectacular success against U-boats heavily armed with cannon and machine-guns for resistance on the surface, but HMS *Fencer* escorted the force that installed the new RAF Coastal Command base on Terceira in the Azores, and her Seafire fighters operated from there until the first Flying Fortress arrived. HMS *Tracker,* too, had some success against U-boats. By the end of 1943, five US Navy escort carriers had sunk twenty-three U-boats. Aircraft from HMS *Chaser, Fencer* and *Striker* and from the British-built escort carriers HMS *Activity, Campania, Nairana* and *Vindex* shot down shadowers, sank U-boats, and fought savage gales in the North Atlantic and Arctic oceans.

The victory of escort carrier over U-boat was perfectly symbolized on 4 June 1944 when Captain Dan Gallery's

USS *Guadalcanal* and her destroyer-escorts forced *U505* to surrender. The carrier towed the submarine intact into Bermuda, and after the war she was placed on permanent display at the Museum of Science and Industry in Chicago.

What follows is the first account in detail – made possible by special access to previously classified documents – of this Atlantic battle between the CVEs, themselves converted versions of the merchantmen they were protecting, and the expertly handled, often heavily gun-armed submarines of that crafty and resourceful ex-submariner Grossadmiral Karl Dönitz, master of 'wolf packs', 'Belfehlshaber der U-bootë'.

1. 'Suitable merchant ships'

At the age of fifty-two Rear-Admiral Bill Halsey, Commander Aircraft Battle Force, United States Navy, had won his gold wings as a carrier pilot, and had strong views on the importance of naval aviation.

He had watched the Royal Navy's struggle through twelve months of war, and on December 13th 1940 he told Admiral Harold Stark, commanding U.S. Naval Forces, Europe, 'If the U.S.A. is drawn into this war, the Navy's six big carriers will have to go on active duty immediately, leaving no means of training carrier pilots or transporting planes.

'You must find some suitable merchantmen and convert them into auxiliary carriers.'

In London, Captain Matthew Slattery, Director of Material for the Fleet Air Arm, was telling My Lords at the Admiralty that they should fit 'the simplest possible flight deck and landing equipment to suitable merchant ships.'

With the Battle of Britain lost and the invasion of Britain postponed, the Germans had switched to the night bombing of docks and factories and to blockade by submarines and raiding cruisers.

Prime Minister Winston Churchill was also worried about the rate of sinkings by Focke-Wulf Condor bombers, which he called 'the Scourge of the Atlantic.'

Auxiliary carriers, Slattery urged, were the answer.

In Washington, Stark spoke to Chief of Staff Admiral Ernie King. King spoke to the President. Roosevelt, always a Navy man at heart, said, 'Why don't we fit some fifteen-knot merchant ships with short flight decks to operate autogyros or planes with low landing speeds?'

Halsey and Slattery both got their way, and it began to look like a race to build the first auxiliary carrier.

Both projects were begun in January 1941, each with one experimental ship. In the United States, the 13,499-ton S.S. *Mormacmail* of the Moore-McCormack Line was commandeered for conversion. In the Blyth Dry Docks & Shipbuilding Company's yard at Blyth, Northumberland, England, the work of turning the 5,537-ton captured German fruit-passenger ship *Hannover* into an Ocean Boarding Vessel was stopped, and conversion to an Auxiliary Aircraft Carrier begun.

The Americans, with more labour, more time and more space than besieged Britain's cluttered yards, started later, on March 6th 1941, but worked faster, pressurized by the President, who had taken a personal interest.

On both sides of the Atlantic, belief in the merchantman carrier grew. In March the U.S. Navy Board approved the conversion of more C3 merchant hulls, and in April the Royal Navy asked for six of these on Lease-Lend as 'fighter carriers.' The Naval Person at the White House agreed, and the first carrier for the British was started one week later.

On June 2nd Commander Donald B. Duncan commissioned the United States Navy's first auxiliary aircraft carrier, U.S.S. *Long Island*. On June 17th Commander D.W. McKendrick, a former Fleet Air Arm Swordfish pilot, took over H.M.S. *Audacity* for the Royal Navy. By September both ships were ready to begin testing the feasibility of not merely transporting but operating modern aircraft from converted freighters. The difference was that whereas the American guinea pig could make a leisurely shakedown cruise to the West Indies, the little British flat-top had to jump straight into the deep end of the U-boat and Condor-infested North Atlantic.

There were other differences. *Long Island*, with a catapult and a hangar, could operate twenty-one planes. *Audacity*, with neither, carried eight fighters for defence against Condors, all parked out on the wet and windy flight deck. She was to have had Hurricanes, converted from landplanes by the addition of arrester hooks, but these left-overs from the Battle of Britain had too many defects and were not

2

ready. This was a blessing in disguise, as *Audacity*'s little Squadron, Number 802, Fleet Air Arm, was given six American Grumman Wildcats. The Royal Navy renamed them Martlets, preferring the fast-flying bird which in heraldry is legless. Although not the fastest fighters in the world, they were rugged aircraft, with an undercarriage specially built to take the heavy shocks of deck landing, and a battery of six 50-calibre Colt-Browning machine guns. They out-gunned the eight .303s of the Sea Hurricane 11A, and *Audacity*'s Martlet Mk IIs had folding wings.

[handwritten margin note: II, not eleven!]

H.M.S *Audacity*'s shortcomings began to show themselves soon after she left the Clyde on September 13th to escort her first convoy, OG74 to Gibraltar, and plagued her ever after through her short life.

Lack of a hangar complicated every take-off. All aircraft not flying had to be parked as far aft as possible, which still left only about 300 feet in which to get off the deck. For landing on there were only two arrester wires, compared with six in a British Fleet carrier, eight in *Long Island*, and one more last-ditch wire up ahead, which the C.O. John Wintour called the 'Jesus Christ!' wire, though this one had no hydraulic retardation and would hand out a short, very sharp shock to plane and pilot. Beyond that there was a wire barrier, which would stop an aircraft all right, but make a nasty mess of the prop and probably the pilot's face if he hadn't got his R.N.-modified American harness done up properly. And ahead of *that* loomed the other aircraft . . .

The air mechanics cursed her, working out on the open flight deck in the wild Atlantic weather and damp sea air, which jammed throttles, made guns seize up, earthed the firing circuits, corroded gun wells, breech blocks and barrels, I.F.F., switches, sparking plugs, contact breakers and other electrics. After dark you had to use torches masked with blue filters, screened by someone's hand or jacket.

She was makeshift, but she was the best that could be found in a hurry, she and the few Fighter Catapult Ships of the Royal Navy, which operated a single two-seat Fulmar fighter apiece, and the merchantmen, each fitted with a rocket-powered accelerator and a Hurricane, served by the Royal Air Force Merchant Ship Fighter Unit. Condors, which were themselves adapted from commercial airliners and were not really robust enough for combat, had also been shot down by a trawler's machine gun, and the old 3-inch gun of a merchantman.

Audacity had some redeeming features too. The young Royal Naval Volunteer Reserve pilots enjoyed the luxuries of the old *Hannover*'s original passenger state rooms and lounge, which there had been no time to remove. The ship was fitted with the new H.F./D.F.,[1] or 'Huff-Duff', radio receiver which could pick up U-boat signals and turn them into a range and bearing. And there were the excellent Grumman fighters, so tough and tireless. On the last round-trip young Sub-Lieutenant Eric 'Winkle' Brown was flying one with a bent airscrew when he chased a Condor through thick cloud and suddenly found the four-engined machine coming straight at him, head-on, 500 yards away and closing fast. Brown had just had time to thumb the firing button, see the Condor's windscreen shatter and bits fly off the nose, then pull up sharp some seventy feet short of collision, his tail just clearing the top of the cockpit canopy. The big plane hit the water with a shock which tore off the entire port wing. Brown developed the head-on to make up for the Martlet's lack of speed. Another pilot returned to *Audacity* with part of the enemy's W/T aerial wrapped round his tail wheel, and a nasty hole in the fuselage further forward.

Condors were now being used to shadow convoys and home in U-boats, and four more were shot down by *Audacity*'s American fighters, but frustration would set in when a patrolling pair sighted a surfaced submarine, and dived on it with the 'Tally-ho!' which went back through generations of fox-hunting admirals, only to find they were beating up an empty swirl where the U-boat had crash-dived, with nothing more lethal than machine guns. They would then climb and circle over the spot for the ship to get a radar fix on them and alert destroyers. Commander

4

McKendrick longed for a pair of Swordfish T.S.R.s[2]

Commander Walker, the escort commander on *Audacity*'s last trip, often used her fighters, in lieu of T.S.R.s, to search for U-boats. When H.M.S. *Stanley,* formerly the U.S.S. *McCalla,* one of the fifty old 'four-piper' destroyers handed over to the Royal Navy under the Destroyers-for-Bases agreement,[3] sighted a U-boat, he suggested that a fighter should attack the submarine in the hope that she might fight back with her guns and give his sloops more time to reach her. This new tactic worked in that the U-boat was sunk, but the Martlet pilot, Sub-Lieutenant Fletcher, was shot down and killed by the submarine's guns.

On this, *Audacity*'s last voyage, Admiral Dönitz, *Befehlshaber der U-boote* (Flag Officer, Submarines), Brest, had made the carrier the priority target for his wolf pack, and had asked Kampfgeschwader 40, the Condor unit at Bordeaux, for a maximum effort in support.

Walker sank three of the U-boats, *Audacity*'s fighters destroyed two Condors, and the convoy lost only two merchant ships, but the *Stanley* was torpedoed and blew up, and when on the night of December 21st Commander McKendrick decided to take the carrier out of the convoy without an escort screen she was torpedoed twice by U-751, her petrol storage tanks went up and she sank in a matter of minutes, after only two round-trips.

Dönitz reported 'The worst feature was the presence of the aircraft carrier. Small, fast, manoeuvrable aircraft circled the convoy continuously, so that when it was sighted the boats were repeatedly forced to submerge or withdraw. The presence of enemy aircraft also prevented any protracted shadowing or homing procedure by German aircraft. The sinking of the aircraft carrier is therefore of particular importance not only in this case but also in every future convoy action . . .'

On December 7th the Japanese Naval Air Arm attacked the U.S. Fleet in Pearl Harbour. U.S.S. *Long Island* helped to escort a convoy to Newfoundland, then went to Norfolk, Virginia, where she was used to qualify the new wave of

Navy and Marine Corps pilots in deck landing.

The first of the new U.S. West Coast carriers, which were merely hulls on the stocks, were not likely to be in commission before the winter of 1942 at the earliest, so the American Auxiliary Vessels Board took over four Fleet oilers of the *Cimarron* class, already in service, for accelerated conversion into auxiliary carriers, and twenty more new conversions were ordered.

H.M.S. *Archer*, the first of the six converted diesel-engined C3 hulls requested by the Royal Navy from the U.S.A., was in Hampton Roads on her trials, and her air squadron was at Palisadoes Airport in Jamaica practising anti-submarine patrols with four Swordfish. Four more of the carriers for Britain were in East Coast yards, and delivery was anticipated in the spring and summer of 1942. Each was larger than H.M.S *Audacity*, with a catapult, a hangar and twice the aircraft capacity.

It was President Roosevelt's and Admiral King's understanding that these ships would be used on convoy protection in the North Atlantic, which was mainly a British responsibility, as soon as they were ready.

On January 2nd 1942 *Archer* left Hampton Roads en route for southern waters to pick up her Swordfish T.S.R.s. First her gyro compass failed, then one engine broke down. They were the first of many mechanical troubles. Next morning the steering gear broke down, then the gyro failed again. Both were repaired, then the radar gave up, and in the darkness *Archer* collided with a Peruvian steamer. She was towed backwards into Charleston for repairs.

On March 2nd 1942 at Bethlehem Steel, Staten Island, H.M.S. *Avenger*, second of the diesel C3s for the Royal Navy, was commissioned. Down at Palisadoes in Jamaica Number 834 Squadron got their postponed flying orders. In their four Swordfish they flew via Cuba, Miami, Daytona and Jacksonville to join *Archer*, which left dry dock in Charleston on March 7th. 'We had a very pleasant four-day stop at Miami U.S.N. Air Station,' wrote air gunner Peter Jinks, 'where our antiquated Stringbags, seen against the

6

modern U.S. training aircraft, were greeted with awe and incredulity. "Gee, are these operational?"'

Archer weighed from Charleston on March 18th and headed with a task group, not for the United Kingdom, but south to pick up a fast convoy for Freetown, West Africa. Eleven ships had been sunk by U-boats on this route earlier in the month, but *Archer* sailed through the hazy heat of the Doldrums and flew off patrols without seeing any, with the gyro compass and the engines playing up again. The Busche-Sultzer diesels were connected to the propeller shaft by a magnetic clutch, which was continually failing, often when the ship had planes in the air. There would be a tremendous shuddering as the engines raced, and an agitated Chief Engineer McMaster would appear again on the bridge, shaking his head over the unfamiliar, unreliable machinery. In Freetown *Archer* delivered a consignment of Martlets to the big Fleet carrier H.M.S *Illustrious*, ready for the attack on Vichy French Madagascar.

Every day there seemed to be some new mechanical breakdown. Oil fuel got into the fresh water tanks again, and the petty officers were shaving with their morning tea once more. By April 24th the main engines were declared sound, but the auxiliary air compressor broke down.

H.M.S. *Avenger* was having trouble too. Twice she sailed from Brooklyn Navy Yard, twice her engines broke down, but she finally left for Britain on April 30th.

On May Day *Archer* was ready to leave Freetown, but her anti-mine degaussing gear would not work. The heat in the White Man's Grave was intolerable.

On May 6th 1942 Britain's third carrier from the Arsenal of Democracy, H.M.S. *Biter*, was commissioned. Her engines broke down as she cleared the Queensboro Bridge out of New York.

Archer left Freetown on May 15th. There was a hopeful buzz that she was going home to operate with the North Atlantic convoys, a belief shared by Admiral King in Washington, but the Admiralty wanted to send her to the Mediterranean to fight submarines there. She got as far as

Capetown and her engines broke down again. She was clearly in no condition to face the Luftwaffe in the Mediterranean, and the Admiralty asked the U.S. Navy to put the rogue engines right once and for all. They broke down again when *Archer* was in mid-Atlantic, with twenty-six U-boats reported between her and the U.S.A. She got under way, was reported by a British ship as a German raider, and reached New York on July 15th.

Some of her officers went over to Brooklyn Navy Yard to have lunch on board H.M.S. *Dasher,* the fourth of the Lease-Lend carriers, which had commissioned on July 1st. *Dasher*'s engines were 8,000 horsepower Sun-Droxfords, a design which her Chief Engineer did not trust, and which on trial runs in the Navy Yard backfired frequently on starting up, with a shattering explosion, and on one occasion pieces flew out of the exhaust vents.

The first of the twenty C3 steam-powered American West Coast conversions of the *Bogue* class, the U.S.S. *Bogue* herself and H.M.S. *Attacker,* one of ten reserved for the Royal Navy, were nearing completion. In Britain the auxiliary carrier, H.M.S. *Activity* was launched, and the Admiralty was converting two grain ships into Merchant Aircraft Carriers, or M.A.C.-ships, which would continue to carry the bulk of their former cargoes and also operate a few Swordfish in defence of their convoys.

For one reason or the other, however, it did not look as if there would be any British-manned carriers available to fight the very serious U-boat menace in the North Atlantic until the spring of the following year, 1943. My Lords at the Admiralty had formed a very low opinion of the first batch of Lend-Lease 'Woolworth carriers' already delayed by their mechanical troubles, and considered that they needed anglicizing. When *Avenger,* then *Biter,* arrived in the U.K. they were put into dockyard hands for various time-consuming modifications, principally the lengthening of the flight deck by forty-two feet to allow a Swordfish, which could not use the American catapult, to get off the deck safely with a full war load. There was also the fitting of

H.F./D.F. and British radio equipment. Admiral King, no anglophile to start with, thought that all this was just the British dragging their feet. Even when this work had been completed these ships were not going to the North Atlantic for some time. The destruction of twenty-four of the thirty-five merchant ships of Convoy PQ17 to the new ally Russia in early June was largely the result of lack of air cover, and *Avenger* was to be sent with the next convoy to North Russia in September. After that she, with *Biter* and *Dasher*, if they were ready, was to give close air support for Operation Torch, the Allied invasion of North Africa. A M.A.C.-ship conversion took only half as long as an escort carrier, but you had to allow for trials and working up. The new H.M.S. *Activity* was to be used for pilot training.

For the sake of winning the war, not for any love of the British, Admiral King decided to lend a U.S. Navy-manned escort carrier to the Royal Navy for the North Atlantic as soon as he had one he could spare. The four ex-oiler conversions U.S.S. *Santee, Sangamon, Suwanee* and *Chenango* were nearing completion, but they were booked to cover the American landing in North Africa, then to go to the Pacific and the South Atlantic, and it was going to need a special effort if they were to be ready to serve even for Torch. *Santee* was hurriedly commissioned on August 24th and fitted out in such haste that dockyard workmen from Norfolk were still on board during her shakedown training and her decks were piled high with stores. She also carried a load of cold-weather gear, including snow shovels, heavy winter jackets, long-john underwear, gloves and thick pants.

H.M.S. *Dasher,* last of the diesel C3 conversions to be sent to Britain,[4] left Brooklyn Navy Yard in mid-August to pick up a convoy for the U.K. As the convoy sailed, her engines misfired twice, then gave up. Eventually she had to make a desperate full-speed dash through Long Island Sound and the Cape Cod Canal, and caught up the convoy at Boston.

In this autumn of 1942 the Allies were losing the Battle of

the Atlantic. They were sinking U-boats, but German yards were producing new ones twice as fast, and these were adding to the enormous losses of Allied merchant ships, especially in the mid-Atlantic gap where the convoys had as yet no air cover.

In September, with this grim picture in front of them, the Admiralty approved a scheme for tanker Merchant Aircraft Carriers, and in October it was decided to convert six tankers. At the same time the grain ship conversion programme was expanded to six ships. The tankers, unlike the grainers, had no room for a hangar in their superstructures, and could carry only three instead of four Swordfish, all on the open flight deck, *Audacity*-style.

In late October H.M.S. *Avenger, Biter* and *Dasher* left British waters for the Mediterranean to support the landings at Oran and Algiers. U.S.S. *Santee, Sangamon* and *Suwanee,* the cruiser *Cleveland* and the fast 'cans' of Destroyer Squadron 10, together comprising Task Group 34.2 of Vice-Admiral Henry K. Hewitt's Western Naval Task Force, left Bermuda on October 25th, commanded by Rear-Admiral McWhorter in the big Fleet carrier *Ranger.* Steaming westward into battle with only five experienced aviators in her air group, and only a handful of her complement familiar with salt water, *Santee,* having offloaded her decoy cold-weather gear at Bermuda, feverishly prepared for combat.

She had a scare on October 30th. One of the Douglas Dauntless S.B.D.3 scout bombers of her VC29 Squadron coming off the catapult dropped a 325lb depth-charge on to the flight deck. With everyone diving for the catwalk, the lethal lump of Torpex rolled off the deck into the Goofers, then overboard, detonating, as D.C.s will do when dunked in water, thirty-five feet off the port bow, shaking the entire ship, damaging plating, carrying away the range-finder and a searchlight, and dislodging radar antennae. The planes on deck were all manned, and those whose tie-down wires broke were saved from being thrown along the deck by applying the brakes.

On November 7th, with the destroyers *Rodman* and *Emmons* and the minelayer *Monadnock*, she left the convoy and next morning took station off Safi, French Morocco, one of three landing points for the troops of Major-General George S. Patton, and 125 miles south of Casablanca. Beginning on November 8th, when a tidal wave of landing craft, tanks, trucks and men broke over enemy coastal defences, the *Santee*'s planes thundered aloft to hammer nearby Marrakech airfield.

Some eighteen planes took off, made their strike, but could not find the ship again and were forced to land in fields ashore. The area was rain-soaked, and all the aircraft sank up to their axles in mud. There some of them stayed until November 10th or 12th. The Army put down steel mats, and the planes tried to take off from a dirt highway, but there was a cross-wind, and some were blown off the road and into a ditch. The fighter C.O. ran out of gas trying to locate the ship, floated for three days on his life raft, and was picked up and returned to the *Santee* on the 11th. She launched planes and fuelled ships until Friday, November 13th, when she rejoined her task group and returned to Bermuda.

Her fellow ex-oilers also supported the American Torch landings. U.S.S. *Sangamon*'s VC26 flew combat air patrols, anti-submarine patrols and ground support with the Northern Support Force off Port Lyautey, French Morocco. U.S.S. *Chenango* transported Army planes to Lyautey immediately after its capture, and refuelled twenty-one destroyers at Casablanca. U.S.S. *Suwanee*, less than a month after commissioning, joined the big Fleet carrier, U.S.S. *Ranger* off Casablanca to provide C.A.P., A.S.P. and ground support. Her planes flew 255 sorties in four days, lost five aircraft, and made *Suwanee* the first U.S. carrier to sink an enemy submarine, a Vichy French boat.

Operation Torch also brought H.M.S. *Archer* back into the war. On October 29th she embarked thirty-five U.S. Army Air Force Curtis P40 Warhawks and their pilots. On November 2nd she left New York with an American troop

11

convoy bound for Casablanca. On November 14th off the West African coast she began catapulting the Warhawks. Two crashed in the sea, but the remainder flew safely ashore.

Archer, Biter and Dasher all reached the U.K. safely after their involvement in Torch, but Avenger, returning several days later than the others because of more engine trouble, was torpedoed and sunk just west of the Straits of Gibraltar by U-155. The torpedo struck amidships, shattering her thin plates like an eggshell. She jack-knifed immediately and sank swiftly under a column of flame and smoke, with heavy loss of life. The circumstances of her sinking exacerbated the controversy between the two navies over the use of auxiliary carriers. From the reports of the unusually heavy explosion which followed detonation of the torpedo the Admiralty concluded, or perhaps some officers wanted to think, that the aviation spirit stored in unprotected tanks had been ignited, thereby proving the Admiralty contention that the American type petrol system installed in these ships was unsafe and should be replaced by a British system. In fact the first explosion had penetrated the bomb room and set off the explosives there.

In the month of November U-boats sank over 700,000 tons of Allied shipping, 500,000 tons of it in the North Atlantic, the highest monthly figure of the war so far, much of it in the dense mass of shipping backing up the African landings, with escorts spread very thinly.

At the end of November, with Avenger sunk, Biter was in Dundee for overhaul, Dasher in Liverpool for enlargements to her Air Direction Room and scheduled for a Russian convoy run after that, Archer in Liverpool for modifications including the new routine lengthening of her original American flight deck, the newly arrived Bogue class H.M.S. Attacker queueing up for the same treatment.

None of this pleased Admiral King in Washington or President Roosevelt. These American-built carriers were supposed to be out in the Atlantic sinking U-boats. The North Atlantic convoys were in desperate need of air cover.

Exercising off San Diego, California, was the new U.S.S. *Bogue*, launched on January 15th 1942 from the Seattle-Tacoma Shipbuilding Corporation's Seattle, Washington, yard as the S.S. *Steel Artisan*, and the first merchant ship to be converted to a carrier on the West Coast. *Bogue*, named after a sound in North Carolina, was commissioned eight months later, on September 26th 1942, at the Puget Sound Navy Yard, Bremerton, Washington, by Captain Giles E. Short U.S.N. Captain Short had been standing by the ship for some time, as had key men like the Executive Officer, Commander J.B. Dunn, Engineer Officer, Lieutenant-Commander R.A. Fuller, First Lieutenant, Lieutenant-Commander A.A. Goodhue, Navigator, Lieutenant-Commander F.E. Angrick, Gunnery Officer, Lieutenant R.A. Chandler, and Bosun C.W. Ruber. As soon as the commissioning pennant was hoisted the balance of the ship's crew went aboard from the dockside. The new men wandered about the new carrier's empty, echoing hangar, which seemed too lofty, and explored the unfamiliar maze of passages, crew spaces, cabins and mess halls down below the hangar deck. Commander Dunn got all hands turning to, taking on ammunition and stores and cleaning ship. One month later, October 26th 1942, *Bogue* was under way in Puget Sound for the first of her trial runs, and on November 17th she left for San Diego, where she moored four days later in the Naval Air Station dock, North Island.

The ship's company, many of whom were survivors from the famous Fleet carrier *Lexington*, sunk six months previously, May 8th, in the Battle of the Coral Sea, were beginning to learn how to work the new carrier as a ship, but without aircraft she lacked purpose. This was remedied the day after she had come in with the arrival on board of the personnel of Composite Squadron (V.C.9), commanded by Lieutenant-Commander William McClure Drane U.S.N., of Alexandria, Virginia. Two days later their planes were loaded aboard, and the big barn of a hangar filled up with twelve Wildcat F.4F.4 fighters and nine big-bellied, bulky Grumman Avenger T.B.F.1s, with all their spares, which were hung on the hangar bulkheads and stacked in corners.

The following day aircraft training exercises began. Now Commander J.P. Monroe, Air Officer, took the weight, and the Landing Signal Officer, happily named Lieutenant C.S. Friend, took out his red and tan-striped paddles and went to work guiding the pilots through the new experience of landing on an A.C.V.'s short flight deck. Accidents were inevitable. On December 4th there was a tragic collision in mid-air between T.B.F.s 597 and 547. The pilot of one Avenger, Ensign J.O. Pfeffer, parachuted out of his crashing plane, but died after being picked up by *Bogue*'s crash boat, the destroyer *Gillespie*, and his crewmen. C.M. Martlette Jr. and G. Laughlin, were lost.

On December 11th *Bogue*, with the destroyer *Kendrick* in company, sailed for Balboa on the Panama Canal, exercised at drills and training flights all the way, transited the Canal on the 23rd, and on Christmas Day left Colon for Norfolk, Virginia, with the destroyer *Corry*. Drane's men of Compo 9 flew anti-submarine patrols all the way across the Gulf of Mexico and up the coasts of Florida, Georgia and the Carolinas, and *Bogue* arrived at the Naval Operating Base, Norfolk, on December 31st. After an inspection by ComAirLant, Rear-Admiral A.D. Bernhard, she spent three weeks in the Navy Yard at Portsmouth for modifications and adjustments, and passed the first week of February 1943 learning how to refuel the two old flush-deck destroyers *Belknap* and *George E. Badger,* now allocated to her as her screen, in the waters of Chesapeake Bay. Flight operations were also practised, and on the last day of these workouts there was another tragic accident. F.4F. 3440 crashed on landing, killing Lieutenant Friend, plunging over the side and drowning its pilot, Lieutenant (jg) R.I. Steward U.S.N.R. A brief and sad return to Norfolk was followed by another week of exercises in the Bay, dropping the hook there every night.

Then, on February 24th, school was over, and *Bogue* with her two destroyers, was under way for Argentia, Newfoundland, to give air support to the hard-pressed North Atlantic convoys. She anchored at Argentia on March 1st, swung round the hook for four days, and on the 5th was formed, with *Belknap* and *George E. Badger,* into Task Unit 24.4 a Mid-Ocean Carrier Escort Group under Com.Task Force 24.

[1] High Frequency Direction Finding
[2] Torpedo-Spotter-Reconnaissance, also fitted for bombs and depth-charges.
[3] The first eight left the U.S.A. on September 5th 1940. These ships were old but completely refitted and fully stored with shells, torpedoes and depth-charges, sextants and chronometers for the Navigating Officer, paint and cordage, messtraps of silver and china, even a typewriter, paper, envelopes, pencil sharpeners, pencils and ink in the ship's office, with American spiced tinned ham, canned fruit and corn, in fully stocked storerooms. In British service they were re-named after British and U.S. towns and villages with the same names. In return the U.S.A. received ninety-nine-year leases for naval and air bases in Newfoundland, Bermuda, the Bahamas, Jamaica, St Lucia, Antigua, Trinidad and British Guiana.
[4] H.M.S. *Challenger* was retained by the U.S. Navy for deck-landing training.

2. 'Check your switches'

U.S.S. *Bogue*, A.C.V.9,[1] had all the familiar features of the great majority of World War 2 escort carriers. From the first of these conversions, U.S.S. *Long Island*, commissioned on June 2nd 1941, to the last, U.S.S. *Saidor*, handed over to the Navy on September 4th 1945, the deep, blunt-stemmed merchant hull was unmistakeable. Topped off and top-heavy with the long slab of the flight deck, they were not pretty ships, though to see one of them swing into wind and launch planes was to become aware of a certain beauty in motion. Many fish-head sailors and old shellbacks called them ugly, others dismissed them as characterless hybrids, impractical compromises, too slow and poorly protected for ships of war, no longer of any use for carrying cargoes. They forgot that *Bonhomme Richard* was a converted merchantman, and had served John Paul Jones well enough.

Bogue's Captain, Giles Elza Short, born in Lohrville, Iowa, had been a naval aviator for twenty-two of his forty-eight years. He entered the U.S. Naval Academy at Annapolis in 1915, and on graduation in June 1918 he qualified as a Naval Aviator at Pensacola, Florida, served with Scouting Squadron 1, attached to the seaplane tender *Wright*, in Bombing Squadron 5 with the U.S.S. *Langley*, the U.S. Navy's first aircraft carrier, and in June 1943 took command of Patrol Squadron 5, based at Coco Solo in the Canal Zone. Six months later he fitted out and commissioned Bombing Squadron 7 and commanded it aboard the U.S.S. *Yorktown*. He was a carrier air group commander in the *Enterprise* in 1939, then commanded the U.S.S. *Patoka*. At the outbreak of World War 2 he was on the Staff at the Naval War College, and joined the new U.S.S. *Bogue* in the Seattle-Tacoma yard in June 1942.

Long Island and the first two B.A.V.G.s H.M.S. *Archer*
and H.M.S. *Avenger* had been fitted with rudimentary
bridge-flying control positions level with the flight deck to
starboard, balanced by a room full of pig iron on the port
side below decks. From B.A.V.G.3, H.M.S. *Biter,* on-
wards, this spray-lashed open box was developed into the
typical bridge-island tower, with its lattice girder mast and
bird's nest of aerials. The open bridge was the Officer of the
Deck's territory. Here too Captain Short always stood when
the ship was in confined or dangerous waters or operating
aircraft, standing no watches but always on call for
emergencies day and night, and for that reason sleeping in
his emergency cabin just below, whenever the ship was at
sea. This was a simple, two-room suite with none of the
luxuries associated with The Captain's Cabin. A built-in
bunk, chest of drawers, chair and chart table were the
bedroom's only furnishings. A big desk and an easy chair
filled half the dining room, which was also his office.
Though fresh air was constantly blowing in through ducts,
the cabins always seemed stuffy, because scuttles were
permanently secured in wartime. In U.S. Navy A.C.V.s the
Captain also had a shower fitted, but Captain Stephenson
R.N. of the *Bogue*-class ship H.M.S. *Battler* had the shower
taken out and replaced with an outsized bath, preferring the
languor of the long hot soak to the brisk shock of the spray.

To an officer used to a cruiser or a destroyer it seemed
awkward at first to stand on a bridge at the side of a ship,
but from here the Captain, and the Air Officer, who held
sway in the after part of the island, with his telephones and
flags, could see clearly the entire pattern of flying operations and the panorama of the surrounding ocean. Below,
the flight deck stretched like a big pine-planked football
gridiron, with arrester wires and thick barrier cables for
stripes. Along the sidelines, in railed galleries which the
British called The Goofers, were sited *Bogue*'s sixteen forty
millimetre and twenty-one twenty millimetre ack-ack guns,
and there were two five-inch, one in the bows, one tucked
under the round-down astern. Below the bridge was the Air

Office, where the Air Officer and Squadron Commander had desks. Service records of planes and pilots were kept here, separate from the ship's files, so that they could be quickly bundled together and put in a plane when the squadron moved ashore. On the Air Officer's desk was a much used model of the flight deck, with little T.B.F.s and fighters, which would have been best sellers in the toy departments of Macy's, but which the Air Officer played with constantly to improve the spotting of his aircraft on the deck. Next door was the Air Plot, where men kept track of the ship's planes in the air. On the bulkhead a dead-reckoning tracer plotted the ship's course and position automatically. From this office the Air Officer contacted his lonely patrols by radio.

In harbour, with squadron disembarked, the hangar was vast and spacious, big enough for Bob Hope or Betty Grable and a full U.S.O. troupe to put on a show for the whole ship's company. There was also a fully-equipped cinema projection room above the after end. A screen was lowered from the deckhead for'ard so that the men who were going out to fight the U-boats could watch John Wayne or Errol Flynn winning the war.

After the aircraft had flown aboard, this empty hall was packed solid with T.B.F.s and fighters. Even with wings folded there was not enough space for eight big Avengers and twelve Wildcats, surrounded by torpedoes, depth-charges and spare engines, with propellers, wings, rudders, elevators and wheels covering the bulkheads. If for the Hangar Deck Officer there were too many planes, for the Air Officer there were too few, and it was vital to keep as many as possible operational. In the hangar was a complete tool and repair shop. If necessary a badly damaged plane could be rebuilt as quickly as the Navy Yard could do it, and probably quicker.

Below the hangar deck was the mess hall, where the enlisted men stood in line in a cafeteria, filling tray compartments with green peppers stuffed with Hamburg steak, French fried potatoes, fresh string beans, coffee or cocoa, and Mom's apple pie with ice-cream. There was more than enough food in the ship's stores and frozen-food lockers for a growing teenage sailor to go round the buoy as many times as he wanted, even for a sirloin steak. The Supply Officer never ceased to hark back to the Old Navy, when they used to hump sides of beef aboard and cut them up themselves. Now steaks, chops and veal cutlets came cut to size. All they had to do was to open a box and defrost the meat. *Bogue* carried enough staple foods to last for several months without touching port, even though the ship's 890 men ate a ton of flour, half a ton of sugar and a quarter ton each of stewed tomatoes and coffee every week. The officers, who ran their own mess, complained that the men ate better, but they too could eat all the butter, sugar and steaks they fancied, and coffee, hot chocolate and sandwiches were available at all times, day or night, in case anyone felt like a snack. There were ninety-seven officers[2] in this small ship, so many that there were two servings, sometimes three, for meals. After dinner the big tables, covered with green cloths, became a battleground for acey-deucy, cribbage, bridge and poker, with the duty censors in a corner reading the mail.

British sailors in the R.N.-manned A.C.V.s, though they did not eat so well, found the cafeteria system a novelty after their traditional 'cooks of the mess', who drew the food from the galley, prepared it themselves on long wooden mess tables which had not changed much from the days of wooden ships and iron men when Nelson's jack tars had chewed on their hard tack among the guns, then returned it to the galley to be cooked, and collected it again at meal times. They liked the Yankee soda fountain too, the well-equipped barber's shop and the modern laundry, though some R.N. ships were too short-handed to use it. Then ratings had to do their dhobeying in a bucket in the traditional way.

No traditional hammocks were slung in the British or American-manned 'Woolworth carriers'. Men slept in bunks or cots three and four deep, one above the other.

When the bosun's mate's yell of 'Wakey- wakey! Lash up and stow!' in a British carrier or 'Up all hammocks!' in a U.S. Navy A.C.V., rang out, the cots were simply pushed up on their hinges out of the way. One thing most men agreed on, whether they were called gobs or matlows, ratings or enlisted men. It was not easy to sleep so deep down in the ship. Down there it was unhealthy, claustrophobic, and difficult to escape from in a hurry. The bang of water hammer in the pipes each morning when the water was turned on sounded like a torpedo hitting the ship's side. Aircrew preferred to spend their off-duty time in the Ready Room higher up adjoining the hangar and The Goofers. Junior officers' well-equipped cabins were also too deep in the bowels of the ship for peace of mind.

Right up in the eyes of the ship was the sick bay, a miniature hospital with an operating theatre and the latest equipment, including a bacteriological research chest and an X-ray fluoroscope, unheard of in British ships.

Thus *Bogue,* the little merchant warship, untried and unsung but at least well-found and replete with all the material comforts which America could give her fighting men, waited in the wings for her entry into the tragedy of war.

On the other side of the U-boat-ridden North Atlantic two more American-built small flat-tops were preparing for the same battle. H.M.S. *Archer,* with everything to prove, and the already battle-hardened *Biter,* both ships of an older model, were working up with aircraft.

Between British and American-manned vessels there were big differences in equipment. *Bogue,* with her larger hangar, could carry up to twenty-eight aircraft operationally, and was sailing with twenty. *Archer* and *Biter,* with capacity for eighteen, were carrying twelve apiece, a mix of nine Swordfish and three Martlets.

Contrasts in aircraft were spectacular, not so much in the fighters – though the F.4F.4 Wildcat[3] was a more advanced model than its Martlet II brother[4] – but in the age and quality of Fairey Swordfish T.S.R. Mark II versus Grumman Avenger T.B.F.1[5]. The stately Stringbag biplane dated back to early 1933 and was obsolete by 1939. The Avenger was the most modern naval bomber in service, and had only got its name after Pearl Harbour. The Avenger had a top speed of over 220 knots and cruised at 132, a Swordfish with no war load might just manage 125, eighty in cruise. Range of a Swordfish on internal tank at economical cruising speed was 546 miles, 770 with an extra sixty-nine-gallon tank; a T.B.F. could fly 1,105 miles on its basic tankage, 1,390 with two drop-tanks. The pilot, radioman and rear turret gunner of a T.B.F. were accommodated in comfortable closed cockpits, a Stringbag driver sat high in a windy, open office, with the observer (navigator) and telegraphist-air-gunner in a bathtub-shaped open cockpit down behind him. A Swordfish pilot had a slow-firing .303-inch machine-gun in front of him, a .303 Lewis on a Scarff ring mounting aft; an Avenger had a forward .30 and another poking out ventrally for the radioman to use, as well as its big .50-inch in the turret. The Avenger was a strong alk-metal aeroplane with a tough undercarriage for deck-landing; the Stringbag, though rugged enough for its day and protective of ham-fisted rooky pilots, was put together with wood and fabric, and more prone to break a leg in a rough landing.

An Avenger was obviously the latest thing, the Stringbag looked like something from *Dawn Patrol*. Yet the T.B.F. did not have *all* the advantages. Both were easy deck-landers. The Swordfish, so much slower and thus more vulnerable in an approach to a well-defended target, had a better view from its open cockpits and could sight a U-boat sooner. It also had the advantage of better A.S.V. (Air to Surface Vessel) radar than the Avenger. The Avenger could lift four 500-pound bombs, the Swordfish one less, but some of Lieutenant-Commander O.A.G. Oxley's Number 819 Squadron's Mark II Swordfish in *Archer* had had their lower planes especially strengthened to operate the new rocket projectiles, racks for eight of which had been fitted to each machine. It was a Stringbag which had first tested R.P.s for the Royal Navy on October 12th 1942 at

Thorney Island, and *Archer*'s Swordfish were the first naval aircraft to take them to sea. Swordfish working at night had inflicted great damage – at Taranto on the moored Italian battle fleet, flying from Malta against Axis convoys to North Africa. A Swordfish had crippled the mighty *Bismarck* with a torpedo in daylight. Using cloud cover properly, an experienced Stringbag operator might still be effective over the Atlantic, though it was doubtful whether the R.N. ships, with their inferior repair facilities, would be able to keep as high a proportion of their planes in the air. It had also to be borne in mind that, whereas *Bogue* could catapult both her Wildcats and Avengers, ignoring lack of wind and with a full war load, only *Archer*'s and *Biter*'s Martlets could use their American accelerators. Swordfish would have to balance weight and wind over the deck very carefully.

These ships were new weapons in the Battle of the Atlantic, they were all untried, though the Senior Service had the slender tradition of the gallant little *Audacity* in its favour. Between the Captains, upon whom so much would depend, there was little to choose in experience, except, again, that 'Streamline' Robertson of *Archer* and Conolly Abel-Smith of *Biter* had both seen active service in carriers before, while Giles Short of *Bogue* was untested in this form of war.

In February, with the easing of the January gales, sinkings by U-boats began to rise again, from the thirty-seven ships totalling 203,128 tons of January to sixty-three ships (359,328 tons), in spite of individual successes by surface escorts and the patrols of Coastal Command. The increase continued in the first days of March.

Four convoys were to be sailed from North America to Britain at short staggered intervals. They got rough treatment, both from the weather and the U-boats.

The first to sail, S.C.121 from New York, was escorted by the U.S. Navy's Group A3, with Senior Officer Escort in the destroyer *Spenser*. From the 4th to the 12th March this

22

convoy was hammered by south-westerly gales. Mountainous, savage seas scattered ships and put submarine detecting gear in the escorts out of action. Vital H.F./D.F. sets broke down, radars in four out of eight escorts and sonars[6] in three went defective, R./T. was unreliable. Along the 59th parallel, between longitudes 19 and 38 West south of Cape Farewell, Greenland, the U-boats gathered, and when the winds were not blowing Force 10 they struck. The heaviest attack was made on the night of March 9th-10th. A weak escort of Coastal Command aircraft had a difficult job, with ships scattered all over the compass. Twelve ships were sunk, and Commodore Birnie killed.

The remaining three convoys were re-routed to pass 350 miles further south of Cape Farewell, but Dönitz learned the change of course from intercepted signals, and thirteen U-boats of the *Neuland* group, plus five more outward-bound boats and others temporarily re-routed, were heading towards a confrontation on the 50th parallel.

The second convoy to sail was H.X.228, bound for Britain from Halifax, Nova Scotia, and it was in support of this convoy that U.S.S. *Bogue* became the first of the new Allied auxiliary carriers to operate on the North Atlantic shipping lanes.

Escort Group B3, comprising the British destroyers *Harvester* (Senior Officer Escort) and *Escapade* and the corvette *Narcissus,* the Polish destroyers *Garland* and *Burza,* and the Free French sloops *Aconit, Renoncule* and *Roselys,* left St John's, Newfoundland, at 6.45 p.m. on March 5th. They met the convoy at ten o'clock on the following morning, and at 1.45 in the afternoon *Bogue, Belknap* (Lieutenant-Commander Doyle M. Coffee U.S.N., Screen Commander) and *George E. Badger* (Commander W.H. Johnsen U.S.N.) came up with them.

The two old U.S. destroyers were of a distinctive flush-deck types laid down in 1918, of which the U.S. Navy had eighty-three on strength in 1940, most of them having spent from twelve to eighteen years laid up in reserve. Fifty of these were handed over to the Royal Navy under the Destroyers-for-Bases agreement. Of the remainder, some had been converted in 1939-40 to Light Minelayers, Fast Minesweepers, Transports and Aircraft Tenders. U.S.S. *George E. Badger,* named for a North Carolinian lawyer and politician who had been President Harrison's Secretary of the Navy in 1841 and an opponent of secession, had been converted into seaplane tender A.V.D.3 in the autumn of 1940, and had tended her planes, based at Argentia, Newfoundland, and Reykjavik, Iceland, until the spring of 1942, before reverting to destroyer duty to escort convoys along the eastern seaboard of the U.S.A., in the Gulf of Mexico and to Recife and Rio de Janeiro, then returning to Norfolk, Virginia, to be fitted out for Atlantic escort duty. As part of *Bogue*'s Task Group 24.1, although re-classified a D.D., she still retained her mutilated A.V.D. form, with her two for'ard funnels missing, and reduced armament of two four-inch and one three-inch guns and two machine guns, although carrying depth-charges for anti-submarine work. The old 'four-stackers' or 'four- pipers', as the U.S. Navy called them, formed the screens for the U.S. Navy escort carrier groups in the Atlantic for some months and, along with their R.N.-manned sisters, became a familiar sight there, with their spindly smokestacks, raking flush-decks and large craggy bridges.

There were sixty-one merchant ships in Convoy H.X.228, disposed in thirteen columns, with Commodore J.O. Dunn, Royal Naval Reserve, in command. *Bogue* took up station in a lane of her own seven cables wide between the fifth and sixth columns. Her escorts reinforced the close escort screen, except when the carrier was operating planes, when the U.S. destroyers were detached again to screen her, with the Polish *Garland* in attendance as well.

Bogue catapulted T.B.F.s for anti-submarine patrols on March 7th between dawn and dusk, then the convoy made a forty-five degree turn to starboard to avoid a reported concentration of U-boats ahead.

Bad weather prevented flying on the 8th and 9th, but on

the 9th the escorts' H.F./D.F., with which *Bogue* was not fitted, reported U-boats signalling a long way off in a northerly direction.

The first sign of a tangible threat came at 2.32 a.m. on the 10th with the convoy some 700 miles east-nor'-east of Newfoundland and 900 miles to the west of Ireland, when the sharp-eared Huff-Duff reported U-boat signals twenty-five miles away on a bearing forward of their port beam. This was in fact Kapitänleutnant Hunger's U-336, the southernmost boat of the *Neuland* group. As the first to sight the convoy, Hunger's job was now to maintain contact with it and home in the rest of the group. Commander 'Harry' Tait, S.O.E. in *Harvester,* requested *Bogue* to fly off aircraft to investigate as soon as possible.

As light crept over the eastern horizon, the four-ton thrust of *Bogue*'s catapult hurled a T.B.F. into the sky. Two hours later the plane reported a sighting. *Harvester* and *Escapade* ran down the bearing given for eight miles, then received the signal 'Negative' from the T.B.F. *Harvester* returned, leaving *Escapade* patrolling fifteen miles ahead of the convoy.

It was misty and raining slightly when Lieutenant (jg) Alexander C. McAuslan was launched from *Bogue* at 9.18 a.m. in T.B.F. No 7 on anti-submarine patrol. They were flying one of the legs of their zig-zag search pattern about ten miles on the port bow of the convoy at 12.26 when McAuslan sighted a black spot about two miles on their starboard bow which on closer investigation turned out to be the conning tower of a U-boat with decks just awash heading north on an opposite course to their own.

McAuslan called up the ship to make a contact report but could get no acknowledgement.

He opened to full throttle. The steady throb of the big fourteen-cylinder Wright Cyclone rose to its full-throated roar as the Avenger increased from its 140-knot cruising speed and the deep-bellied bomber in its duck-egg green top decking and off-white under-surfaces turned sharply to attack.

Radioman Newman and turret gunner Bill Boyd were both at the centre station. McAuslan said over the talkback, 'This is it. Man the turret. Check your switches and break out the camera.' Boyd climbed up through the small doorway and hunched himself in the perspex bubble of the ball turret, knees up to his chin, the breech of the big 50-calibre machine gun under his left hand. He swung the turret to check for freedom of movement. Newman checked all the armament switches, then got his small K2 camera and climbed down into the belly to position himself for photographs at the after window, next to his .30 belly gun. They were the first crew from aU.S. Navy escort carrier to sight a U-boat, and McAuslan wanted to be the first to score a kill.

He was aiming to come in on the U-boat's starboard quarter, losing altitude in a steady power glide so as to reach his release point at fifty feet from the water.

In U-336 Hunger was too intent on keeping in touch with the convoy to be keeping a sharp lookout for aircraft, and the T.B.F. was on its approach before it was sighted. She crash-dived at once, and the conning tower submerged about one second before McAuslan reached the release point.

He pressed the release button, but nothing happened, the D.C.s did not drop. He tried again. Still they would not go. Frustrated and angry, he steered the plane round in a sharp turn to starboard for another try, cutting the approach short to take the sub from where her starboard bow should be, under the swirl. It would have to be a quick shot anyway, as he was getting very low on gas, and there were now other planes nearby. He pressed the button, but again nothing happened. After that there was only just enough time to fly to the nearest destroyer and direct her to come to the scene, then he returned to the carrier, where the T.B.F. crashed on landing. The failure of his D.C.s to release was put down to faulty loading drill.

The destroyer *Escapade* was switched from her position fifteen miles ahead of the convoy to a station on the port beam to cover any more potential attacks from that direction. Other aircraft patrolled the area to continue McAuslan's good work in keeping the hungry Hunger down and thus far less able to close the convoy. A plane was launched at 1.35 in the afternoon to make one circling sweep round the convoy.

Lieutenant Howard Roberts was returning off a patrol and was preparing to jettison his unused depth-charges before landing on. He had flown past the port side of the ship from bow to stern and was circling about half a mile astern to run back over the flight deck and look for the signal to come aboard, when his turret gunner shouted on talkback that he had seen a swirl in the water on their port beam and about two miles from the ship on her port quarter. Roberts had a look and saw a huge patch of agitated white water, fanning out from a point where small waves suggested the presence of a submerged submarine.

Roberts opened the throttle and continued on his turn to port, pressing the release button as he crossed the track of the target. Only one D.C. fell, hitting the water about a hundred feet ahead of the swirl directly on the path of the target. The charge took a long time to explode, and threw up only a feeble plume of spray. Roberts circled and saw the typical greenish-brown D.C. slick on the water but no sign of a damaged submarine. Unaware that he had only dropped one D.C., he closed the bomb bay doors. He dropped two smoke pots, flew over to the ship to warn her of a U-boat, then came back to the swirl. As he circled he opened the bomb bay doors to make absolutely sure that both D.C.s had gone, and the second charge of the first stick fell out of the plane. He returned to the carrier, where there was another inquest on the failure of his depth-charges. A defective fuse had probably caused the first one to go off with a whimper instead of a bang. The second charge had hung up initially because the solenoid had received too weak an impulse to trip the release mechanism, partly caused by the low air temperature. It was a cause for concern as it was only one of a crop of similar teething malfunctions which were plaguing the squadron in these early days of operations. U.S.S. *Belknap* was despatched to

27

the scene of the abortive attack. She made no sonar contacts with submarines but sighted a school of porpoises in the vicinity.

At 4 p.m. the carrier and her escorts left the convoy to return to base. Compo 9's few hours of uncertain sightings and two abortive attacks had been very much a preliminary canter.

But their presence had been noted uneasily by Oberleutnant Langfeld in U-444, which had taken over as stationkeeper from U-336, and it was not until the carrier was well over the horizon four hours later that, in the fading twilight just as the remaining escorts were taking up night stations, Oberleutnant Trojer's U-221 came in from ahead submerged and torpedoed the two freighters *Turinca* and *Andrew F. Luckenbach.*

Tait put his helm hard-a-port. *Harvester* raced back through the convoy columns and, just as the third ship, the S.S. *Lawton B. Evans,* was hit by a torpedo which failed to explode, attacked a submarine contact near the torpedoed ships.

The destroyer was still hunting just over an hour later when Huff-Duff reported more U-boat signals twenty-five miles away in the north-east. Three hours later U-336, back in touch, U-86 and U-406 attacked the convoy from both beams. The American *William G. Gorgas* and the British *Jamaica Producer* were hit and left stopped and damaged. *Harvester* sighted a submarine on the starboard beam of the convoy. The U-boat dived but Tait's determined depth-charging blew her to the surface where he rammed her at twenty-seven knots, seriously damaging both vessels.

Lieutenant de Vaisseau Levasseur in F.F.S. *Aconit,* closing *Harvester,* saw a surfaced U-boat, opened fire with his Oerlikons, transfixing the German with his biggest searchlight and tossing five depth-charges at her for good measure, and rammed her amidships. The U-boat sank about half a mile from the stricken *Harvester.*

Towards the end of the middle, the graveyard watch, with light creeping over the horizon, there was a third attack on the convoy, from starboard, by U-757. The munitions ship

Brant County was hit, burned furiously, illuminating the convoy and escorts, then blew up in a huge sheet of flame. Her attacker was damaged in the explosion, but torpedoed and finished off the disabled *William G. Gorgas.*

Two Coastal Command Liberators joined the convoy escorts at dawn on the 11th and made numerous U-boat sightings from ten to forty miles away from the convoy. During the afternoon *Harvester,* now completely disabled, was torpedoed twice by Kapitänleutnant Eckhardt's U-432, and sank rapidly, taking Commander Tait with her.

The aggressive Levasseur, sighting on the column of black smoke from the sinking destroyer, steamed up at full speed, got a resounding ping three miles from the gallant Tait's funeral pyre, and sank his killer.

Convoys S.C.122 from New York and H.X.229 from Halifax ran into very heavy concentrations of U-boats, and with no mid-ocean air support and very few surface escorts, suffered severely. H.X.229 was joined by a land-based aircraft on the 17th. This conscientious pilot was a thousand miles from base when he picked up the convoy. He made six sightings of U-boats, attacked three of them, and frightened them from repeating the previous night's heavy attack. Generally, however, this convoy was attacked further west than the others, and could not get air cover in the most critical period. Twenty-one ships, a total of 140,842 tons, were sunk in the two convoys, with one U-boat destroyed by land-based aircraft after the end of the convoy battle, and another damaged.

[1] A. for auxiliary, C.V. for aircraft carrier. The original designation was A.V.G., and the first six American conversions for the Royal Navy were B. (for British) A.V.G.s. Thus U.S.S. *Long Island* was A.V.G.1, H.M.S. *Archer* B.A.V.G.1, H.M.S. *Avenger* B.A.V.G.2, H.M.S. *Biter* B.A.V.G.3, H.M.S. *Challenger* B.A.V.G.4, H.M.S. *Dasher* B.A.V.G.5, H.M.S. *Tracker* B.A.V.G.6. All U.S. Navy auxiliary carriers were re-classified A.C.V. on August 20th 1942. U.S.S. *Bogue,* A.V.G.9, became A.C.V.9, etc.
[2] and 921 enlisted men.
[3]. Maximum speed about 280 knots at 18,800 feet, 242 at sea level, 140 in cruise.
[4] Maximum 254 knots at 5,400 – 13,000 feet.
[5] Torpedo bomber. *Bogue's* T.B.F.s carried depth-charges at this stage, which the U.S. Navy also called depth-*bombs.*
[6] Acronym for Sound Navigation and Ranging, the U.S. Navy's echo-sounding submarine detection system, similar to the Royal Navy's Asdic (Allied Submarine Detection Investigation Committee.)

3. 'Shall I run interference?'

Ten days after she had left·H.X.228 *Bogue* was ready to accompany S.C.123. A meeting was held in the carrier at Argentia, Newfoundland, just before the escorts left to rendezvous with the convoy, with Captain (Destroyers), Argentia, and S.O.E. of B.2 Escort Group, Commander Donald MacIntyre D.S.O. R.N., as British representative.

The American *Commander Task Force Twenty Four Tentative Doctrine For Use Of A.C.V.s In Escort Of North Atlantic Convoys* was discussed. There was a difference of opinion as to the best place for the carrier at night if an attack on the convoy was likely, when, the *Doctrine* suggested, the A.C.V. with her escorts might well operate thirty to fifty miles from the convoy. MacIntyre, seasoned destroyer captain and U-boat fighter, a big man with a positive and decisive manner, had not forgotten that *Audacity* had been sunk in a manoeuvre like this. He said carefully, 'It is my opinion that the carrier should remain in the lane left for her in the centre of the convoy. In this position she is in danger only from the submarine which enters the convoy to make a deliberate attack on the carrier herself, as she is out of range of a torpedo fired from outside the convoy.'

'If, however,' he went on, 'the carrier decides to leave the convoy, I consider that she should put a hundred miles *at least* between herself and the convoy, as the area for fifty miles around is likely to be fairly thickly populated by U-boats when a massed attack is brewing.'

The Americans looked dubious about that. But did not the *Doctrine* urge that 'The C.O. A.C.V. . . . . should be strongly influenced by the advice of the S.O.E. Escort by virtue of the latter's experience and his probable thorough information on the subject'?

The three old V-and-W class destroyers *Whimbrel,* *Whitehall* and *Vanessa,* contemporaries of the American four-pipers, and the corvettes *Gentian, Sweetbriar* and *Heather,* of B2 Escort Group, sailed from St John's at 10.30 p.m. on March 20th, with MacIntyre in *Whimbrel.* The corvette *Clematis* had gone on ahead to round up the wandering S.S. *Shickshinny* and escort her to the convoy. The main section of the Group and *Clematis* with her charge all met the convoy at 8 a.m. the following morning, with the four-stacker destroyers H.M.S. *Salisbury,* ex-U.S.S. *Claxton,* and *Chelsea,* the former U.S.S. *Crowninshield,* of the Western Support Group, joining at the same time.

The convoy had already lost the Panamanian S.S. *Pacific* and the British *Vera Radcliffe,* which had returned with engine trouble, as well as the Panamanian *Santiago,* which, with westerly gales threatening the convoy, had been unable to keep up even in the good weather enjoyed so far. This left forty-six merchantmen, with Captain M.E.P. Magee D.S.O. R.N. as Commodore in the S.S. *Umvuma.*

Bogue, Belknap and *George E. Badger* of TG 24.4 were on their way from Argentia. As they steered for the rendezvous on the forenoon of the 21st visibility was some twelve miles, the sea was smooth, but the wind could not make more than four knots, insufficient for Avengers and Wildcats to land into. Just after twelve noon they joined the convoy. *Belknap* and *Badger* joined the convoy close escorts, one to each flank, *Bogue* steered into her special lane and took station in the centre of the convoy, with ships of various nationalities boxing her in, the British *Empire Pibroch* and *North Britain* flanking her, the French *Il de Re* on her port bow, the Greeks *Panos* and *Agios Georgios* on her port quarter, the American *Western Queen* to starboard. The carrier's watch officer kept his eye on the quarter. Greek ships were generally poor station keepers and inclined to straggle. And there were a few Smokey Joes in this convoy, including the American S.S. *Tachee,* just ahead of *Bogue* to starboard. When cautioned, her Master blamed a faulty arrester on his steam pipe for the smoke.

31

Empire Barrie, two columns to starboard of *Tachee* on her beam, had a bad bout of heavy smoking, but her Master promised an improvement once her bunker of Durban coal was empty. The Captain of the *Ivan Topic*, two places away to starboard of the Commodore, said 'I'm doing all I can to keep it down. It's this bloody awful Bitumarian I took on on New York.' The Master of the *Campus*, out on the port wing, said that it was wet coal due to a leak in the bunkers that was writing his and the convoy's signature in the sky.

In the afternoon the fickle weather changed its face. Visibility shrank to three miles, the sea worked up a swell, clouds hung heavy at 1,500 feet and shook out flurries of snow but the wind, though variable, rose and blew up and down the scale from eight to twenty-one knots. *Bogue* launched a T.B.F. at four o'clock, another half an hour later. The two planes covered an area all round the convoy at a radius of thirty miles, but had to be recalled just after five o'clock when the weather worsened.

That night the air grew very cold, and lookouts reported ice ahead, much further south-west than the ice bulletin had forecast. For some two and a half hours the convoy picked its way through wide fields of pancake ice, with heavy drifting floes and several small growlers. Of the five corvettes, which had fixed underwater sonar domes, only *Clematis* lost hers in the ice, and the S.S. *West Maximus* had rudder damage. Later, luckily in daylight, big craggy bergs were sighted and passed down the convoy lanes. Shortly after dawn wind and sea started to rise menacingly and a Force 8 gale which blew all day and most of the night from the north-west ruled out all flying.

The weather seemed to have moderated with the morning, March 23rd. Waves and swell had flattened, the wind had sunk to a reasonable blow. Heartened, Giles Short sent off a T.B.F. just before ten o'clock. Fuel consumption was worrying the small ships of the escort, especially the thirsty destroyers, and an anxious *Salisbury* used the lull to close the tanker *British Prestige* and weigh the chances of topping up from her. But the oiler had no buoyant hoses for refuelling from astern, which might have been possible had the weather stayed quiet, and she could only transfer by the trough method, with the two ships side by side. But the sea started to get up again, and Commander de St Croix decided it was too dangerous. *Bogue* had to recall her T.B.F. after twenty minutes flying, as the visibility suddenly closed in.

Short tried again at 1.43 p.m. with two T.B.F.s launched for all-round coverage of the convoy at a distance of thirty miles. On recovery at 3.12 p.m., the first plane to come in, Ensign Harry Fryatt's T.B.F., bounced over the barriers and disappeared over the bows. Everyone held their breath, then the heavy plane climbed laboriously into view again. Another Avenger was launched at five o'clock, made one complete sweep round the convoy, and returned aboard.

The 24th dawned murky and uncertain, with rain and a moderate sea and wind, just good enough to launch a T.B.F. at half-past six. The weather grew ugly again while it was searching round the convoy and it was recovered at 7.45 p.m. The gale blew hard for three hours, then moderated, and a T.B.F. got off at 10.46 p.m. But it was only a short breather. Cloud and rain closed in, and when the plane was recalled it had to fight its way down on to the deck against a forty-knot wind. *Salisbury* and *Chelsea* reached their prudent fuel limit at two o'clock in the afternoon. *Bogue* had extra fuel, but it was too rough for Short to think of trying to top up even the destroyers of his own screen, which had practised the drill with him, and the British-manned four-pipers left the convoy to return to base.

Within four hours of their departure the wind rose to Force 8, and a full gale with raging seas battered at the ships throughout the night of the 24th-25th and into the daylight. Gusts of swirling snow lightly carpeted *Bogue*'s gyrating flight deck, cloud lay at a hundred feet, and there was no question of flying.

Operating conditions were still bad at dawn, with the carrier pitching badly and rain and snow hanging about, though the visibility was clear and unlimited in between squalls. Then conditions improved and at 7.35 a.m. a T.B.F. left *Bogue*'s catapult, followed by a second at eight o'clock. These two planes searched an area of forty miles round the convoy with their A.S.V. radar but reported no contacts. They were recovered at 10.45 a.m. and two more launched at 11.30 for another all-round sweep. Again nothing was seen of the enemy. Rain and snow increased around mid-day, and they had to fight high winds to make it to the deck when they returned at half-past two. Two more were launched just after three and searched all round the ships for fifty miles ahead and thirty miles on the flanks and rear.

By now the tanks of *Bogue*'s old destroyers were almost at the point of no return. It was still too rough for refuelling, and at five o'clock, some 150 miles south-east of Cape Farewell, Short recalled the two T.B.F.s from their empty orbits round the convoy, and took his three ships out of their stations to return to Argentia.

Just twenty-eight minutes later, with *Bogue* still in sight from the convoy, MacIntyre's Huff-Duff man in *Whimbrel* picked up a U-boat signalling from a position within thirty miles to the north-west of the convoy, and the destroyer *Vanessa* was ordered to investigate. Ten minutes later a transmission in German naval Enigma code was picked up about the same distance to the south, and *Whitehall* was sent on a hunt.

Whimbrel signalled *Bogue* with the news at 5.42 p.m. Three minutes later *Vanessa* signalled MacIntyre that she was in contact with a submarine at a range of seven miles. She made another signal, but it was too mutilated to be readable in *Bogue*, which was having difficulty in picking up communications between the convoy escorts as she drew further away from them. Then at 6.20 she overheard *Vanessa* report to S.O.E. that she had lost contact with her U-boat.

Twenty minutes later an anxious Short, considerably frustrated at having to leave the convoy with the enemy in the offing, asked MacIntyre if he had had any more news from his two hunters. A few minutes later *Vanessa* burst in with 'Sub in sight on my starboard side . . .!'

The old V-and-W crashed through the heavy seas, catching sight of a conning tower intermittently over the crests. Huff-Duff in *Whimbrel* was also picking up the German's Enigma, and from the hurried way the operator was stabbing his key it looked as if he was rushing to get his sighting message out before the boat was forced to dive. This was true enough. Not only had the U-boat commander seen *Vanessa* coming for him with bow wave curling, he was also worried that the carrier and her escorts, which he had seen steering away from the convoy, was also off on a hunt, and might be back.

In fact Short was losing touch with the situation. Messages between the convoy escorts were becoming more and more garbled, unintelligible and faint. A signal to *Whimbrel* from *Vanessa* reporting an attack with D.C.s at 7.25 p.m. and a report of a second attack twenty minutes later were the last decipherable clues to the situation *Bogue*'s operator could extract from the weak crackle in his ears, then the sounds of battle faded altogether. Worried about the critical fuel state of his destroyers, and feeling vulnerable with only the two of them to screen the carrier, Short went to General Quarters and worked the ship up to sixteen knots as she zig-zagged on irregularly changing courses.

Meanwhile *Vanessa*'s U-boat had dived when the destroyer closed to three miles. In four runs over the target *Vanessa* dropped forty-seven depth-charges, the last pattern including one special heavy charge set for a very deep explosion, which damaged the submarine.

MacIntyre realized they were passing through a U-boat patrol line. But the submarine attacked and damaged by *Vanessa* had been the pack organizer, and the convoy steamed on unharmed through that night and the following day. Late in the forenoon, after six frustrating hours trying to contact two Liberators from Iceland which were looking for them, one of the aircraft appeared.

Rough weather prevented the homeward-bound *Bogue*

from launching any aircraft for two days, and the wind was blowing very hard on the 29th, but at nine o'clock in the morning a T.B.F. was launched to patrol round Convoy O.N.S.1, heading for Halifax, Nova Scotia, from Britain. In the afternoon thick fog blanketed the sea. There were no more flights that day or the next, March 30th, with the carrier pitching badly, visibility almost zero, and ice on the flight deck. They reached Argentia later that day, and Task Group 24.4 was dissolved.

Weather had restricted *Bogue*'s contribution to convoy defence, but such conditions were normal for March in the North Atlantic, and Donald MacIntyre was 'pleasurably surprised by the heavy weather in which this small carrier was able to operate', and thought 'the operation proved a most useful test of this class of vessel.'

March saw sinkings by U-boat rise to the horrifying total of 108 ships (627,377 tons), two-thirds of these in convoy. The Germans, recorded the Admiralty, 'never came so near to disrupting communications between the New World and the Old as in the first twenty days of March 1943.' 'It appeared possible,' the Naval Chief of Staff recorded, 'that we should not be able to continue convoy as an effective system of defence.'

On March 27th the newly repaired H.M.S. *Dasher*'s Swordfish and Sea Hurricanes had finished a full working-up programme for the day in the Firth of Clyde and were being refuelled in the hangar when the whole ship gave a shudder, followed by a tremendous explosion. Men in *Dasher*'s escorting destroyer saw the carrier's lift soar into the air, and the ship sink rapidly by the stern. Half her officers and two-thirds of her ratings were drowned, or burned to death by flaming petrol on the water.

The Board of Enquiry attributed the explosion to the igniting of petrol fumes from a leaky valve in a petrol compartment, badly located below a messdeck, by a carelessly dropped cigarette end, and blamed the American safety arrangements, 'by our standards practically non-existent,' for stowing volatile high-octane fuel in ordinary tanks. American experts blamed British inexperience with the system, which was revised after the *Dasher* disaster on British lines in the R.N.'s American carriers. Solid ballast was also added for stability, in preference to the American practice of filling empty fuel tanks with salt water. This further increased the delays in getting new ships to sea, which in turn angered the Americans.

However, on April 14th the first grainer M.A.C.-ship *Empire MacAlpine* was commissioned, while H.M.S. *Biter* was on her way to support Convoy O.N.S.4 to Argentia, with No. 811 Composite Squadron of Swordfish and Martlets.

There was no proper understanding between Donald MacIntyre as S.O.E. and Conolly Abel-Smith in *Biter* on operating policy for this, the first Royal Navy carrier to work with a North Atlantic convoy since December 1941, and they had different ideas.

MacIntyre, with his belief in keeping an escort carrier snug inside the convoy when not operating aircraft, was expecting *Biter* to join him with the convoy on April 22nd, but Abel-Smith intended to operate the carrier and her escorts as an independent unit, a separate hunting group which could also cover the convoy at a distance. With their greater flexibility they could intercept U-boats before they attacked, and give support to other convoys within aircraft range, like one of the separate surface support groups, with the additional facility of the aircraft.

Instead of joining O.N.S.4 *Biter* shadowed it at a distance, maintaining strict radio silence, and S.O.E.'s signal on the 22nd requesting the carrier's position was not answered. By this time a spate of U-boat signals intercepted by MacIntyre's H.F./D.F. set indicated a U-boat patrol line close ahead, and he badly wanted *Biter*'s Stringbags so that he could make the most of Huff-Duff's magic.

On the afternoon of the 23rd the crew of a *Biter* Swordfish, freezing in their open cockpits as the slow biplane battled on through heavy snow, sighted a surfaced U-boat. They dived towards it but it had disappeared before

37

the Stringbag could get into an attacking position.

MacIntyre was not told about this sighting, but later he saw *Biter*'s unmistakeable silhouette through the swirling snow. Then she hauled off and vanished again. Huff-Duff began picking up signals from a U-boat, obviously calling in others. MacIntyre took *Hesperus* and *Clematis* off on a hunt down the H.F./D.F. bearing, sending a 'Come in, come in, wherever you are!' signal to *Biter* requesting the co-operation of her aircraft, but the carrier was fifty miles away by then. *Hesperus* sighted the U-boat, dropped D.C.s, fired a salvo of her new Hedgehog missiles, and sank U-191 with all hands. Shortly afterwards a Swordfish approached, 'indifferently briefed', MacIntyre complained, 'and too late.' He seemed to have proved a point, but Royal Ingersoll, U.S. C. in C.Lant, read the report of Abel-Smith's experiment with particular interest, as he himself had been thinking on similar lines.

While O.N.S.4 and its standoffish satellite headed along their northern route, on the watch for icebergs and wolf packs, *Bogue* and the old destroyers *Belknap, Greene, Lea* and *Osmond Ingram*[1] of the newly formed Task Group 92.3 were threading the swept channel out of Argentia, heading for a rendezvous with Convoy HX235, which had been routed further south than either of *Bogue*'s two previous convoys.

On April 24th pairs of T.B.F.s flew round the Group all forenoon in clear skies, and in the afternoon four Avengers were launched to locate and cover the convoy. They found HX235 at 2.45 seventy-five miles from the carrier, and set up Viper[2] patrols right away round Commodore Anchor's thirty-five ships.

The position of the convoy as reported by the T.B.F.s was forty-five miles further to the north-east than Atlantic Fleet and C-in-C Western Approaches said it was, and Captain Short did not know who to believe. Eventually he put his faith in his pilots. What had started as a leisurely cruise southwards to make an easy interception in the morning turned into a hectic tail chase through the night, delaying the time of joining and burning up fuel.

During the night, S.O.E. in H.M.S. *Churchill*, ex-U.S.S. *Herndon*, another old American destroyer in R.N. hands, reported U-boats twenty miles south of the convoy's track, and asked *Bogue* to launch an early search. She put up a Python[3] patrol at dawn, and finally joined the convoy at noon some four hundred miles east-by-south of St John's, taking station in her allotted place between the sixth and seventh columns of merchantmen. Her four D.D.s joined the convoy's close escort.

It was mild weather, and the T.B.F.s flew regular patrols ahead of the convoy and off each bow to a depth of fifty or sixty miles, and 360° sweeps right round the ships at visibility distance. There seemed to be little use for the fighters. In fact before this cruise Compo 9's Wildcats had been reduced from twelve to six, their nine Avengers increased to twelve, though Short would actually have traded three of his modern T.B.F.s for a trio of old Swordfish. His aircraft relied heavily on the catapult, which made him uneasy. Catapults could break down, and there would be near-windless days when a light Stringbag could lift off the deck but a heavy Avenger would be grounded. In these conditions or at the other extreme of sudden gales, the Swordfish, again, might make it down, but the much faster Grumman find itself in trouble. And the otherwise obsolete British machines could be used for night operations, which they had already proved, when their hooded exhaust flames would be an asset. A slow aircraft at night had a better chance of spotting a submarine than a fast one.

The weather also allowed *Bogue*'s escorts, parched after their unscheduled stern chase, to be refuelled. Short's memory of his enforced premature departure from SC123 still smarted, and he had afterwards spent some time in Placentia Bay practising the topping-up drill.

Even in this calmer southerly weather fuelling by the trough method was a complicated evolution, demanding good seamanship and accurate ship-handling, with the ever-present fear of collision and court martial. U.S.S. *Lea* was the first to come in for a drink. Lieutenant-Commander Thomas inched his way up the carrier's starboard side, keeping a good ship's width distance from the gently heaving steel cliff of the *Bogue*'s side, until the pelorus on his bridge was about abreast the winch on the carrier's for'ard sponson, then slowed his speed to *Bogue*'s cautious eight knots. The monkey's fist of a heaving line, bent on to the light messenger line, came snaking over from *Bogue* – in rough weather it would have been a gun line. Seamen heaved in the messenger, rove it through a snatch block and as a precaution made a few turns round the capstan. Another heaving line started through the air, fell short, was hauled in and hurled over again, this time connecting, bringing over another messenger, which was connected with the four-inch Navy Standard Fuel Hose already rigged on the carrier's starboard sponson, and the heavy black snake of the hose started swaying on its way across the sixty-foot channel. Meanwhile the towline messenger had brought over the phone line with it. A phone set came over in a canvas bag, and communication was established between the bridges of the two ships. As the towline reached *Lea*'s deck its eye was secured over the after bitts. A distance line was rigged from the carrier's well deck to the destroyer's foc'sle, marked every twenty-five feet so that *Lea* could maintain the forty to sixty-foot clearance between ships. With the towline secured, the fuel hose was taken aboard and brought to the open tank top, and fuelling began. It was an anxious fifty minutes for the destroyer skipper, with constant adjustment of engine revolutions to keep station, trying to maintain position without riding on the towline, which was really only there as a backup.

Lea took aboard 16,402 gallons, then cast off her umbilical lifelines and gave way to Screen Commander Doyle Coffee's *Belknap*, which took on 21,279 gallons in some seventy-one minutes. This represented a rate of 300 gallons a minute, which was not fast enough for Short's liking. For *Osmond Ingram*, next in the queue, he ordered two hoses rigged so that the destroyer could top up her fore and aft tanks at the same time. Before he came alongside, Lieutenant-Commander Sampson and his Chief Engineer had to work out a computation whereby the existing levels of fuel in both fore and after tanks were adjusted so that both pumps could finish at the same time, bearing in mind that the after hose would be making a heavier delivery than the for'ard one. All went well. Sampson, a good ship-handler, held the ship steady so that heaving lines hit first time, the men were able to work both sets of messengers in parallel, and the operation went through smoothly. Ingram took aboard a satisfactory 33,620 gallons in just over an hour. Meanwhile the tubby Avengers kept up their clockpit orbits round the horizon.

Further north in less obliging weather the *Biter* group was still holding aloof from the main body of O.N.S.4 and conserving aircraft for the big occasion, though flying patrols round the convoy, when asked by S.O.E.

On the afternoon of April 25th, Easter Day, Swordfish L sighted a surfaced U-boat about eight miles from the carrier, and Abel-Smith detached the destroyer *Pathfinder* from *Biter*'s screen to hunt it down. Meanwhile the Swordfish dropped two calcium sea markers and guided *Pathfinder* to them. The destroyer got a ping, and after two hours and five separate attacks, U-203 reared up above the surface and her crew began to abandon ship.

For the first few halcyon days of her southerly cruise *Bogue* had had pleasant flying weather. Compo 9's only difficulties had been the light airs prevailing, but for a fully loaded catapult launch a T.B.F. only needed sixteen knots of wind, an F.4F. a mere six knots, and this *Bogue* could always provide. But after the Group turned north and crossed the 49th parallel a gradually worsening swell set in, and the wind dropped. As the flight deck pitched more and more violently, the risks of operating planes increased. The auxiliary carriers, with their light merchant hulls and heavy superstructure were very susceptible to pitch anyway, especially after they had emptied their tanks into the greedy guts of their escort brood.

41

There was haze on the water but the skies were clear when Lieutenant Roger Santee and his T.B.F. crew, radio-man Frank McDuffer and turret gunner Frank H. Sherwood, were cruising at 150 knots on the return leg of their anti-submarine search at 4.40 p.m. on April 28th in mid-ocean between Newfoundland and Ireland. About four miles ahead of them Santee, an experienced Navy regular, sighted a fully surfaced U-boat, about fifty miles from the convoy, making about eight to ten knots. He overtook the submarine and pushed over in a 200-knot dive, still unobserved from the target.

He dropped four depth-charges, and as the plane banked away Sherwood strafed the sub with his fifty-calibre. He hit the conning tower, but when the D.C.s hit the water they ricocheted before exploding off the U-boat's bow. The closest was seventy-five feet off to starboard about level with the stem, the last 150 feet ahead of the first, the other two in between. There was no evidence of any damage to the U-boat, but the escort *Restogouche* sent to investigate found no trace of it, and nothing more was seen or heard of it. S.O.E. in *Churchill* signalled to *Bogue,* 'Please thank pilot whose excellent attack certainly prevented interception of the convoy by this U-boat.' It was nice to be appreciated, especially by these salty and superior British sea hunters.

On the night of the 29th it looked as if the convoy would soon cross the tracks of homeward and outward-bound U-boats. In the sleepless hours of the graveyard watch Giles Short pondered what his group could best do to protect the convoy. Should he push ahead and look for the enemy, or stay where he was, with his escorts helping to swell the convoy screen? There seemed little likelihood of a pack attack from the rear or quarters – these areas had been covered by Lizard[4] patrols.

Surely the convoy's greatest danger lay in accidental contact with U-boats ahead? Well, it was no time for pride. The British S.O.E. in the old American destroyer could help him make up his mind.

Bogue signalled to *Churchill,* 'In bucking possible U-boat line tonight which do you think best – to run interference on ahead with my screen and radar and sweep back by morning or remain in convoy? Any other suggestions welcome.'

The British S.O.E. may not have been familiar with American football terminology, but he got the gist, and thought boldness was the right tactic. He replied, 'I think it would be best for you to go ahead and rejoin after flying off the dawn patrol.'

So *Bogue* and her braves ran on independently ahead of the convoy for a distance of fifty miles. As soon as light crept into the sky at a little before five o'clock a patrol of four T.B.F.s was launched to fly back to the convoy, then search ahead and on its bows to a depth of sixty miles, finally to establish a 360° patrol round the ships to visual distance, with one Avenger prowling round the carrier herself as she returned to the convoy.

In the interval between launching and landing planes the wind dropped to a three-knot whisper, and a heavy swell rose, producing just about the worst sea and wind conditions for recovery.

The first T.B.F. was in the circuit at half-past eight. After many nerve-racking wave-offs three planes were recovered. The fourth aircraft to come in caught the eighth, and last, arrester wire with its hook and crashed into the barrier and bridge island, badly damaging itself and the barrier. While the wrecked plane was being cleared off the flight deck and down into the hangar on the for'ard lift, the remaining two T.B.F.s were ordered to jettison their depth-charges. They were then brought down safely, watched with fellow feeling by the crews of an R.A.F. Coastal Command Sunderland flying boat and a Liberator which had arrived from their English base to give cover. In the circumstances S.O.E. agreed to suspend all carrier flying until the heavy swell subsided.

The sea remained angry but S.O.E. warned of the presence of U-boats and the possibility of attacks by enemy aircraft. *Bogue* flew off a T.B.F. anti-submarine patrol and established a Combat Air Patrol with two F.4F.s over the convoy. This pleased the bored fighter pilots, but their hoped-for Jabos[5] did not materialize. Task Group 92.3 left the convoy on the night of April 30th and steamed ahead, as on the previous night, 'running interference' along the convoy's track, making for Londonderry and Belfast. *Bogue* was to have H.F./D.F. fitted at Belfast while her air squadron attended a fortnight's course at the R.A.F. Coastal Command Anti-Submarine School at Ballykelly.

Bogue was in dockyard hands on May 8th. To the many survivors from the *Lexington* in her crew this was a special, and a solemn anniversary. It was one year to the day since the great and legendary Lady Lex had gone down in the Coral Sea battle, first engagement in history between two carrier air fleets. They remembered, and told their green shipmates, how she had sent her planes over the 12,000-foot mountains of New Guinea to swoop on the Japs at Salamaua and Lae, sinking three cruisers, how she had in that lovely South Pacific dawn of May 7th launched an armada of seventy-six S.B.D.s, T.B.F.s and F.4F.s to clobber the big new flat-top *Ryukaku* into a sinking wreck with bomb and torpedo. They were less keen to swing the lamp about those flaming minutes just before noon when forty Jap planes found them and put two tinfish and a 1,000-pound bomb into the ship, when they had fought the fires for five hours until, racked by gasoline explosions, the great ship died, and they had to leave her.

Here, in this cold grey northern British port many thousands of miles from the blue and gold Pacific, the little half-merchantman *Bogue* came off badly against the memory of the mighty fighter *Lex* with her eighty planes. Some men found the comparison odious, and despised, or affected to despise, their 'Woolworth' boat. Others put the pride they had had in the old ship into the new, quietly determined that, if they had anything to do with it, she should not disgrace the dead.

Of course, everyone aboard, from the Captain down to the youngest seaman, wanted the ship to score. Three trips with no kills was hard to explain away, especially when you ran into British gobs in the boozer, full of beer and bullshit, and the most bloody-minded were the aircrews.

In fact the passage of H.M.S. *Biter*'s O.N.S.4 to Argentia without loss and with the destruction of two U-boats, one shared by a carrier-borne aircraft, reflected the turn of the tide in Dönitz's spring offensive. A combination of changes in convoy routing, the efforts of surface escorts and long-range land-based aircraft, and the introduction of escort carriers had reduced sinkings in April to fifty-six ships, a total of 327,943 tons, sunk by U-boats, a little over half the figure for bloody March, and eighteen U-boats had been sunk, almost matching the rate of production.

In spite of these losses, however, on May Day sixty U-boats in four groups had gathered south of Cape Farewell in the gap between air coverage from Iceland and New-foundland. Perhaps the unblooded *Bogue* and her frustrated aviators would get their chance there.

[1] Named after Gunner's mate 1st Class Osmond Kelly Ingram, first U.S. Navy enlisted man to be killed in action in World War 1, when jettisoning ammunition to save his ship, the destroyer *Cassin,* from destruction by a torpedo. U.S.S. *Osmond Ingram* was converted to a seaplane tender in 1940, serving as such in the West Indies, the Pacific and the Galapagos Islands, before returning to destroyer duty in 1942.
[2] A patrol round a convoy at visual distance in bad or variable visibility when U-boats were known to be in the vicinity.
[3] A search down a bearing for a specific distance provided by H.F./D.F. with a twenty-minute square search round the position of the U-boat.
[4] A search of a sector where U-boats were suspected, to a specific depth.
[5] Junkers 88s

4. 'Sub is coming up!'

May 21st was a lovely summer's day, an aviator's day, wind fifteen knots from the east, ceiling unlimited, except for a few scattered clouds at 3,000 feet – useful for cover – right up to the roof of the wide blue sky.

Bogue and her screen, flush-deckers *Belknap, George E. Badger, Lea, Greene,* and *Osmond Ingram,* forming Task Group 21.12, were steaming south-by-west, five hundred miles south-east of Cape Farewell. On the horizon was the wispy smoke from the thirty-eight ships of westbound convoy ON184 and the eight destroyers of their close escort. *Bogue* and her D.D.s were on their own, unbloodied hunter-killers getting hungry for a fox, after three blank outings. *Biter* had come in just before they left. The British had been in several firefights with U-boats, had lost two Swordfish and three ships from their convoy and helped surface escorts to sink two subs, all in fog, lashing rain and heavy seas.

It was still fine and clear at five in the afternoon when *Bogue* got ready to launch the last patrol of the day. C.O. Bill Drane's bulky T.B.F. in its duck-egg blue-and-grey camouflage was poised on the catapult for'ard, belly strapped down, tail tied to breaking ring, engine idling, big prop turning lazily, sun glinting off the long canopy and the sphere of the ball turret aft. Forward in the green leather armchair which Avenger pilots enjoyed, the C.O. was checking his clocks. Behind him in his roomy quarters radioman Bob Egger was also looking over his radios, telephones, dials and levers. Down below him in the belly tunnel the .303 ventral gun poked its muzzle aft. Up above it gunner Chester McKinley climbed through the small aperture leading up into the turret, where he wedged himself in beside his big fifty-calibre machine gun, facing

46

the tail in a small cupped seat with his parachute pack for a cushion, legs drawn up, head almost touching the roof of the perspex, in the pre-boosting foetal position. Then the big fourteen-cylinder Wright Cyclone burst into its full deep roar. The plane shook and thrust against the brakes. Drane said, 'Here we go,' and Egger and McKinley braced their heads against their arms. The heavy plane shot forward. All three felt the now familiar tremendous prolonged push, like the shove of a giant hand. Drane's body tried to ram itself through the back of the seat, the turret gunner's head jammed against his arm, his doubled-up legs and feet pushed against the turret. Then he looked up and already the bows of the ship were far astern, and the carrier got smaller and smaller.

They were flying the second leg of their patrol about ten minutes past nine, cruising at 145 knots, when Drane sighted the wake of a U-boat about sixty miles off the convoy's starboard beam, heading towards it.

Drane immediately increased speed to 200 knots, and started to circle so as to approach the submarine from dead ahead to avoid ack-ack from its conning tower guns.

As they approached he called up the carrier. 'U-boats in sight Green nine-, distance eight miles, speed ten knots, course one-two-o True, sixty-two miles from convoy.' It came through loud and clear to the carrier, but Drane could not make out her acknowledgment. As he was speaking he was losing height so as to be at fifty feet when he let go his depth-charges. He noticed then that there was no gunfire from the submarine. Then he was lowering his wheels, cutting his speed down to try and avoid the ricochet which had spoiled Roger Santee's attack. At the release point – still no flak – he could see the U-boat's entire length quite plainly and had a quick impression of a very large boat with a big high conning tower rounded in front. Then the four depth-charges were gone and he stayed on course for some ten seconds to let the gunner and radioman get some photographs.

McKinley in the ball turret had the best view. He saw the

water flung up by the four explosions as one towering mass of white foam and spray. It was right on the U-boat's course, but of the submarine itself there was no sign, and none of them saw it again. If the geyser from the explosion had hidden it, it must have made the fastest crash-dive in the history of submersibles. McKinley saw a swirl where the U-boat had probably gone down, but there were no traces of oil or anything else, although they circled low over the torpex slick for a good two minutes. Drane then climbed to seven thousand feet and tried to contact the ship, which had meanwhile sent the U.S.S. *Osmond Ingram* and H.M.C.S. *St Laurent* to hunt the contact. Drane's aircraft was getting low on fuel. He circled for fifty-five minutes, still trying vainly to get an answer from the ship, but her signals were too weak to be understood. He had to leave the scene, having dropped sea markers, before the destroyers arrived, and had only thirty gallons of fuel left in his tanks when he rolled to a stop on *Bogue*'s flight deck once more.

Osmond Ingram and *St Laurent* arrived at the position of Drane's attack at one o'clock in the middle watch on the morning of the 22nd. They searched throughout the hours of darkness but the U-boats were lying low, and they returned to the *Bogue* group at dawn.

Bogue's westbound ON184 and *Archer*'s eastbound HX239 were now drawing close to one another, the former to the north. At first light weather around HX239 was better. *Archer* left her cosy spot in the centre of the convoy and turned into wind to test conditions for flying. There was still a lot of movement on the ship but it looked promising.

Bogue too found the early morning clear. It rained intermittently, but there was some quite useful broken cloud at 1,500 feet and you could see for fifteen miles. The dawn patrol was launched smoothly into a sixteen-knot wind, with the ship fairly stable on the gentle swell, to recce ahead and around the convoy.

Just after half-past six, Lieutenant (jg) Roger Kuhn's T.B.F. No. 2, radioman M.S. Gos, turret gunner D.A. Smith, was cloud hopping at 140 knots about fifty-five miles south-east of the carrier, when Kuhn's eye caught a dark spot on the surface of the sea about three miles away just off his port bow. Then he saw it was a U-boat[1] surfacing.

He climbed to 3,000 feet and made his report to *Bogue,* then began stalking the target through the cloud, losing height all the time.

When the heavy plane burst out of the cloud the submarine was fully surfaced and immediately opened fire with twenty-millimetre cannon. Kuhn triggered his own light cowl gun and kept on firing in the teeth of the tracer curving up round him. When he was about a quarter of a mile away he pushed over into a dive, gradually increasing the angle, plane and U-boat still firing at each other.

Plunging at 180 knots, still firing, two seconds from release, Kuhn's bullets hit the U-boat's twenty-mm crew and the barrage stopped. At 150 feet he let go three Mark 44 flat-nosed Torpex-filled depth-charges and one Mark 17 T.N.T. They were all set to splash at eighty-foot intervals, C.O. Drane's compromise between BuAer's fifty feet and the one hundred feet R.A.F. Bellkelly had recommended, but Kuhn's dive was steep, and Smith in his ball turret saw them go in about a plane's length apart, to plunge eighty feet and explode in great geysers of white water, the second one almost directly under the submarine's stern. Kuhn flew down the U-boat's side for a few seconds while Gos at the side window of his greenhouse quickly photographed the sub, the D.C.s exploding, the Torpex swirl behind the boat. He saw men run to replace those shot at the twenty-millimetre on the conning tower, and as the T.B.F. climbed away flak came up at them again. He heard Smith's fifty-calibre open up.

Then they were out of range and circling to see what damage their bricks had done. Kuhn had time to study the submarine. It was black, about 200 feet long, with the twenty-millimetre in a sort of big steel basket on the after part of the conning tower, and there was another gun of about three-inch calibre on the deck casing aft.

She couldn't hit them now but still she didn't dive, and

must have been hit. She was moving very slowly, no more than two knots, and virtually spinning in a small circle. Perhaps the second charge had damaged her rudder or screws. As they watched she suddenly blew off a tall spout of compressed air or steam from the hull aft, like a whale sounding. As she circled she began to trail a big bluish oil streak. Then, about half an hour after their attack, there was a sudden flash of intense white light from her stern, about four feet in diameter. Kuhn at first thought it was a signal, that the U-boat was flashing a Tare at him, but the German made no further attempts to communicate, if that was what he was trying to do. The light was much too intense for an Aldis Lamp, anyway, and no submarine would carry a searchlight as big as that.

The sub went on circling for about an hour, making broken, over-lapping white rings on the blue water, then finally stopped moving entirely and began to sink stern-first. At last only the conning tower remained above the surface. A minute later this too disappeared.

By now Kuhn was wondering why no reinforcements had arrived from *Bogue*. In fact the position he had given was wrong, and he was also in a 'null' area, not covered by the ship's radar, so neither the relief T.B.F. nor the convoy escorts H.M.S. *Woodstock* and H.M.C.S. *St Croix,* which had been despatched, could find him.

Lieutenant Dick Rogers was launched at 7.15 a.m. in a Wildcat to assist the relief T.B.F. With no radar in the plane, he had only his fighter pilot's navigation to rely on, but after he had been flying for about fifty minutes he sighted a long, wide wake about eight miles away from him and thirty-five miles ahead of the convoy. He used cloud cover to get in close, then dived at full throttle, but the submarine, Kapitänleutnant Rudolph Bahr's U-305, crash-dived when he was about a mile away from her. He could still see her shape just below the surface but didn't think a shadow was worth wasting fifty-calibre bullets on. He spent five minutes circling round the spot, flew off, came back again half an hour later, circled for a few minutes, saw a swirl and a bluish oil slick, but the U-boat did not reappear, and he was recalled to the ship.

At 10.45 a.m., fifty miles away to the south-east, *Archer*'s Swordfish A flew off on a Cobra patrol to circle HX239. On one of their circuits round the convoy this crew sighted the ships of ON184's screen, about thirty miles to the north-ward. They did not see anything of U-305, which was between them and the westbound convoy, though they were well aware, from the heavy R./T. traffic and the numerous Huff-Duff interceptions of U-boat signals to the northward of their own convoy that ON184 was being shadowed by a large pack.

Rudolph Bahr had stayed down until he was sure Dick Rogers's F.4F. had gone for good, then surfaced and continued his pursuit of the convoy.

He and the lead ships of ON184's screen closed one another head-on, and they were about eighteen miles apart when Rogers's shipmate Stewart Doty, patrolling through a rain squall in a now overcast sky in his T.B.F. No. 6, sighted U-305's long conspicuous wake about nine miles off his port bow.

The young ensign immediately climbed into the cloud layer and began a high-speed approach at 190 knots to overtake the U-boat from astern. He came out of the cloud to find the submarine dead ahead of him, about a mile and a half away. She was on the convoy's starboard bow and with her present course and high speed would intercept in about an hour.

Having eluded one aircraft, Bahr's vigilance had slackened off. Doty could see men on deck and in the conning tower. For some fifteen seconds after he had emerged from cloud they did not see him, then he saw a man run to a twenty-mm gun on the conning tower and open fire. Doty hung on in a long power glide at full speed, then reduced to 200 knots as the submarine grew large under the T.B.F.'s nose, to cut down the possibility of ricochet. In the last few hundred yards he lowered his wheels to slow the bulky machine down even more, then quickly raised them again to

51

clear radioman Pollock's tunnel window for photographs, and pressed the bomb release button, holding steady on the point of aim for a few seconds and pulling the emergency release in case the four D.C.s were still aboard.

To Pollock, clicking the shutter of his K2 down in the tunnel window, the four charges seemed to go off all in the same spot, very close on the U-boat's port quarter. Her stern jerked violently to port and the whole boat lurched to starboard. She slowed to a stop, apparently completely out of control, buffeted about by the waves. About a minute and a half later she slowly settled below the surface. Out of the swirl where she sank the ocean belched up a huge bluish oil bubble about fifty feet in diameter. About two minutes after this, part of the conning tower and some twenty feet of the bow reappeared on an angle of forty-five degrees, then slowly settled again, stern-first, until there were only about eight feet of the bow above the surface. The bow hung there for some twenty seconds, then slid below. Another big blotch of oil rose straight up from the apparently dead, motionless U-boat. T.B.F. 6 circled the spot for fifty minutes. Its excited crew were pretty certain they had made a kill. Then the two spindly stacks of *Osmond Ingram* came in sight, and they flew back to *Bogue*.

In fact U-305 was hurt, but not dead. One of Doty's charges had ruptured the pressure hull, but all was not lost. Bahr dived as deep as he dared and, with *Osmond Ingram* rumbling about distantly above, made temporary repairs, and surfaced again. In the time he had lost, the convoy had passed him by, and he shaped course to overtake it.

But Giles Short believed in reinforcing success, and there were more planes in the air. U-305 got to within twenty-six miles of the convoy's starboard quarter when Lieutenant R.L. Stearns in Compo 9's T.B.F. 5, circling the convoy at 1,200 feet, sighted her long dark shape and white wake ahead.

He opened the throttle and dived towards her. About 750 yards away he fired a burst from his cowl gun. The submarine replied with twenty-millimetre fire. The Avenger held on and Stearns released his four D.C.s in salvo – set shallow, as the U-boat was still fully surfaced, moving slowly ahead. Stearns fired two more bursts with his for'ard .303. His turret gunner fired five rounds from his fifty-calibre, then the gun jammed, but he saw one explosion just off the U-boat's stern. Pilot and radioman saw a second charge go off twenty-five feet from the sub's port bow, the spray hiding the whole fore part of the boat.

The battered U-305 submerged again. Two destroyers hunted her with sonar, which Bahr managed to elude. But this time, after more emergency repairs, he admitted defeat, and limped eastward for Brest.

The battle with the *Donau-Mosel* boats was far from over. Next it was *Archer*'s, and No. 819 Squadron's turn.

When Swordfish F flew off at 1.15 p.m. to relieve Swordfish A, the wind over the deck had sunk to seventeen knots, and F could carry only two depth-charges. After flying out twenty miles on the convoy's port beam her crew sighted two corvettes from ON184's screen. Five minutes later they saw another wake about ten miles astern of the corvettes and on the same course. A closer look revealed a U-boat on the surface, which sighted them and immediately reversed her course. This was Roger Kuhn's old opponent U-468, which was now looking for Convoy HX239.

Using cloud cover, F approached to within two miles ahead of the submarine's new course. As the Stringbag made its pass from dead ahead, the submarine, showing no signs of diving, started to zig-zag. The Swordfish then received a signal from *Archer* to say that a second Swordfish and a Martlet were on their way. The pilot of F remembered his doctrine and waited for reinforcements. Then after remaining on course for about two miles, the U-boat started to dive. The Swordfish immediately dived and made an attack from the bow. Her two charges exploded twenty seconds after the submarine had disappeared, a hundred yards ahead of her departing swirl. A few minutes later the Martlet arrived, followed by the second Swordfish, and the two aircraft remained on the scene until 3.40 p.m., when the destroyer *Onslaught* homed in on a smoke float dropped by the Swordfish. Two Swordfish and one Martlet remained on patrol.

At 5.23 *Bogue's* new Huff-Duff picked up a U-boat transmission twenty-three miles off the convoy's port quarter. Half an hour later Lieutenant (jg) William F. Chamberlain U.S.N.R., with James O. Stine as his radioman and Donald L. Clark in the turret, was launched in the refuelled and rearmed T.B.F. No. 6, flown by Stewart Doty earlier in the day, to chase it up, and the convoy made an evasive change of course. Chamberlain climbed into the cover of cloud at 1,500 feet and headed down the bearing at 160 knots. Seven minutes after take-off he sighted the telltale wake of U-569.

He circled in the broken cumulus to make an undetected approach from the submarine's stern. Diving and increasing speed, he got right down to a hundred feet and let go four T.N.T.s. As the Avenger turned away, Jim Stine got pictures showing men in the sub's conning tower apparently still unaware of the plane's presence. Don Clark got off a burst of fifty-calibre from the turret gun as the U-boat dived, and saw the four charges score a perfect straddle, two on each flank of the boat, forty feet apart.

Chamberlain called up *Bogue,* and ten minutes later Howard Roberts was launched in T.B.F. No. 7 to follow up the attack.

Roberts was on the scene in five minutes, homing in on Chamberlain's smoke bombs, and Chamberlain flew back to *Bogue.* He was over the ship when he heard Roberts' voice in his earphones.

'Sub is coming up!'

Chamberlain immediately turned the T.B.F. round and in a few minutes was back at the scene of action.

The U-boat was steering down the glittering path of the westering sun, and Roberts' plane was diving on her, at a very steep angle. At 600 feet his four D.C.s began to fall away from the plane's belly, one after the other.

Roberts moved quickly, left hand to the trimming tab

wheel, right hand pulling on the stick, left foot pushing on the rudder bar. The Avenger was down to a hundred feet before it pulled up and round to port, ending up at about 800 feet, nose high and almost stalling. The centrifugal force after pull-out pushed the radioman's camera away from the tail window but he and the turret gunner both saw spray rise on either side of the submarine's stern and form an arch over her hull.

U-569 rose out of the water, sank, rose again, this time on its side, sank again and came up for the third time, now on an even keel.

As men started leaping up out of the conning tower hatch and into the sea, Roberts' turret gunner and Don Clark in Chamberlain's T.B.F. opened up on them, to try to drive them back into the boat and thus be unwilling to open the sea cocks. From the beginning of the war escort commanders had been urged to make every effort to capture a U-boat intact, for its valuable technology, signals, orders and code books – especially its Enigma machine and set of daily rotor settings.

The hail of fifty-calibre seemed to be having the desired effect. No more heads appeared out of the conning tower hatch, and the submarine seemed to have got some buoyancy on her stern and was staying up.

Then the T.B.F.s ran out of ammunition. While the turret gunners were changing their ammunition cans about thirty men came out on the conning tower and some of them waved a white table cloth.

The T.B.F. gunners opened up again. Some of the submariners dropped back down the hatch, others jumped overboard with life jackets on. Those still on the conning tower waved the improvised white flag again. With their last few rounds the Avenger gunners drove them back through the hatch.

The two planes circled impotently, waiting for more reinforcements. Then the raking flush-deck and four thin funnels of H.M.C.S *St Laurent,* foaming white at her narrow, knife-like bows, were sighted. The old destroyer slowed and stopped within fifty feet of the U-boat's beam, boarding party ready to go.

There were still some dozen men on board the submarine. One of them was the Engineer Officer, who slipped below and opened the flood valves. The submarine began to sink, and in a few minutes was gone. The Canadians hauled twenty-four survivors out of what was by now a very rough sea.

U-569 would have made a glittering prize, but at least she had been destroyed. She was the first U-boat to be sunk by aircraft from an auxiliary aircraft carrier. The Americans had won that particular race.

Meanwhile U-218 had picked up *Archer*'s convoy, HX239, 700 miles north of Flores in the Azores, and informed Dönitz. Most of the *Donau-Mosel* group, which had never had time to combine properly anyway, were scattered and out of touch. The only boat which might have a chance of success was Kapitänleutnant Karl Schroeter's U-752, and he was directed towards HX239.

Schroeter's two previous patrols had been barren, and he was keen to make a killing. He pressed on at full speed throughout the night, and just before dawn signalled to U-boat Headquarters in Berlin. H.M.S. *Keppel*'s Huff-Duff intercepted the signal and produced a range and bearing. Commander Evans went a-hunting at full speed and asked Streamline Robertson in *Archer* to fly off patrols to search a fifty-mile sector round the quarter. Two Stringbags obliged him, but found nothing. A Very Long Range Liberator which was weaving to and fro ten miles ahead of the convoy, alerted for U-boats, was also drawing a blank. Then H.F./D.F. came up with another range and bearing, the Liberator attacked the U-boat which it found at the end of the track, and the destroyer *Onslaught* was diverted to the scene.

At eight o'clock Swordfish F, a busy aircraft, took off with orders to patrol right round the convoy's port flank. A quarter of an hour after she had left the deck, *Archer* received good H.F./D.F. bearings from *Pelican* and *Faulk-*

nor, producing a good fix on the convoy's port quarter at a range of twenty miles, hauled the Stringbag back to the ship and packed it off to investigate.

At 8.55 p.m. F sighted a U-boat on the surface almost directly ahead making about ten knots. The Swordfish climbed into the cloud base and crept closer. The U-boat dived, but visibility was good, and F's crew could clearly see the sharply white feather trailing from her periscope, which was trained on the Liberator circling to the northward. At five past nine the Swordfish pushed over and made its attack. The observer and air gunner saw the periscope feather pass between the two centre bursts of their stick of four D.C.s. The Swordfish remained circling round the spot but saw no signs of a score.

At 9.15 p.m. Swordfish G and Martlet B took off from *Archer* to follow up F's attack. Twenty minutes later both crews were looking out for signs of Swordfish F when they sighted a U-boat fine on their starboard bow, heading straight towards them, its foaming wake indicating a good twelve knots. This one was an unusual off-white colour, with a particularly large conning tower. It was a milch cow heading for a refuelling rendezvous.

There was no cloud cover and both aircraft attacked at once. The U-boat lookouts saw them, she turned hard-a-starboard and began to dive. The Martlet was just in time to fire eight hundred rounds of fifty-calibre at the stern gratings and the after end of the conning tower.

Swordfish G flew over the swirl a few seconds after the submarine had disappeared. The first depth-charge fell on the edge of the swirl and the remaining three to starboard of the U-boat's track.

At 9.58 p.m. Swordfish B, armed with eight of the new British rocket projectiles, was flown off with orders to circle the port quarter of the convoy and await instructions.

Twenty minutes later this Swordfish, pilot Sub-Lieutenant Harry Horrocks R.N.V.R., who had distinguished himself flying an Albacore T.S.R. from Malta against the Italian Fleet, observer Sub-Lieutenant W.W.

Noel Balkwill R.N.V.R., telegraphist-air-gunner Leading Naval Airman John W. Wick R.N., was flying at 1,500 feet when a U-boat was sighted at a distance of about ten miles. It was Schroeter's U-752, heading at fifteen knots for the convoy.

Horrocks immediately turned to port into cloud cover. Balkwill passed him a course of 195°, which he calculated would take them into a good position for a surprise attack.

Horrocks flew on blind for four and a half minutes, then Balkwill said, 'Break cloud now, Harry. She ought to be dead ahead, range just over a mile.'

The Stringbag nosed out of the cumulus at 1,500 feet and there she was, fine under their port bow, about a mile away. Horrocks dived in a copybook Macrihanish[2] attack, angle of dive 20°, target held steady in the Swordfish's old ring-and-bead gunsight.

He fired the first pair of R.P.s at eight hundred yards. They lanced into the water about 150 yards short of the unsuspecting U-boat. Schroeter hastily triggered off the squawking klaxon and the sub's bows plunged in a crash-dive.

Four hundred yards. . .Horrocks fired the second salvo. The two small splashes went up thirty yards short of the conning tower. Three hundred yards. . .The third pair shot on firework trails of flame from their launching rails under the lower wings. . .Just abaft the conning tower, ten feet short.

The U-boat was tilted steeply, only her stern clear of the water, when the fourth, and last, pair of R.P.s scored a bullseye.

Two 25-pound solid heads, fired at 200 yards, smashed through the submarine's hull on the waterline about twenty feet ahead of the rudders.

U-752 continued downwards at the same steep angle for a few minutes, then gradually rose to an even trim and surfaced. It began to circle to port, gushing oil. The conning tower hatch opened, men leapt out and rushed to man the twenty-mm gun in the rear of the conning tower. Schroeter was going to make a fight of it. If he could not bag a merchantman or an escort, he might still be able to nail the victorious Swordfish.

Horrocks opened the range and requested *Archer* for fighter assistance. He had shot down a Macchi fighter in the Mediterranean with the little front gun of a T.S.R., but he saw no point in tackling a twenty-mm cannon in a slow-diving Stringbag if he had better fire power on call.

The pilot of Martlet B, on his way back to the ship from the scene of Swordfish G's attack, heard Horrocks' call, turned back, and in not more than a minute was over the damaged U-752. He fired his remaining 600 rounds of fifty-calibre in one burst into the conning tower, killing Schroeter. The twenty-mm crew fired a few rounds at the Martlet, then tumbled down the conning tower hatch. The fighter flew over to the destroyer *Escapade*, which the pilot had sighted about ten miles away, and directed her towards the U-boat.

At 10.50 p.m. the submarine's crew started to come up on deck, and took to the water as the boat sank beneath them, taking the ambitious Schroeter's body with her on her deep six. *Escapade* arrived a few minutes later and picked up thirteen survivors. Ten more men were rescued some hours later by U-91. Her report made gloomy reading in Brest and Berlin. *Archer*'s U-boat was the first to be sunk by an auxiliary carrier's aircraft using R.P.s, and Harry Horrocks had dealt the death blow to the spring offensive.

[1] U-468
[2] Royal Naval Air Station in Scotland.

5. 'To you, Lily Marlene. . .'

'The situation in the North Atlantic now forces a temporary shift of operations to areas less endangered by aircraft,' signalled Admiral Dönitz on May 24th to all his U-boat captains.

Forty-five merchant ships were sunk in May by U-boats, eleven fewer than in April's good returns, and these were almost balanced, ship for ship, by the forty-one U-boats destroyed during the month. During the whole period of the U-boat spring offensive, February-May, only two ships were sunk in convoy in the Atlantic while air escort was present.

Increasing help for the convoys was coming from the cryptanalysts of the British Government Code and Cipher School housed in a mansion at Bletchley Park in Buckinghamshire, and from Admiralty Cipher specialists. Signals in the German Enigma codes from various commands were picked up by listening posts and relayed to Bletchley Park, where a machine known familiarly as The Bomb would decode them. Warnings of some important enemy movements by land and sea had been picked up in this way, though the Allies had not always had the means to act upon them.

Anticipating U-boat movements had been greatly helped by the capture of an Enigma coding-decoding machine and a set of daily rotor settings from U-110, commanded by Kapitänleutnant Lemp, notorious for sinking the liner *Athenia* just after the outbreak of war. With this and coding documents captured from the weather ship *Munchen* the cryptanalysts were able to crack the *Kriegsmarine* M-Home Waters, or Hydra, code used for radio communication with U-boats. In February 1942 the Germans, realising that Hydra had been broken, replaced it with the new Triton code for messages to and from U-boats, which Bletchley struggled for several months to crack, though Hydra was still in use by escort vessels, and some information on U-boat strength and concentration was still available. The break-through was finally made in December 1942.

Secret teleprinter lines from Bletchley Park would deliver Special Intelligence, or Ultra, derived from decoded signals passed between U-boats and U-boat headquarters in Brest or Berlin, to the Admiralty, and with increasing frequency it was becoming possible to warn convoys and escort commanders of the positions of U-boat concentrations, and enable Commander Roger Winn's Submarine Tracking Room to re-route them clear of the danger zone. Sometimes, when an Enigma signal from a submarine could not actually be decoded in time, it was possible, even for the ship whose H.F./D.F. had picked up the signal, to tell from the particular pattern whether the U-boat was merely reporting its position or shadowing a convoy.

Sometimes Ultra had become inaccurate and misleading by the time escort and convoy commanders received it. In June 1943 British Intelligence realised that the Germans had cracked the British Naval code used to brief convoys on the location of U-boats. The codes were changed at once, and the Germans never cracked the new ones. But local conditions often changed, and the escorts had to fall back on the faithful Huff-Duff, which was the main means of locating U-boats by their signals, and the electronic whiskers of radar and sonar, as well as the alertness of their aircrews and lookouts.

The signal of May 24th by the German Commander-in-Chief And Admiral Of Submarines admitted defeat on the America-UK convoy routes. The 'areas less endangered by aircraft' were the Central and South Atlantic and the Indian Ocean.

The Central Atlantic was the U.S. Navy's responsibility, Through this vast blue desert of water steamed big convoys of troopships, tankers and freighters heading for Gibraltar, North Africa and Malta, fattening the build-up for the scheduled invasion of Sicily in July and Italy in September.

Until now they, like the earlier North Atlantic convoys, had had no air cover, and with the main U-boat blitzkreig being mounted in the north, had made do without it. Delicate negotiations were still going on between the British and Dr Salazar, Prime Minister and Dictator of Portugal on the use of the Azores for a British air base. Salazar would not treat with the Americans, and Admiral Ingersoll had wanted to send the first U.S. Navy escort carriers on these central routes. But with the British North Atlantic convoys taking such a beating, and in the continued absence of British carriers, he had been forced to divert *Bogue* there to help out.

Meanwhile, the next of her class, Captain Isbell's U.S.S. *Card*[1], was ready for duty in the Central Atlantic. Arnold Jay Isbell was an Iowan, like Giles Short. He was forty-four, and was being groomed for flag rank. At Annapolis 'Buster' Isbell had excelled in athletics, football, wrestling, and lacrosse, and had a brilliant Service record. He graduated as a Naval Aviator in 1924. There followed a year with the catapult unit in the battleship *Tennessee,* two years at the Postgraduate School for Aviation Ordnance Engineering, two years with Torpedo Squadron 1B in the *Lexington,* two years of shore duty in the Bureau of Ordnance, a year fitting out and flying from the new Fleet carrier *Ranger,* two years as Gunnery Officer to Commander Aircraft, Battle Force, in *Saratoga.* After two years as an instructor at Pensacola, in May 1939 he was given command of Patrol Squadron 54 at Norfolk, Virginia, and won the Air Medal while surveying future U.S. bases. 'Skilfully manoeuvering his plane' the citation read, 'while en route in an attempt to evade a hurricane. . .he was finally forced by exceptionally strong headwinds to effect a night landing on Prince Edward Island. Menaced by the hurricane centre, which was about twenty miles distant, he took off before daylight in fog and violent winds and reached his destination without mishap. Successfully completing the inspection tour over uninhabited regions and seacoast areas, he returned to carry out the first aerial survey ever made of Argentia, Newfoundland. . .' Service with patrol wings on North Atlantic convoy escort was followed by command of the *Card*. Isbell was the complete naval aviator.

When *Card* finished her shakedown cruise in early May the situation up north had improved sufficiently for her to be sent with the U.S.–Gibraltar convoy U.G.S.8A. There was a big meeting of ships off the Virginia Capes, with *Card* and her D.D.s *Bristol*, *Ludlow* and *Woolsey*, and nine close escorts riding herd on seventy-eight merchantmen and twelve tank-landing craft.

Ingersoll now favoured the idea of using his escort carriers as the nuclei of detached Support Groups, after the *Biter,* and later the *Bogue* model, which, with numbers still limited, could cover more than one convoy at once and go where the U-boats were concentrated, but with *Card* so green and vulnerable she was hidden in the middle of the merchant ships, with the Avengers of Lieutenant-Commander Carl E. Jones's Composite Squadron 1 giving air cover.

The T.B.F.s not only flew patrols all day and every day, but Isbell, a great sailor and aviator, starred commander and aviation expert, had them operating on moonlit nights as well. There were no U-boats in these water yet, but they practised hard.

When fifty-one more merchantmen and ten extra escorts joined off the Pillars of Hercules, U.G.S.8A became in tonnage the biggest convoy in history. U.S.A.A.F. Liberators from Port Lyautey, Morocco, took over from *Card*'s T.B.F.s, and the carrier group switched to westbound Convoy G.U.S.8. Troopships which had brought G.I.s to the Mediterranean were returning with German prisoners of war. Tanned Afrika Korps tankers were astonished to sail through an empty, peaceful ocean. Stuffed with Göbbels' propaganda, they were wryly resigned to being sunk by one of their own submarines.

The middle sea was not empty for long. On May 26th the Grand Admiral ordered the *Trutz* Group of seventeen

U-boats to form a north-south barrier down the 43rd line of longitude with the northernmost boat patrolling on the latitude of New York and the Azores, and the southernmost on the lattitude of Bermuda and Madeira. This order was not locked in Enigma for long. Washington got it through Bletchley and the Admiralty, and the U-boat battle simply shifted south.

Bogue was ordered to leave Argentia and come south to provide *offensive* support for Convoys G.U.S.7A, U.G.S.9 and Flight 10 against the *Trutz* line. No longer would Giles Short have to ask local permission to 'run interference.' Now quarterback Royal Ingersoll had called that very play. Ingersoll was able to move *Bogue* from the bloody seas off Cape Farewell with an easier mind now that the British were putting their new M.A.C.-ships on the northern convoy routes. On May 29th the first Merchant Aircraft Carrier, the grainer *Empire MacAlpine,* sailed from Britain with Convoy O.N.S.9 for Halifax, Nova Scotia, four Swordfish in her hangar.

Bogue left Argentia as the flagship of Task Group 21.12 on May 30th with her screen, four-pipers *Clemson,*[2] *George E. Badger, Greene* and *Osmond Ingram,* the latter three old friends by now.

Drane's T.B.F. crews were looking forward to better flying weather as a welcome change from the rain and rough seas of northern waters. Short, now his own man, had a complex commitment. With his small group he had to cover both the areas where the maximum concentrations of U-boats were likely and those in the vicinity of the most endangered convoys, placing himself in the densest U-boat gatherings, which were constantly changing, but in positions relative to the convoys so that he could give help to them, and continue operating to the absolute limits which logistics allowed. Here, fuel for his destroyers was the biggest problem. He decided that Task Group 21.12 must be as self-supporting as possible. *Bogue* would top off the D.D.s whenever practicable. Any fuel they could get from convoy oilers was a bonus. The bottom line was that they must be maintained with enough fuel on board to enable them to reach port or intercept a convoy in the event of *Bogue* being sunk.

When the Group reached its first patrol station 300 miles to the south-sou'-east of Argentia on June 1st the weather was disappointingly bad, with fog, cloud, and visibility no more than two miles. But by eleven-thirty the visibility had opened up to some fifteen miles, with scattered stratus cloud between 3,000 and 5,000 feet, and a brisk north-easterly blowing at twenty knots, veering round into the west at noon, the sea light with a moderate swell. At 5.30 p.m. a T.B.F. was catapulted off to search ahead and on the port bow for seventy-five miles, with the possibility of sighting one of the most northerly *Trutz* boats at the limit of the patrol. The T.B.F. was recovered at half-past seven with nothing to report.

By evening *Bogue* had reached the latitudes of the *Trutz* line and was in the north-west sector of a 300 mile circle within which the U-boat group was concentrated. The westbound convoy G.U.S.7A was uncomfortably close to the southern end of the *Trutz* line, U.G.S.9 and Flight 10 a good 400 miles to the west. Short debated whether to veer east towards the centre of the circle of U-boat concentration, then take a southerly course and aim to be in a good position to help the eastbound U.G.S.9, if necessary, later, or continue on a southerly course through the western part of the circle towards the area where U.G.S.9 and G.U.S.7A would pass close to one another, in which case he would be able to give direct support to either convoy, or both, on the morning of June 3rd. As G.U.S.7A seemed to be in more imminent danger of attack, he decided on the second alternative. This plan also gave an opportunity of fuelling the escorts. So *Bogue* carried on south, with the five ships' combined radar, sonar and aircraft sweeping a path 120 miles wide through the western part of the *Trutz* hunting grounds, and *Bogue* topping up the thirsty destroyers as they went.

The weather was good all through the 2nd, and patrols

were flown all day. As June 3rd dawned it looked as if
G.U.S.7A was in the clear, and Short thought about turning
east soon and steaming slightly ahead of U.S.G.9 to try and
flush any U-boats lying ahead of the eastbound convoy.
First he satisfied himself that the Flight 10 convoy was safe
and sound by sending a T.B.F. to pick it up to the west and
keep it in sight for a while. Then during the night he altered
course to the north-east, looking for trouble at what he
thought must be the centre of the pack.

Weather was good on the 4th, with visibility twenty miles.
Flying started at 8. a.m. with patrols ahead and around the
ship. At 6.15 in the evening five T.B.F.s of E Flight were
launched to search a wide sector from north to south.

Half an hour later the T.B.F.s of Lieutenant (jg) Harry
Fryatt, with O.L. Scholl as radioman and H.E. Dokken as
turret gunner, and Lieutenant E.W. Biros, radioman L.G.
Murray, gunner L.E. Emmitt, were flying together at 2,500
feet investigating a suggestion by Huff-Duff, Fryatt slightly
behind and to the right of Biros, when Fryatt saw a U-boat
broad on his starboard bow, about a mile off. He signalled
to Biros and nosed over to attack from the U-boat's stern.
Biros followed him down.

There was no flak, and Fryatt saw astonished, frightened
faces turned towards the roaring plane from the conning
tower. He went so low that they must have wondered
whether he was going to pull out, and released his D.C.s in
salvo. Scholl took pictures as they splashed and exploded in
line with the conning tower, ten feet apart, Dokken fired a
burst from his fifty-calibre at the men in the conning tower.
The sub turned violently to starboard when Fryatt's D.C.s
went off, and Biros had to swerve in his dive to get her back
in his sights. His charges seemed to go in and explode in the
spray from Fryatt's, and debris flew through the air. The
submarine's bow reared up about five feet out of the water
just as the spray cleared, then she sank quickly stern-first.

At 7.15 p.m. Ensign Ted Hodgson's Avenger was on a
return leg of his regular patrol when he saw 'a huge grey
object on the surface' about three miles dead ahead which

turned into a surfaced U-boat on the same southerly course as his own, ten miles from Convoy Flight 10 and fifty miles from *Bogue* and T.G.21.12.

He immediately dived to the attack and, with no sign of any opposition from the submarine's guns, had time and leisure to level off at fifty feet and drop his D.C.s in level flight. Then a twenty-mm gun opened up on them. Hodgson made a circuit of the sub on the starboard tack so that radioman Al Pacyna could take photographs of the spray-blown U-boat gleaming in the sun and the glittering patch of sea around her pocked by turret gunner Morrison's bullets, as he returned the U-boat's fire. Then Hodgson roared low over the sub, firing on it with his thirty-calibre cowl gun. As he circled for another strafing run the U-boat made what looked like a normal dive and disappeared, leaving a swirl.

Meanwhile a more stubborn battle was developing closer to the task group. Alert radioman Wojcik in Lieutenant (jg) Bill Fowler's T.B.F. sighted a submarine twenty-five miles from *Bogue,* the first time in fourteen U-boat sightings by Compo 9's planes that the target had been seen first by a radioman, who was not ideally placed to sight one, housed as he was right over the wing.

Fowler immediately pushed over into a diving run to approach from out of the strong sun on the U-boat's port quarter, but when he reached the release point he felt that the plane was going too fast for accuracy so, as there was no flak, he pulled out to go round again. The sub's guns opened fire as he flew over it and continued to put up a hot and heavy barrage as he dived on his second run. Only two depth-charges left the plane, although he hit the emergency release. They splashed in a few feet off the starboard bow of the submarine, silvery-grey in the sunlight. She either would not or could not submerge, but circled slowly, down at the stern, then gradually began to pick up speed.

Meanwhile Bill Drane had been launched from *Bogue* to follow up Fowler's attack. He and his turret gunner C.T. McKinley both sighted the sub's circular wake at about the same time, ten minutes after leaving the ship.

Drane turned immediately towards the enemy and dived on her port quarter. Her cannoneer was very good, and the T.B.F. shook as the shells tore past the fuselage and canopy. Fowler dived to try to divert the gunners while Drane came in, and had his I.F.F. aerial shot away.

Drane's charges raked the U-boat's stern. She came out of her perpetual circle, steered straight for 200 yards and dived at a sharp angle. The T.B.F.s circled for some ten minutes and were then recalled by the ship. Everyone in the two aircraft considered that the U-boat had been sunk, though there had been no signs of damage. In fact the aggressive U-641 got away.

Aboard the carrier the positions of all the U-boats attacked were plotted, and Short found that he had there the skeleton of a patrol line extending almost exactly north-south. If there were any more boats out there to the south of those plotted, U.G.S.9 would very likely run into them next day, and Short intended to send his T.B.F.s out to find them in the morning. Meanwhile, after Drane and Fowler had been recovered at dusk, he retired westward, then doubled back at dawn to resume searching in the area of the previous evening's attacks before continuing on south towards the convoy.

At half-past seven in the morning five T.B.F.s and one F.4F were brought up from the hangar and the first plane ranged on the catapult, its crew briefed to search a wide arc to port of the carrier. By eight o'clock they were all out of sight of the ship.

Lieutenant Alex McAuslan's T.B.F. had been paired with Ensign Dick Rogers' F.4F in case they met another gun-slinger like U-641. They were on a return leg to the ship when at ten minutes to nine McAuslan reported sighting a submarine heading west at high speed.

McAuslan signalled to Rogers to strafe the U-boat and clear her decks. Rogers peeled off at once, dived flat-out, and bored in on the sub's port quarter, firing with his six big fifties. The U-boat's gunners started firing on him from long range but when he opened fire four or five men in the conning tower threw up their arms and fell into the water, and the guns were silent.

As Rogers came back to strafe again the submarine suddenly turned hard-a-starboard, and he found himself heading at twenty-five feet for her port beam. The tubby Wildcat roared over the sub's conning tower, its belly almost scraping the periscope standard, banked and did another beat-up from the opposite beam. The fire in the conning tower was out by now, but no-one had appeared on deck to replace the dead gunners, so Rogers hauled off for McAuslan to make his bombing run.

The T.B.F. dived out of the sun on the U-boat's port bow, cowl gun rattling, and threw its D.C.s from a hundred feet. Radioman Ellingsworth and turret gunner McLemore saw the four charges straddle the enemy halfway between her bow and conning tower, the first very close on the port side, the others going over in line. In the cascading spray the submarine tilted backwards below the water, bows high in the air, and Rogers' fighter bored in again, its bullets zipping over the water to clang off the mottled grey hull and race up the conning tower.

McAuslan hung around for another fifty-five minutes, watching the slow, inexorable spread of the huge bluish oil slick which rose to the surface, not fanning out as it would have done behind a boat which still lived and had way on her, but just seeping steadily straight upwards from the deep where her bows had disappeared. This foul venal haemorrhage marked the destruction of U-217 and the grave of her crew.

Still probing for the southern limit of the *Trutz* line, *Bogue*'s H.F./D.F. picked up a possible U-boat signal to the southward of the one previously attacked, but the T.B.F.s could not find any more targets that afternoon, and Short decided to continue on to the southward, make direct contact with U.G.S.9 and give it close cover that evening and the following day.

T.G.21.12 steamed on with the convoy throughout the 6th, flying off patrols but making no contacts. Short thought they had probably got past the southern end of the *Trutz* line, leaving the ten boats remaining in the pack away to the north-west, but he could not be sure that they had not been spotted. The U-boat skippers had become very mean with their signals to H.Q. and they could well be heading south or south-westward for the convoy. He left the convoy that evening and steered a north-westerly course so that his T.B.F.s could search in that direction at dawn, then doubled back eastward when they found the ocean bare, sweeping along the 30th parallel, watching the whole port flank of the convoy with his T.B.F.s.

The next day, June 7th, also passed peacefully, largely because the *Trutz* boats were heading north-west to refuel from the milch cow U-488. Short intercepted the convoy on the 8th, making a thorough search to the northward and round the flank as they were joining U.G.S.9, as he still feared that submarines might be trailing the convoy on its port quarter or rear. Huff-Duff was busier now, and he was concerned to keep the subs down and stop them from overtaking and forming concentrations which could grow into a pack attack on the convoy. Some of the latest transmissions were probably aircraft sighting reports. The enemy must know where they were, but they could only get together on the surface.

The 8th was clear and calm, with a glassy sea. If there was a periscope feather within range Drane's pilots would see it, though the cautious U-boat skippers were not about to offer them much.

The forenoon passed, and *Trutz* had shown no sign. Then at three o'clock H.F./D.F. picked up a transmission to the south-west. Lieutenant Balliett's T.B.F. was launched to investigate.

He found nothing on the given bearing and proceeded on regular anti-submarine patrol. At five o'clock Balliett was ten miles to the south of the convoy when the ship called him up and ordered him to rejoin in twenty-five minutes. He had just finished acknowledging the message when his radioman Jack Finch, who was keeping a lookout down in

70

the rear window in the belly, shouted,

'Ship on port beam. . .about two miles! Looks too big for a sub, Skipper. What the hell is it?'

Balliett took a look. It was certainly big, at least 300 feet long, and fast, doing a good eighteen or twenty knots and leaving a long, wide, white wake. 'I think it's a destroyer.' But when they got closer they could see it was a submarine, bigger than they had ever seen before.

The U-boat was heading directly for the convoy. Balliett circled to attack from the sun, and had to make a very steep dive to reach the sub from where he was at 5,500 feet. When the Avenger was down to 1,000 feet and about 1,000 yards from the U-boat, guns in her conning tower opened fire, and a lot of unusually thick tracer started to scrape their paint. Balliett held on, lowered his wheels to steady up, and let go his four D.C.s at 200 feet. They straddled the boat midway between stern and conning tower. The third charge exploded right underneath the hull, lifted the stern fifteen feet in the air and blew men off the conning tower into the water.

Balliett circled and made another run to strafe and take pictures. Goodwin in the turret got off a good long burst. The men in the water swam frantically away from the boat to escape his first bullets. Then he hit their reliefs at the twenty-millimetre. The guns fell silent, but the sub did not dive, presumably damaged in a vital place. Balliett stayed with her, circling.

Bill Fowler was launched at 5.36 p.m. to relieve Balliett, followed off the catapult by Lieutenant Fogde's T.B.F. and Lieutenant Phil Perabo's F.4F.

Fowler sighted Balliett's Avenger and their quarry ten minutes after launching. He reported the submarine now steady on a southerly course.

U-758's Kapitänleutnant Helmut Manseck was a hard man, and far from giving up. Balliett's D.C.s had shaken them up somewhat, but the Kapitänleutnant had no intention of diving and giving up his chance of a shot at the convoy. If the Americans tried again he would fight it out.

71

Fowler dived to attack on the U-boat's starboard quarter. After Balliett's report of the accuracy of these German gunners, he tried now to cut down the odds by taking evasive action as he came in, swooping back and forth, diving and climbing.

Manseck, with fresh guns' crews, held his fire until the Avenger was about 250 yards off and would have to steady up ready to release its D.C.s, then opened up with all his conning tower weapons. There seemed to be at least two heavy-calibre cannon – twenty-mm or bigger – and three or four smaller guns. Solid sheets of tracer seemed to fan out from the conning tower. Machine-gun bullets pinged off the diving plane's metal flanks, explosive shells burst around it.

They were too accurate to miss. The cowling and engine were hit, one cylinder holed, air intake lines and an oil line cut. Shells tore off the tip of the tailplane, punched a big hole in the starboard wing and punctured the tyre on the starboard wheel, and another tore through the bomb bay, mercifully not hitting the depth-charges but wounding radioman Wojcik in the foot with jagged splinters, putting him out of action for the time.

Fowler knew they were badly hit but he pressed home his attack and hit the release button at a hundred feet. There was a fault, and only three D.C.s went down, but they exploded under the U-boat's stern. Then he headed straight for the ship. The cockpit was full of smoke and the engine leaking oil badly, and with the obvious fire hazard he flew low at one hundred feet. Even though a forced landing into the sea seemed imminent, turret gunner Bucholtz got down into the rear cockpit and, working without a safety belt, not only tended the injured Wojcik but took over his duties as well until he felt fit enough to resume, and they reached the ship safely.

Meanwhile Fogde's T.B.F. had arrived over the U-758. Knowing how roughly Balliett and particularly Fowler had been handled, he waited for Perabo, who had been cata-pulted some minutes after him, to come along and deal with the gunners. The F.4F. did not appear for another twenty-five minutes, with Fogde impatiently circling. Balliett, with only twenty gallons of petrol left, returned to the ship, where he landed with empty tanks. When Perabo did arrive he immediately dived on the sub, taking no notice of the very heavy flak, his own fifty-calibres blazing, and hitting in and around the conning tower, silencing the gunfire.

Perabo made two more strafing attacks, with no opposition from the U-boat's guns. As Fogde dived to attack, the submarine began to go down. Fogde's D.C.s exploded to starboard of the swirl where she had been, and Falwell in the turret fired at the shape below the surface.

About eight minutes after the U-boat dived a big air bubble rose about half a mile ahead of the swirl. Some 150 yards further on the U-boat's bows rose high out of the water, hung there for a moment, then the whole boat surfaced, the guns were manned again, and opened up the heaviest fire yet experienced on the circling planes. Fogde counted as many as twenty black bursts of powder erupting at the same time, and thought that the submarine must be using twenty-mm guns in twin mounts plus some fifty-calibre machine guns. Balliett felt she might have a pom-pom. She was certainly a fighting boat.

The submarine now ran on the surface for about ten minutes, trailing oil, with Perabo's Wildcat strafing her again twice. She went about a quarter of a mile, then disappeared slowly beneath the surface on an even keel. There was no swirl, but oil bubbles continued to rise.

The cocky young Compo 9 pilots had already signalled *Bogue* that no assistance would be needed from the salt-horse Navy, and *Badger*, *Greene* and *Osmond Ingram*, which had been heading for the battle, were recalled. But there were now only four serviceable T.B.F.s available, with the evening patrol ahead and round the convoy still to put up, and to Drane's frustration Short refused to send any of these spoken-for machines to pursue the belligerent *unterseeboot*. He despatched Yancey's *Clemson* instead.

Down below, U-758 was still very much alive, though Manseck was glad of the suddenly bare sky and the silence from above. For forty minutes he glided along, making minor repairs, and adjusting the trim to compensate for the flooded tank ruptured by one of the depth-charges, then he heard the growing rumble of *Clemson*'s engines above him. The destroyer made an attack, which kept U-758 down until midnight. Then she came up to breathe and recharge, and in the early hours of June 9th stole away homewards to fight another day.

Compo 9's evening patrol on the 8th sighted no U-boats ahead or flanking the convoy, but the onset of dusk, which drove them back to the ship, was the time of the day when U-boats came up out of the depths to send Enigma, and the spate of signals suggested that a pack could be forming ahead to attack on the night of the 9th or 10th. *Bogue*'s aircraft tracked down every H.F./D.F. bearing received during those nights and patrolled out to seventy miles from beam to beam ahead, thirty miles astern, but their searches led to nothing, and the ships of the task group could not leave the vicinity of the convoy yet to add their radar and sonar to the hunt. All this was accomplished with depleted numbers of aircraft due to the wear and tear of combat and intensive flying, and increasingly tired aircrews. Lieutenant Puckett's F.4F. cracked up on landing on the 10th, and Stewart Doty made a heavy landing with hydraulic trouble.

Then, before dusk on the 10th, the expected Army Liberator from Morocco arrived over the convoy. As soon as the dusk patrol had been recovered the task group left the convoy and turned back westward along the 30th parallel towards the centre of the reported concentration of U-boats, hoping to spring their patrol line.

On June 11th *Bogue* maintained a good position relative to the centres of estimated concentrations. The submarines seemed very alert to the dangers of aircraft, either remaining submerged or surfacing just long enough to transmit a brief message. Anyway, they were not to be found.

The hunt began again at dawn on June 12th. The first Avenger was launched a few minutes before seven o'clock, and four T.B.F.s, each paired with a fighter, between them covered a broad sector seventy miles deep round the bow and the reciprocating sector out to thirty-five miles astern, with a patrol round the convoy at visual distance. Nothing was stirring this morning. At noon four T.B.F.s and three Wildcats were catapulted on a similar programme, with a broader, beam-to-beam coverage ahead, but at only half the range.

Half an hour after launching, Biros' Avenger returned with generator trouble. Scattered all round the compass the other six vigilant Grummans flew through a clear, cloudless day with the sun glittering off a smooth, polished sea.

At a quarter to two Lieutenant Stearns' T.B.F. No. 12 and its partner Lieutenant (jg) R.J. Johnson's F.4F. were twenty miles out on the carrier's starboard quarter when Stearns sighted a surfaced submarine lying stopped in the water about a mile ahead of them to starboard.

They had found a milch cow, Kapitänleutnant Czygan's big 1,600-ton U-118, a combination minelayer-supply boat from the 12th Flotilla at Bordeaux. Built, like so many other German submarines, in the Germania yard at Kiel, she had commissioned on December 8th 1941, but did not leave Kiel for her first operational patrol until September 1942, when she operated as a supply boat west of Madeira. She arrived at Lorient at the end of October 1942 and left on her second patrol in mid-November to work as a milch cow in pastures round the Azores. She returned to Lorient in mid-December but air raids drove her out and she took refuge at Brest, leaving there for her third patrol on January 25th 1943.

During the first week of February she laid mines across the mouth of the Straits of Gibraltar between Spanish Tarifa and Tangier on the African side, and refuelled eight other U-boats off the Azores. She was back in Bordeaux on February 28th, and her crew rotated for leave, one week with the boat on repair and maintenance, one week's local leave, and one week in Germany. In the bars of Bordeaux they sang,

'If we should sink to the ocean floor

We still shall walk to the nearest shore,
To you, Lily Marlene,
To you, Lily Marlene. . .'

and there were Madame and her girls at the Casino bar,
though they had to watch what they said there as it was
supposed to be a pickup for Allied Intelligence. U-118 left
on her fourth patrol on May 27th. On June 9th she took on
oil from Kapitänleutnant Mohr's supply U-boat. Next day
she met Manseck's homeward bound U-758, and her doctor
went across to treat eleven men wounded in the battle with
Bogue's planes on June 8th. Four days later here she was,
about to find out what that was like for herself.

Stearns called up the carrier to report, but got no
response. His radio was dead, and he could neither transmit
nor receive. He signalled Johnson to make a strafing run
and the Wildcat dived straight at the U-boat's stern, firing
all the way down from 3,000 feet, levelling off at fifteen feet
from the water to roar low over the sub, his 50-calibres
stitching up the boat from stern to bow.

Stearns was diving too, firing his cowl gun. At a hundred
feet he lowered his wheels to check the rush, levelled off for
an instant, then dived again and dropped four D.C.s in
salvo. The U-boat was at conning tower depth when they
exploded across its swirl in a perfect straddle. The boat
continued to dive but resurfaced almost at once on the edge
of the depth-charge slick at right angles to its original
course. She went ahead very slowly, decks just awash,
trailing oil, for about seventy-five yards, then sank to a
shallow depth. The water was so clear that she could still be
seen, trailing oil and air bubbles.

Other T.B.F.s on patrol had picked up Stearns' call, and
about five minutes after Stearns had attacked, Fowler's
Avenger and Lieutenant Tennant's Wildcat joined him.

Fowler dropped four depth-charges on the submarine just
as she was breaking water to surface for a second time. It
was his third attack on a U-boat in eight days. The charges
fell in sequence over the boat along the line of its course.

One hit the deck and rolled off to starboard, exploding alongside midway between the conning tower and the bows. The other three fell fifty feet apart directly ahead.

The boat stayed on the surface, and Tennant strafed it twice, then circled for the next move. He saw men come up out of the conning tower hatch and rush to the guns. There were four machine-guns mounted on the solid coamings of the forward part of the conning tower, and a twin twenty-mm mounting aft of that in a round railed-in 'bandstand'. Tennant dived and opened up on them. With all that artillery the boat could have put up quite a fight, but Czygan was no Manseck, and the keepers of this mild milch cow abandoned their guns and hit the deck. When the fighter zoomed away they scrambled to their feet again and made for the guns, but the aggressive Tennant was back before they could pull the trigger. Every time he saw someone going to a gun he strafed him, and the man would tumble below or rush for the shelter of the lee coaming under the roaring fighter and its six flashing guns.

Fowler joined in this grim game. He got on one side of the U-boat, Tennant on the other, and they chased men back and forth across the top of the submarine. Fowler let fly with his cowl popgun and turret gunner Tucker got in some very accurate bursts. When they had had their turn, Johnson's F.4F. joined Tennant in some combined strafing, each converging on the sub from opposite sides. No one on the boat could man a gun, and some of the men could be seen putting on life jackets.

Johnson ran out of ammunition and left the scene. Five minutes later Harry Fryatt's T.B.F. arrived. Tennant made one more run on the sub, then Fryatt dived and got a close straddle with two D.C.s a few feet aft of the conning tower. The U-boat listed to starboard and started sinking slowly by the stern. Fryatt started to make another run to drop his remaining depth-charges but there were now seven other aircraft, including two more T.B.F.s and two F.4F.s milling about and he could not find a path. By the time he did manage to find some clear air he saw that men were

77

beginning to jump overboard from the sub, and her stern was so low in the water that he felt any more pounding was unnecessary. Tennant made a strafing run to clear the decks for him but when Fryatt did not follow him in he made another pass. This time his hot guns jammed.

Newcomer Bill Chamberlain saw the smoke and spray rise from the target but remembered his Navy doctrine about not letting up until the enemy was destroyed, and signalled his fighter escort, the experienced strafer Dick Rogers, to make sure no one down there got a sudden urge of heroics. Rogers made one run, then Chamberlain's Avenger plummetted down. His first stick of two D.C.s exploded right underneath the battered boat, lifting her up out of the frothing sea. She had hardly settled again when the T.B.F. dived out of a sharp left-hand turn and came in to drop its two other charges. To the surprise of the spectators and the discomfort of the man with the ball, flak curled up from the sub. Lieutenant Heim, who had arrived last on the scene with Stewart Doty's T.B.F., silenced them with his F.4F.'s fifties.

Chamberlain persisted, and released his remaining D.C.s. This pair were even better than the first. Both burst right under the U-boat's hull, and one of them penetrated a mine compartment where some six to a dozen mines were lying. The U-boat blew up with a tremendous explosion, hurling big pieces of metal and debris into the air. Huge gushers of oil also rose as if a main and vital artery had been cut.

There was nothing left for Doty to drop his charges on. The spray subsided, and there were survivors and bodies floating in the water. Fryatt flew over them and dropped his rubber boat. Some of the swimmers clasped their hands over their heads and waved their thanks.

An oil slick three miles long and one mile wide wrote the epitaph of this luckless boat. All stages of her agony were recorded by the cameras in the attacking planes. The pictures taken by Fryatt's radioman Scholl from the belly of the T.B.F. showed her most vividly in her death throes at the end of a snaking S-trail of seeping oil. Of her fifty-five officers and men, all the officers, including Czygan, were killed in the final attack, and *Osmond Ingram* rescued seventeen men from the water, of whom one died on board.

As far as Giles Short knew, the sunken U-boat had been one of the *Trutz* patrol lines. The prisoners would not or could not put him right, and at half-past three in the afternoon he started launching four overworked T.B.F.s and three F.4F.s to search the northern sector, beam to beam, for sixty miles. When they had gone, the first of three more Avengers and two Wildcats were launched to cover an overlapping sector in the west and the reciprocal sector to the east, but U-118 had been a camp follower, though a very valuable one, on the perimeter of the battle, and they sighted nothing.

Short decided to carry on westward during the following day, June 13th, so that he could refuel his destroyers in a quiet area away from U-boat Alley. This he did, and steamed south-east for the rest of the 14th to cover the central and westward parts of the likely area, throwing out air searches all day, and one attack team at dusk to investigate an H.F./D.F. bearing fifty miles to the northward.

Now that his D.D.s had got their wind back he intended to steer southward during the night, then head eastward again in the morning across the southern half of the danger area. But after the dawn patrol had been launched the catapult officer reported that cracks in the sheaves were enlarging with every boost and making the catapult dangerous to operate. *Bogue* had relied almost exclusively on her accelerator for launching, with average winds of no more than eight knots, and the carrier managing to raise another ten or twelve knots for landing. A T.B.F. with four depth-charges and enough gas for a three-hour flight needed a minimum of twenty-eight knots of wind to take off from the deck.

They could continue offensive operations in the area, hoping there would be enough wind over the deck for take-off with reduced loads, but they would be unable to plan any flights with certainty, and the sort of coverage they had been giving would be impossible. The aging destroyers also needed repairs. Supplies would run out in another four or five days. Short for once decided to pass the buck to C.in C.Lant, and the task group steamed all night waiting for Ingersoll's reply. In the morning *Bogue* was ordered to Bermuda, the destroyers to Hampton Roads. The light and fickle winds permitted two sectors searches by pairs of T.B.F.s and four circuits of the group by a single aircraft on June 16th, and they managed to put up an extra quartet of T.B.F.s and F.4F.s on the 17th. On June 20th *Bogue* entered harbour. Ingersoll signalled, 'Well done. Results indicate hard work and thorough training.'

The general reaction in *Bogue* was 'You can say that again."

[1] Card Sound was a continuation of Biscayne Bay, south of Miami.
[2] Launched September 5th, 1918, the name ship of her class, at Newport News, Virginia, de-commissioned in Philadelphia Navy Yard June 30th 1922, re-commissioned July 12th 1939 as an aircraft tender. Re-converted to a destroyer in the spring of 1943.

6. 'Hold your bombs, she's finished'

U.S.S. *Santee*, C.V.E.29[1], was a big girl among escort carriers. Sixty-four feet longer than *Bogue*, she had room for more aircraft, and was currently operating thirty-four to *Bogue*'s twenty. As a former tanker, she also carried more spare fuel for topping up escorts.

Her three sisters *Sangamon*, *Suwanee* and *Chenango* of the oiler conversion quartet had gone to the Pacific, but *Santee*, pushed so hastily and unceremoniously into action as a Torch bearer in the autumn of '42, was an Atlantic boat.

After her stint for General Patton off Casablanca, she steamed back to Norfolk Navy Yard for repairs, and Christmas Day there, then left with a hungover crew on Boxing Day for Port of Spain, Trinidad, the faithful D.D. *Eberle* in company. Arriving there on New Year's Day 1943, there were only two days for rum and Coca-Cola, then the little task group acquired their second tin-can, *Livermore*, and headed for the coast of Brazil to join Rear-Admiral Read's lonely cruiser, *Savannah*, whose Task Group 23.2 of the South Atlantic Force[2] had been watching for blockade runners for some months, and in November had taken a particularly valuable prize in the German freighter *Anneliese Essberger*, sixteen days out of Bordeaux bringing rubber from Japan's newly acquired Southern Resources Area, but had so far failed to track down her consort the *Kota Nopan*.

For two months T.G.23.2 patrolled off the Brazilian coast. *Santee*'s Dauntless, Avenger and Wildcat crews saw a lot of sea, and followed up many fruitless submarine contacts.

In Recife bad fruit was thought to have been the cause of a three-day bout of ptomaine poisoning which sorely afflicted the *Santee*, including S.B.D. plane captain Walter Skeldon. . .'It is nothing for a sailor to be walking along and have the man ahead of him suddenly double up and lie on the deck groaning with stomach cramps. You just walk around him. In a few minutes it might be your turn. . .The heads are loaded with diarrhoea cases, men throwing up, but the work has to go on, so you do the best you can. I often wondered how the pilots made out.'

One morning, just after sunrise, four S.B.D.s were ranged for patrol. The first plane was deck-launched, rolled down the deck, sank off the bows and into the sea. The second and third Dauntlesses followed. Neither could get enough lift, both went in.

The bull-horn blared. 'If there is any doubt of this plane getting off safely we will catapult it.' The pilot gave the thumbs-up for a deck launch, S.B.D.7 roared down the deck and disappeared. The whole ship seemed to catch its breath, then, after an eternity, the plane came in sight. The Flight Deck Chief watched it climb away. 'One out of four. It's a great way to run out of airplanes.'

At one point *Santee* had half her S.B.D.s grounded on the hangar deck for lack of spare tyres. A Dauntless did not glide well, and when the Landing Signals Officer gave the cut, it fell like a rock. If the deck was also falling away it was a long way to fall, and tyres would blow out. This happened too often, and they ran out of tyres, until fresh ones were specially flown out to their base near Recife.

While operating out of Brazil the crew had one liberty a month. In March they spent some nine days ashore at the base, living in typical tropical type 'open' barracks, enclosed on three sides by green jungle, ten miles from Recife. Work uniform there was undershorts and shoes, the latter because the sandy soil was red-hot.

Below the hangar deck *Santee* retained an open well deck from her time as an oiler. Crewmen going to chow had to cross this area, and if there was a beam sea running it was advisable to pick out a girder in the overhead to jump for as a wave would hit and roll over the well deck. Those left stranded on deck were soaked, or worse. There always seemed to be someone with cracked ribs. Later some of this open deck was closed up.

The flight deck was no place to goof off, either, when planes were operating, hurtling down the deck with lethally flailing props. One day an S.B.D. landed, taxied forward of the barriers towards an almost full deck parking area, and its plane captain Walter Skeldon was standing on the wing getting the pilot to sign the 'OK' sheet, when a Wildcat touched down and his six fifties opened up. Everyone scrambled wildly in all directions. Skeldon scuttled under a few tailplanes and tried to drop into a forty-mm gun tub, but his cameo ring caught on the deck edge, leaving him dangling in agony two feet from the gun deck. The ring twisted and cut to the bone, and required careful removal in sick bay.

On March 10th a *Santee* plane sighted a ship flying the Dutch flag about 650 miles east of Recife and seventeen miles from the task group.

Going to flank speed, *Savannah* and *Eberle* reached the stranger in half an hour. She was at first identified as the Dutch *Karin*, then someone recognised the unique pointed masts. *Savannah* flag-wagged to *Eberle*.

'Never mind the Dutch flag. Pile in there. This is a runner.'

Read fired warning shots across the fugitive's bows, but saw the Germans getting into their boats, and ordered *Eberle* to prepare a boarding party. The runner started to burn, and was well alight when *Eberle*'s boat went alongside. As it did so, explosives placed by the abandoning crew went off and killed eight of the boarders. The ship was the elusive *Kota Nopan,* the ex-Dutch *Kota Pinang,* with rubber and tin for Germany.

Santee left station off Recife on March 15th, and anchored in Hampton Roads on the 28th. On June 13th, the day after *Bogue*'s Compo 9 had destroyed the milch cow U-118, then left the hunting grounds for repairs at Bermuda, *Santee* got under way from Norfolk with the four-stackers *Bainbridge, Overton* and *MacLeish* to take over the escort carrier presence in the Central Atlantic. Aboard were the thirteen Avenger T.B.F.s and nine Dauntless S.B.D.5s of VC29 Squadron, commanded by Lieutenant-Commander W.R. Staggs, and the twelve Wildcat F.4F.s of VF29, under Lieutenant H.B. Bass.

Santee's skipper Harold Foster Fick was forty-four, the same age as Buster Isbell, and had just about as varied a record as a Navy flier. Missouri born, he entered the Naval Academy on appointment from the Eighth District of Louisiana in June 1916, saw active service as a midshipman, and completed flight training in June 1923. Like Giles Short he was with the U.S.S. *Wright,* mother to Patrol Squadron 6, then helped to set up Observation Squadron 6, first unit to take planes aboard battleships of the U.S. Atlantic Fleet. Two years instructing at Pensacola, and he was back to flying from battlewagons, the U.S.S. *Tennessee* and *California*, then it was Pensacola again, Torpedo 2 in *Saratoga* as Exec., Fighting 2 in *Lexington,* two years in the Plans Division of BuAer, Division Tactical and Gunnery Officer in *Yorktown* under Bill Halsey, then command of a seaplane tender, the converted destroyer *Childs*, in the Pacific.

There followed some important shore duty. Fick helped establish the new Naval Air Station at Corpus Christi, Texas, where many naval fighter pilots, including Royal Navy fliers trained initially at Pensacola, were to be given their specialist training, and where Fick supervised training until October 1942, with an interesting break as U.S. Naval Observer (Air) in London, England. From December 1942 until May 1943 he was Chief of Staff in the Training Command at Pensacola. After he had joined his new command, U.S.S. *Santee*, he received a letter of Commendation, with Ribbon, which testified that 'As a result of his efficient planning and untiring effort, Captain Fick was instrumental in the creation of the new Intermediate phase of flight training, involving improvement and standardization of training syllabi, equalizing of student loads, procurement and assignment of aircraft and the construction of additional facilities. Faced by numerous handicaps in organizing the programme at a time of sudden expansion, Captain Fick displayed a thorough comprehension of the problems involved and, by his aggressive initiative, contributed to the efficient, economical and superb training of our Naval Aviators during a period of vital and grave importance. . .' Pilot and planner, Harold Fick well understood the problems of young naval aviators. He himself was glad to be at sea again. He reckoned he had had enough shore duty, and counted on the wild Atlantic to tint the pallor and lay the dust of offices.

Thanks to Allied Intelligence and Giles Short's tactics, the *Trutz* group had lost one boat and scored no kills. Now Dönitz re-formed the group further to the southward in a concentration of fifteen boats in three north-south patrol lines twenty miles apart with their centre 850 miles east of Bermuda. Manseck had brought his damaged but undefeated U-758 into port. His and his crew's accounts of their determined and successful battle against American T.B.F.s and fighters stiffened the sagging morale of the U-boat crews, and confirmed the *Befehlshaber der U-Boote* in his tactic of arming his submarines heavily with single, twin, even quadruple twenty-mm quick-firing cannon and heavy machine guns to fight it out with the Allied planes at sea and as they crossed the Bay of Biscay on transit, where R.A.F. Sunderlands, Wellingtons and Halifaxes and U.S.A.A.F. Liberators were making life dangerous for the submariners.

But Allied Intelligence and H.F./D.F. had given the Admiralty and the U.S. Tenth Fleet the rough position of the new *Trutz* concentration. The *Santee* group was routed south to latitude 22 North to give cover to eastbound convoy U.G.S.10 as it shaped to go round the new barrier. It was a sloppy convoy, with bad station-keeping and straggling and there was one serious collision. Ships would not douse their lights, and smoked to Heaven during the day. There was also an enemy agent aboard one of the ships, armed with a radio transmitter. This man got out a signal which was picked up by Oberlautnant Gunther

Kummetat's U-572, outward-bound for South America to hunt tankers off the Antilles. Kummetat homed on the signal, got through the convoy screen and sank the Free French naval tanker *Lot* in three minutes.

But the rest of the convoy, as well as westbound G.U.S.8, got through. Isbell in *Card* was supporting G.U.S.8, with orders stating that 'it was not necessary to keep a continuous umbrella over the convoy, and that we could operate independently against any reported concentration (of U-boats) within striking distance, as long as we could get back to the convoy before the concentration could reach it.' *Card*'s T.B.F.s searched the area where *Trutz* had been reported on the evening of June 21st but Dönitz, disgusted by their repeated failure, had ordered them eastwards to try their luck with a new barrier south of Flores in the Azores.

Santee and her group reached Casablanca on July 3rd and left four days later with G.U.S.9, a convoy of empty freighters, tankers and troopers returning to the Americas for fresh loads. The carrier's planes sighted no U-boats. After two westbound convoys had slipped past the new *Trutz* concentrations, Dönitz had dissolved the group on June 29th. One of *Santee*'s Avengers made a forced landing in Spain, where its crew was interned.

The new Bogue class escort carrier U.S.S. *Core*[3] had left Chesapeake Bay on June 27th on her first operational cruise, with Composite (VC) 13's twelve T.B.F.1s and six F.4F.4s, under Lieutenant-Commander Charles W. Brewer, and the destroyers *Bulmer*, experienced Atlantic boat *George E. Badger* and *Barker*.

Core's Captain was an experienced sailor too. Marshall Raymond Greer was a Southerner, born in Riverside, North Carolina, educated at Pikeville College Academy, Kentucky, prior to attending the Naval Academy. He graduated from Annapolis in 1918, saw war service on escort duty aboard the battleship *North Dakota,* became a Naval Aviator in 1921 and served in the Pacific and Asiatic Fleets and Combat Squadron 3, Spotting Squadron 3, Observation Squadron 2, Torpedo and Bombing Squadron

2, and Torpedo Squadron 20. After two years as a flight instructor at Pensacola he flew catapult planes from the cruisers *Memphis* and *Raleigh,* received a Commendation for success as a recruiting officer while commanding a Naval Reserve aviation base, and in 1934 was commanding Scouting Squadron 3 in *Lexington,* being commended again when the Squadron won that year's gunnery competition. Before commanding Cruiser Scouting Squadron 7 in the U.S.S. *San Francisco* in 1937 he was Inspector of Naval Aircraft at the Wright Aeronautical Corporation, Paterson, New Jersey. Two years' duty as Aviation Officer to Commander Cruisers, Scouting Force, in the U.S.S. *Chicago,* was followed by spells in Naval Intelligence, as an Advisor to the Argentine Navy and when the U.S.A. entered World War 2, as Captain of the U.S.S. *Wright.* Up to that point it had been, to say the least, a varied career. In September 1942 he was ordered to Tacoma to take over the new U.S.S. *Core.*

Core remained within visual distance of the big west-bound convoy U.G.S.11 until July 11th, when it was 700 miles south of Sao Miguel in the Azores, then Greer was ordered to relieve the *Santee* group in support of G.U.S.9. The changeover was made on July 12th, and Fick's more experienced group was sent to scour the waters south of the Azores.

The discredited *Trutz* group had been re-formed into four small, four-boat packs and stationed off the Portuguese coast and south of the Straits of Gibraltar, but there were sixteen independent boats south and east of the Azores, some passing through on their way to or from South American waters, some refuelling from milch cows.

On the afternoon of July 13th the *Core* patrol team of Lieutenant Robert Williams' T.B.F. and Lieutenant (jg) Earl H. Steiger's F.4F. were on a return leg of the first area search flight ahead of the convoy. The weather was variable, with visibility ranging from eight to fifteen miles, the sea was smooth with occasional white caps. They were flying at 7,000 feet, where there was some fluffy white cumulus cloud drifting along on the light airs. When the visibility closed in Williams used his radar. Towards the end of the leg the sun was lighting up the whole vast seascape. The radar was secured, and both aircraft dropped down to 5,500 feet to avoid plunging into a cloud layer. About eight minutes after levelling off, at 3.21 p.m., they were flying some 720 miles south-sou'-west of Fayal with the bright sun behind them when Williams' turret gunner, M.H. Paden, shouted, 'White wake ten miles on the port quarter!'

Now they were glad of the drifting cloud. Hopping from one woolly white bank to another Williams stalked the boat. As they got above the wake they could see that the U-boat, a dirty dark brown or black, was a big one, probably a 1,600-ton milch cow, cruising at about twelve or fourteen knots.

They were right. Down below, the crew of the tanker U-487 were sunning themselves. Some of them were fooling about trying to haul on board a floating bale of cotton drifting from some torpedoed freighter, when there was a rising roar on the starboard bow and Earl Steiger's Wildcat came at them, guns flaming.

That was the end of the cotton picking. Some men rushed to the guns, the others dived below or crouched in the conning tower for shelter from the F.4F.'s zipping bullets. Behind it came the T.B.F. at 220 knots. About ten seconds after Steiger had pulled up and away, Williams dropped his four depth-charges, fuses set for twenty-five feet, catching out of the corner of his eye a man running along the casing of the submarine towards the forward gun.

The line of charges raked the sub's bow, the first and second straddling, third and fourth exploding off the port side. Both planes pulled up to 3,500 feet and circled to observe results. The U-boat immediately went into a right-hand circle and gradually slowed down, leaking oil so that the whole patch of water it was enclosing was covered with it. The gunners started shooting. Puffs of black smoke blossomed below and behind the aircraft, still revolving as if attached to a giant carousel.

Williams reported the situation to *Core* and signalled to

Steiger to make another pass over the U-boat so that the T.B.F. could follow and take more pictures.

Meanwhile *Core* had catapulted four more T.B.F.s piloted by Lieutenants (jg) Jim Schoby, C.E. Lair, W.V. Wilson, and Bob Hayman from Red Wing, Minnesota, followed off the catapult by C.O. Charles Brewer's F.4F. and had ordered the destroyer *Barker* to the scene.

There, Williams noticed a surge of white water at the U-boat's stern. He called up Steiger in the Wildcat.

'Have you got enough ammo to make another run and see what's going on?'

Steiger's voice crackled in his ears. 'I've only got one gun left, but here we go. . .'

The fighter dived on the U-boat, but when he was only a few hundred feet from the enemy's port quarter the Wildcat swerved to port, the nose dropped and it plunged into the sea about a hundred feet off the submarine's port bow.

Charles Brewer on his way from *Core* saw him splash and heard Williams say, 'The sub's gotten one of our planes.' Brewer called to the following T.B.F.s that he was starting his own strafing run. Approaching the target from cloud, down-sun, he dived and fired over a thousand rounds of fifty-calibre at the big sub.

Another Wildcat now arrived off regular patrol, got ready to strafe, but had to hold his fire as the two newly arrived T.B.F.s were attacking the target. The first of these dived from the sub's starboard bow and dropped four D.C.s from a hundred feet.

All exploded close aboard or underneath the boat. The upsurge of water lifted the submarine about ten feet before completely enveloping it. When the deluge cleared, some thirty feet of the boat was sticking up out of the water at a sharp angle. Five seconds later it slid under the surface leaving several dozen men swimming in the sea, most of them making for two dark grey life rafts. There were two more almost submerged life rafts, but very little debris. An hour later an oil slick a mile square in area covered the sea. Mixed in was a patch of dark brown D.C. scum and an oval of light apple-green marking the spot where U-487 had submerged for the last time.

Two aircraft remained over the area to guide *Barker* towards the survivors and provide air cover – German submarines had been known to fire at Allied ships slowing down to rescue their U-boat colleagues from the water. There was no trace of Steiger, and he was never found.

A medical officer interviewed the four officers and twenty-nine ratings hauled from the oily sea. The first attack had taken them all by surprise. 'Before we knew it,' said one, 'a plane is directly overhead and a bomb is striking the deck and exploding.' This charge definitely disabled the boat. An oil fire started below decks. This was soon put out but the smoke in the boat was almost unbearable. Many men had been so stunned by depth-charges exploding close aboard that they did nothing to help themselves when the coup de grace was given. The submarine was sunk, not scuttled, and her captain went down with her.

A T.B.F./F.4F. attack team from *Santee*, which was patrolling south of the Azores with D.D.s *Bainbridge*, *Overton* and *MacLeish*, was flying about 150 miles north of the carrier at eight o'clock next morning, July 14th. The big C.V.E.'s fighter leader Lieutenant H. Brink Bass was cruising a mile and a half out on the starboard beam of Lieutenant (jg) John Ballantine's T.B.F., when the latter, who kept a very sharp lookout, sighted a submarine twenty-one miles away. He immediately turned towards it and signalled Bass by rocking his wings.

Bass dived ahead and strafed the submarine from the port bow. The U-boat started to crash-dive, with Ballantine still two miles away. But the T.B.F. had a new weapon in its bomb bay, an acoustic torpedo, known officially for security reasons as a Mark 24 mine but more familiarly in service as Fido or Wandering Annie. Armed with Torpex, Fido homed on the noise made by the vessel's screws churning the water, via a hydrophone in its head, shielded so that it did not home on to its own propeller effects. When dropped, Fido dived and levelled out at a pre-set depth, and was designed to detect prop noises up to a range of 1,500 yards, but if no sound was picked up by the hydrophone the torpedo would make an upward circular search, which it could maintain for fifteen minutes. Good results were hoped for against submerged U-boats under way, especially just after a submarine had crash-dived, when it would probably make a violent change of course at full speed.

Bass turned and attacked from the starboard beam, his Wildcat roaring low over the submarine as its conning tower started to submerge. Ballantine, flying past the sub's port beam, saw his tracers hitting the base of the conning tower. The U-boat disappeared as the T.B.F. was doubling back, lowering its wheels to lose airspeed for the torpedo drop, which had to be made slowly from a low height. Coming in from behind where the submarine went down he released the Fido at 250 feet, 200 yards ahead and about a hundred feet to starboard of the swirl. Ballantine circled to port and saw 'a pronounced shock in the water.' A moment later a ring of foam nearly twenty feet in diameter rose to the surface, followed by a brown mine slick. There was no debris to be seen, but it was the end for U-160 and all her crew.

At 8.42 next morning, with *Santee* steaming in good weather 165 miles due south of Santa Maria, Lieutenant (jg) Claude Barton in T.B.F.12, with Ensign Anderson in a Wildcat a hundred feet out on his port beam, sighted another sub.

Anderson dived and strafed, turned and strafed again, and came back for a fourth run. He raced low over the target just as her conning tower disappeared. Barton dropped his Fido ahead of the swirl, and he and his radioman Bobbie Taylor and turret gunner Dean Fintner saw a shock wave erupt in the water from a hit, followed by a heavy bubbling swirl streaked with oil and brown scum marking the end of U-509.

Core's Bob Williams had the dawn patrol next day, July 16th. He was launched into a rather cloudy sky, and his T.B.F. had just emerged from cloud on the fifth leg of its search when Williams sighted a U-boat on his port bow, about nine miles off, twenty-seven miles from the convoy.

He hugged cloud cover until he was about two miles from the enemy, then pushed over and dived at 260 knots, dropping four D.C.s from 400 feet. The first exploded under the submarine about fifty feet aft of the conning tower, the others on the port side. As the tower of water crumbled Williams saw that fifty feet of the sub's bows were tilted in the air, and blue, irridescent oil was spreading around her, followed by crates, planks, and the same ring of pale green water they had seen when U-487 went down. Against the vivid holiday blue of the ocean around it, it made the grim fact of the death of a crew unreal.

The destroyer *McCormick* picked up three survivors, a lieutenant, a coxswain and a seaman, from a small rubber boat, two others having died from shock, wounds and choking oil half an hour earlier. The commander, Oberleutnant Gunther Muller, had gone down with his ship. Survivors revealed that the boat, U-67, had been looking for a milch cow, after seventy days at sea and a fruitless patrol between the Caribbean and Chesapeake Bay.

Captain Greer naturally thought that he had found the U-boat patrol line reported by C.in C.Lant, but after searching for five days neither *Core* nor *Santee* could find any submarines round the Azores. Spanish ships had warned the U-boats patrolling south of the islands of the presence of Allied carriers. This had been forcefully confirmed by their losses, and they had pulled out to the north.

But there were single U-boats in the Central Atlantic. *Bogue*'s Task Group 21.13, with her old friends *Belknap*, *George E. Badger*, *Osmond Ingram* and *Lea*, but with a new C.O., the carrier's erstwhile Exec., Joe Dunn, had left Norfolk on July 12th to support Convoy U.G.S.12 in its passage to African ports.

Joseph Brantley Dunn, son of a judge, was born and raised in Europa, Mississippi, graduated from Annapolis in 1922, and was unique among carrier captains and naval aviators in having been a submariner before he was a flier.

He served in the submarines R2 and R8, and commanded the R10 until being switched to aviation training at Jacksonville, Florida, via a stint as Instructor in electrical engineering and physics at the Academy. He then had sea duty, commanded a training squadron at Pensacola, then went back to sea to fly from the U.S.S. *Ranger,* commanded a patrol squadron at Coco Solo and a seaplane squadron at Jacksonville, where he stayed, first to command Cecil Field, then as Superintendent of Aviation Training, before joining *Bogue* as Exec. in December 1942 and taking over command from Giles Short in July 1943. With his background Joe Dunn was especially qualified to operate aircraft against submarines.

Bogue joined U.G.S.12 next day. On July 21st Com.in Ch.'s daily submarine estimate warned of a U-boat concentration ahead. Dunn decided to pull out and try to break it up. Having found no contacts during the day, he swung south during the night, meaning to head north again at dawn and return to the danger area ahead of the convoy for another search before rejoining U.G.S.12 at noon.

He was on his way southward when Huff-Duff started picking up U-boat signals to the north of him, near the convoy. One of these messages, picked up at 10.47 p.m., was recognisable from its Enigma groupings as a sighting report. A U-boat had seen the carrier on a south-easterly course and jumped to the conclusion that she had left the convoy altogether on another mission. The message which came back from the German shore control station looked ominously like detailed instructions for an early attack on the convoy, with *Bogue* and her planes away to the southward.

What the Germans did not know was that as soon as the U-boat signal had been recognised as a sighting report *Bogue* immediately reversed course to the north, and later north-west, towards the convoy. Captain Dunn made a mental note of the necessity for operating aircraft at night to catch U-boats sneaking up after sundown to contact headquarters, thinking all Allied planes were by then asleep in the hangar. He gave orders to ready three T.B.F.s and three F.M.1s[4] to take off at dawn.

But when first light came it was dim and murky, with cloud right down to seven hundred feet. Below that, rain squalls lashed the sea, and there was only eight knots of wind. The choppy sea was a good place for periscopes to hide. Even ducks wouldn't fly in this.

'That's what the Germans will think,' said Dunn, and the first T.B.F. in its new 'Atlantic camouflage' of grey, blue and white was launched off the bow.

He was proved right when, at one minute before eight o'clock, Doty in a T.B.F. and Donahoe in his fighter escort both sighted a fully surfaced grey-green U-boat at diving trim only eleven miles dead ahead of *Bogue* and fifty-five miles off the port bow of the convoy. The sub was steering 260°. *Bogue* was on 270°. From this position the U-boat could have closed the convoy in about two hours, and she might well have gone undetected in the rain and darkness below.

The submarine was about three miles ahead of the two planes. Donahoe was flying about 500 feet on Doty's starboard beam. They immediately climbed, the Wildcat to 1,200 feet, the T.B.F. 300 feet higher, increased speed and headed directly for the enemy, with the fighter pulling ahead. When he was about a mile from the target Donahoe started a shallow dive, opening up with his fifty-calibres when he was 800 yards from the boat and strafing on down so low his tail wheel almost scraped the periscope standard as the submarine dived.

Doty dived steeply right on his tail and his D.C.s went in together about 150 feet ahead of the U-boat's exposed rear diving planes and screws. A gush of oil came up.

Bogue, which had swerved north to avoid closing on the U-boat, returned to her south-westerly course to meet the convoy at noon. Two T.B.F.s, an F.M.1 and the *Osmond Ingram*, sent to follow up Doty's U-boat, sighted nothing but angry sea, but at 9.27 a.m., when the Group was 194 miles south-west of Sao Miguel, *George E. Badger* reported a sonar contact with a U-boat about 4,000 yards on *Bogue*'s port bow. The carrier swung again out of the way but reversed course when *Badger* lost the contact.

She picked it up again at eleven o'clock. Again Dunn took avoiding action and ordered *Badger* to pursue the enemy. This left the carrier with only one escort, *Clemson*.

Lieutenant Tom Byrd, *Badger*'s aggressive young captain, held on to the U-boat, sonar pinging, fading, pinging, fading. Down below at the other end of the probing sound wave, U-613, originally outward bound for the Florida coast to sew a barrier of mines off Jacksonville harbour, twisted and turned. For two hours the old flush-decker D.D. kept up the hunt, rivets squealing, engines giving their all as the telegraphs clanged for flank speed, then slow, then full again. At last, after four attacks and forty depth-charges, grim scraps of debris began to appear, splintered planking, empty life jackets, clothing, mattresses, mutilated and dismembered corpses. From somewhere below, a steady stream of small bubbles also rose like carbonated water. The fathometer registered sharp echoes at 125 feet, Out of the sonar issued a loud howling noise. This increased in intensity for a few seconds, to be followed by intermittent bubbling and hissing sounds. The ship stopped, and all hands were able to identify the wreckage and human remains which continued to bob to the surface in a thin film of sharp-stinking diesel oil. It was just part of the terrible price which German sailors, along with the soldiers in Russia and the civilians in the cities of the Fatherland, were now paying for entrusting their destiny to a demented demagogue and his criminal gang. The last piece of evidence picked up out of the water was a German translation of Poe's *Murders In The Rue Morgue*.

Thinking no planes could fly in the murky weather, the U-boats moved in for attack on the convoy.

Bogue had changed to a south-easterly course to join U.G.S.12, and at two in the afternoon Stearns' T.B.F. was flying down a rain and fog-filled corridor, cloud a hundred feet above them, choppy sea below, when his turret gunner

E.L. Myers sighted two white wakes about fifty yards apart on parallel courses to their own about five miles astern, at the extreme limit of visibility.

Between the two submarines stretched a black oiling hose, through which Kapitänleutnant Herbert Uhlig's 740-ton U-527, tanks nearly empty and crew exhausted after a cruise in the Gulf of Mexico, was sucking fuel for her return to Bordeaux. On sighting the planes, which no one had expected to see in this foul weather, Uhlig cast off, recapped, turned hard-a-starboard and ran for a fog bank about half a mile away, as the milch cow U-648, a 500-tonner acting as a relief supply boat, battened down swiftly and dived.

Stearns was already diving on U-527, and as it nosed into the fog bank let go four D.C.s from a hundred feet. Uhlig made no attempt to dive but opened fire. The exploding charges covered his stern in foam and blew one man overboard. Smoke rose from abaft the conning tower as the U-boat circled slowly to starboard, with men jumping overboard. Then her bows rose vertically in the air and she plunged below. *Clemson* rescued thirteen survivors, including Uhlig.

Santee went to the support of westbound convoy G.U.S.10,. At 4.45 on the afternoon of July 30th Lieutenant (jg) Robert Richmond's T.B.F.13 left the catapult, followed by Edward Van Vranken's Wildcat, for an anti-submarine search of 150 miles on the convoy's starboard beam.

It was a hazy day, with quite a bit of cumulus and some white caps on the sea. They had been flying north for about half an hour when Van Vranken wobbled his wings and flew ahead, drawing Richmond's attention to two white wakes some ten miles away on their starboard beam. Both planes altered course to intercept.

When they had about halved the distance they clearly identified two submarines about 1,200 feet apart steering south in the direction of the convoy. While the T.B.F. stayed in the base of the cloud, Van Vranken climbed until he was at 1,500 feet and ahead of the enemy, then dived and strafed the leading boat, the minelayer U-43, on a mission to mine Lagos harbour. Levelling off at fifty feet he opened up on the second sub, U-403, the larger of the two, which had been preparing to take aboard fuel from U-43. As he was finishing this run, Richmond pushed over for a D.C. attack on the same boat, and dropped two charges from 400 feet, with the sub now beam-on to him. They splashed some forty feet abreast of the conning tower. U-403 kept on turning until she steadied on a northerly course and dived, leaving an oil slick.

The smaller sub was turning to port and submerging, and Richmond slowed and lost height to drop his Fido on her. His turret gunner Enoch Tarsillia got off a short burst and the torpedo exploded two minutes later. Oil gushed up, bringing with it splintered wood, paper and what looked like pieces of cork. Down below, U-46 had disintegrated, destroyed finally by her own mines. After this loss, Dönitz warned his captains of the 'new, more dangerous bombs.'

Card, still commanded by Captain Arnold 'Buster' Isbell, and with the same Composite Squadron 1, had left Hampton Roads on July 27th with a new screen, the old flush-decked four-pipers *Barry, Goff* and *Borie*. She took on more fuel at Bermuda, joined eastbound U.G.S.13, topped off her D.D.s, and took her Task Group 21.14 off to look for U-boats. The concentration south-west of the Azores had been so roughly handled by the *Core, Bogue* and *Santee* groups that it had dispersed, and aircraft from Gibraltar and the Moroccan Sea Frontier had broken up the packs off Portugal, but there were many U-boats crossing the U.S.A.–Africa sea routes on their way to or from the American coasts, where twenty ships had been sunk in July, ranging from a freighter off Boston to a schooner near Trinidad, though the U.S. Fourth Fleet had sunk two-thirds of the South American U-boat group; from the Ivory Coast, where the U-boats were having the most success; and to and from the Durban-Mozambique area and the Indian Ocean. There were no U-boats in the North Atlantic.

The veteran Kapitänleutnant Friedrich Markworth's U-66 had sunk two ships off the American coasts in a fourteen-week patrol and was homeward bound 457 miles west-sou'-west of Flores when it was sighted by *Card*'s Lieutenant Richard L. Cormier U.S.N.R. leading an attack team in his T.B.F.

Cormier's F.4F. wingman strafed the submarine and fatally wounded the officer of the deck. Men on the conning tower pressed the klaxon button. This only brought an angry Markworth rushing up the ladder from below. He belayed the order to dive, and shouted at the men to man the guns. The U-boat bobbed up again, survived two attacks by Cormier, one with two depth-charges, one with a Fido. But Markworth himself was badly wounded by fifty-calibre bullets, and his First Officer took the boat down. They surfaced cautiously that night as dusk closed in, and radioed Dönitz for assistance, including fuel. U-66 was ordered to rendezvous with U-117, the nearest milch cow. The two submarines met just before midnight on August 6th, and Oberleutnant Ererks came on board to relieve Markworth.

The following morning was clear and cloudless, with a light wind. Lieutenant (jg) A.H. Sallenger U.S.N.R. was on a routine search at 4,500 feet in his T.B.F. Radioman John H. O'Hagan and turret gunner John D. Downes were in the midships cockpit enjoying the view when Sallenger's voice came through the inter-com.

'White object bearing fifteen degrees on the starboard bow, about twelve miles. Man the turret. Check your switches.'

O'Hagan checked the bombing set-up and reported, 'All ready, sir.'

Downes climbed up into the turret. 'What is it, sir? Looks like something big.'

O'Hagan said, 'It's a destroyer.'

'Looks more like a freighter to me,' the pilot said.

As they drew closer the blurred white 'object' separated into two U-boats, fully surfaced and lying close together, cruising very slowly with neither wake nor bow wave, white-painted hulls gleaming in the sun. It was U-66 and her milch cow.

Sallenger called the ship, eighty miles away, and made his report. Isbell ordered two more T.B.F.s and two Wildcats launched to assist Sallenger, who had no fighter with him.

Sallenger said, 'This is it. Stand by with the camera.' Fighter or no fighter, he could not let this pair get away.

They were almost abreast of him now, no more than 200 feet apart, with no sign of any refuelling operations. There was no cloud for him to hide in, but they did not seem to have seen him.

He broke off and manoeuvred to make his attack down-sun from astern. Picking up the submarine nearest to him and slightly astern of the other, he dived on her at 220 knots.

The lookouts did not wake up until Sallenger was 400 yards away, then the fire from the multiple cannon came up thick and hot. Sallenger dropped two depth-charges from 125 feet, and banked to port so that O'Hagan could take pictures. The radioman recorded two explosions on film, both close aboard the submarine, one on the starboard side aft, one just forward of the conning tower to port. There was a vivid flash of flame from the stern of the boat and dense black smoke started pouring out. As Downes strafed with his fifty-calibre he could see about twenty men on deck, one leaping down the conning tower hatch. There seemed to be two batteries of guns firing on them, and he concentrated his fire on the machine-guns on the bridge.

Sallenger withdrew out of range and reported his attack to the ship. 'Damaged sub is manoeuvering very erratically. Her steering gear may be out of control. Second sub is following her.'

About ten minutes later U-66, the undamaged boat, submerged, leaving the big milch cow alone, unable to dive but with plenty of fire power to defend herself.

Sallenger dived and aimed to drop his homing torpedo fifty yards to starboard and 150 yards ahead of the swirl left by the submerged boat. To do this he had to fly slowly at 200 feet directly past the conning tower of the surfaced submarine and ran the gauntlet of point-blank fire. But the aim, Sallenger thought, was 'rotten, all around us, but no hits,' and the 'mine' was dropped as planned. They left the angry sub spitting fire and still smoking aft, and climbed to 6,400 feet so that the relief planes could be vectored on them.

About twenty minutes later two T.B.F.s, flown by Lieutenant C.R. Stapler U.S.N. and Lieutenant (jg) J.C. Forney U.S.N.R., arrived, with Lieutenant N.D. Hodson U.S.N. and Lieutenant (jg) E.E. Jackson in two F.4F.s.

They pushed over in a gentle dive. Forney slid over to Stapler's port side and followed him in to the attack. The U-boat was taking evasive action, and Stapler swerved as they approached, to keep the target ahead. Their last turn put the blazing sun behind them.

About five miles away Stapler signalled Hodson to make a strafing run. The Wildcat roared on ahead. Hodson fired a test burst when he was about two miles away but the bullets fell well short, and he held his fire until he was within range. Diving through the intense flak he beat up the enemy from the starboard quarter, then came back and strafed from the opposite side.

Stapler came in behind him, steadied down for the drop, fired a burst from his cowl gun to ease his passage, and dropped two depth-charges from 185 feet.

The sub had turned more sharply than he had anticipated and was steering to port, and the D.C.s splashed very close aboard the port side, the explosions sending up huge geysers of spray which obscured the boat. Stapler's gunner Bill Hutchinson got in one good burst at the conning tower. Radioman Wellington Potter's camera recorded the great white towers of water between the sub and the plane, the sun glittering off the sea and the spray-lashed after deck of the boat. He was so preoccupied with his photography it was difficult to grasp that they were in the midst of a firefight.

ve: The first US conversion – USS
Island, originally the 7,680-ton
pe cargo-passenger ship
nacmail. Flying operations on such a
flight deck were difficult and only a
aircraft could be kept on deck during

take-off and landing activities. (US Navy)
Below: USS *George E. Badger*, one of the
'Flush-Deck' destroyers. Originally con-
verted as a Seaplane Tender, she was
further adapted as a High Speed
Transport. (US National Archives)

Below: USS *Bogue* (laid down as a merchant vessel, *Steel Advocate*), in November 1942, a few months before the start of her successful hunter-killer operations during which her aircraft sank seven U-boats. (US National Archives

Inset: One of *Bogue*'s victims, U-118, here being depth-charged (note depth charge in the the air in the bottom lef photograph) on 12 June 1943. (US Na

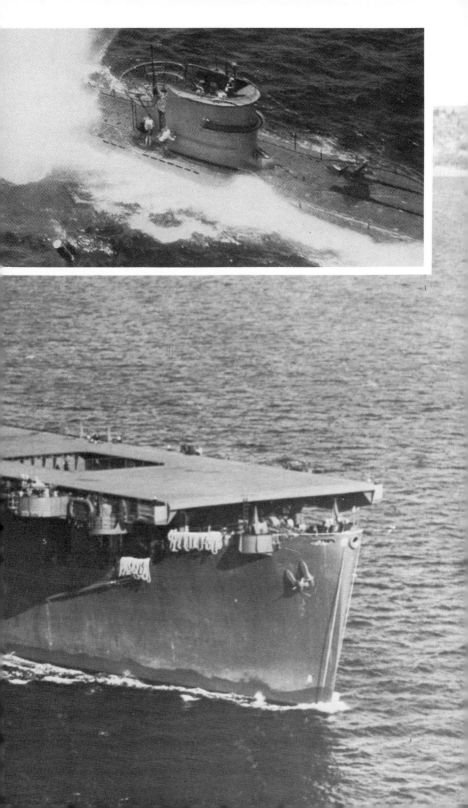

Above: The 'Ready Roo[m]'
Pilots await take-off fro[m]
USS *Santee* for an attac[k]
on French North Africa[,]
November 1942. (US
Navy)
Left: Anxious moments [for]
this crew of a Grumma[n]
Avenger after it had
ditched on take-off.
Right: The steadfast
destroyer USS *Borie*
abandoned after her ep[ic]
battle with U-405, 1
November 1943. Crippl[ed]
with no hope of being
saved, she was eventual[ly]
depth-charged and sunk[.]
(US National Archives)

Above: HMS *Broadway* (ex-USS *Hunt*), one of the large number of over-age US destroyers that were transferred to the Royal Navy to provide them with much-needed escort vessels. (IWM)

Below: A Fairey Swordfish TSR returns HMS *Tracker* (BAVG6). Nicknamed 'Stringbags', these aircraft were used for reconnaissance and as torpedo-bombers the anti-submarine role. (IWM)

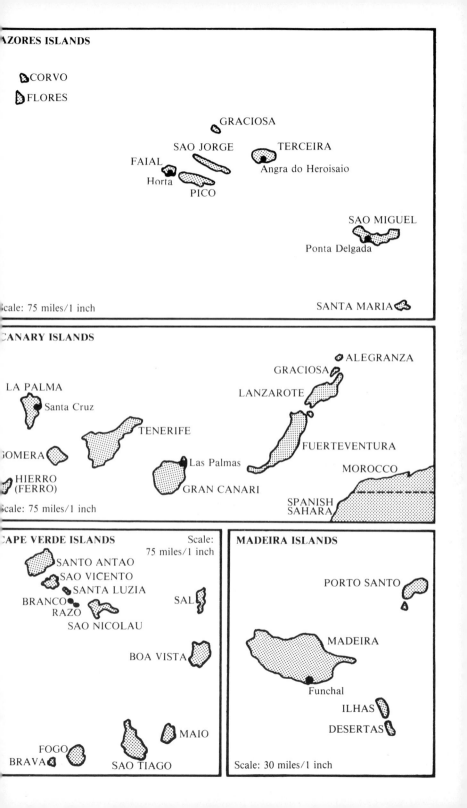

AZORES ISLANDS

CORVO

FLORES

GRACIOSA

SAO JORGE

TERCEIRA

FAIAL

Horta

Angra do Heroisaio

PICO

SAO MIGUEL

Ponta Delgada

Scale: 75 miles/1 inch

SANTA MARIA

CANARY ISLANDS

ALEGRANZA

GRACIOSA

LA PALMA

LANZAROTE

Santa Cruz

TENERIFE

FUERTEVENTURA

GOMERA

Las Palmas

MOROCCO

HIERRO
(FERRO)

GRAN CANARI

SPANISH
SAHARA

Scale: 75 miles/1 inch

CAPE VERDE ISLANDS

Scale:
75 miles/1 inch

SANTO ANTAO

SAO VICENTO

SANTA LUZIA

BRANCO

RAZO

SAL

SAO NICOLAU

BOA VISTA

MAIO

FOGO

BRAVA

SAO TIAGO

MADEIRA ISLANDS

PORTO SANTO

MADEIRA

Funchal

ILHAS

DESERTAS

Scale: 30 miles/1 inch

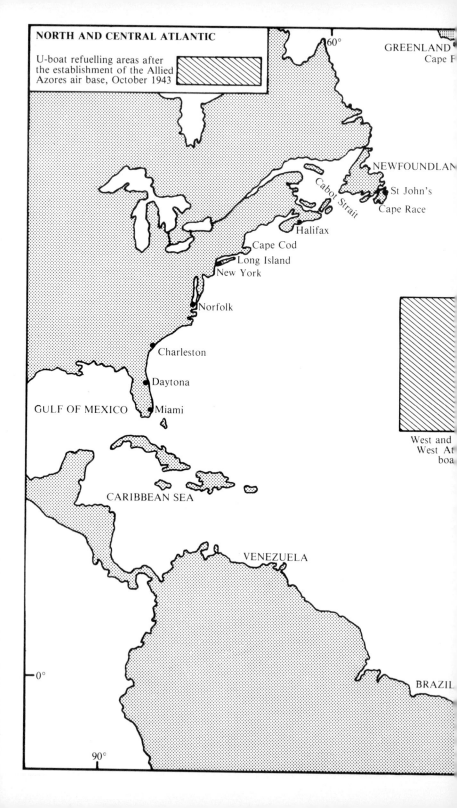

NORTH AND CENTRAL ATLANTIC

U-boat refuelling areas after
the establishment of the Allied
Azores air base, October 1943

60°

GREENLAND
Cape F

NEWFOUNDLAN

St John's
Cape Race

Cabot Strait

Halifax

Cape Cod

Long Island

New York

Norfolk

Charleston

Daytona

GULF OF MEXICO

Miami

CARIBBEAN SEA

VENEZUELA

West and
West At
boa

BRAZIL

0°

90°

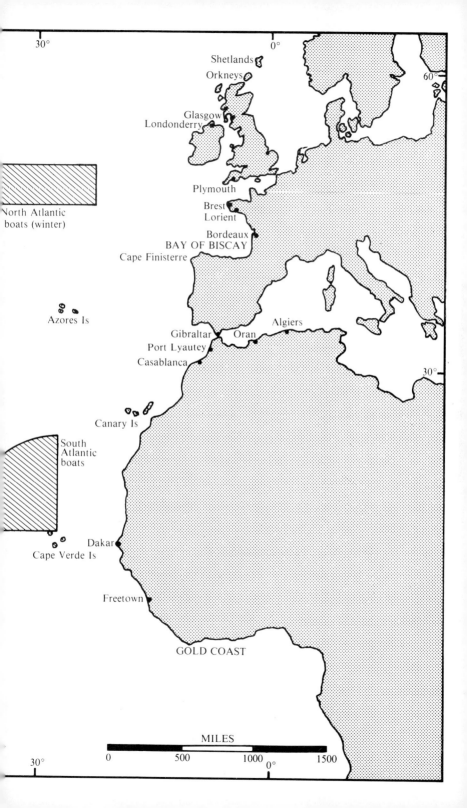

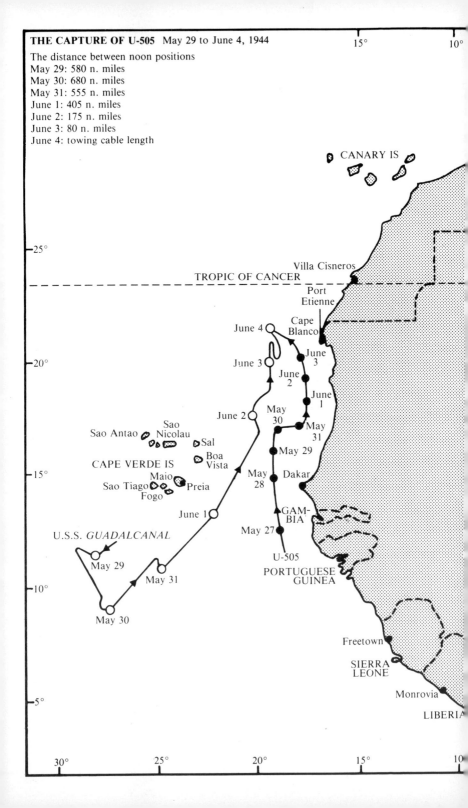

THE CAPTURE OF U-505 May 29 to June 4, 1944

The distance between noon positions
May 29: 580 n. miles
May 30: 680 n. miles
May 31: 555 n. miles
June 1: 405 n. miles
June 2: 175 n. miles
June 3: 80 n. miles
June 4: towing cable length

15°

10°

CANARY IS

25°

Villa Cisneros

TROPIC OF CANCER

Port
Etienne

Cape
Blanco

June 4

June 3

June
3

June 3

June
2

20°

June 1

May
30

June 2

May
31

Sao
Sao Antao   Nicolau

Sal

May 29

CAPE VERDE IS

Boa
Vista

Maio

May
28

Dakar

15°

Sao Tiago   Preia
Fogo

June 1

May
27

GAM-
BIA

U.S.S. *GUADALCANAL*

U-505

May 29

PORTUGUESE
GUINEA

May 31

May 30

10°

Freetown

SIERRA
LEONE

Monrovia

5°

LIBERIA

30°   25°   20°   15°   10°

Right: U-664, a Type VIIC, under attack from USS *Card* (AVG-11), 9 August 1943. The U-boat's 88mm gun had been removed earlier that year. (US National Archives)

Below: U-505 after her capture in June 1944; it was one of only three U-boats captured in the Second World War. The last remaining Type IXC in the world, U-505 is now preserved at the Chicago Museum of Science and Technology. (US Navy)

Top left: Grumman Avenger TBF 1s above their carrier task force. The Avenger became the standard US Navy torpedo-bomber in the Second World War and, after its first operational appearance (at the Battle of Midway), the type took part in all subsequent major air-sea actions. (IWM)

Left: Grumman Wildcat F.4F.4, the standard US Navy fighter in 1942–43. (US National Archives)

Above: Bob Payne, Commanding Officer of the Composite Squadron VC6 aboard the USS *Tripoli*, 1944.

Left: USS *Core*. A successful hunter-killer, *Core* sank two U-boats on her first operational cruise and three more on her subsequent two cruises. She was finally withdrawn from service in 1969.

Below left and right: Deck landings were always a risky business and accidents were inevitable. These two incident happily without casualty, involved an Avenger (below left) and a Wildcat.

Above: USS *Santee*, which was completed as a mercantile tanker (*Esso Seakey*) and taken over by the US Navy in 1940. In 1942 she was converted from a fleet oiler to an escort carrier. After operational duties in the Atlantic in 1942/43, *Santee* saw action in the Pacific where she was damaged by enemy submarine and aircraft torpedoes, October 1944. (US National Archives)

Below: USS *Jenks*, a Buckley class escort destroyer, being refuelled by USS *Guadalcanal*. (US National Archives)

Forney's radioman David Blazer was in the centre bay with his lookout's binoculars round his neck when the pilot called over the inter-com 'There it is. Go aft and get ready for an attack!' He checked the armament switches and broke out the camera. As they went down he lay in the belly facing aft, getting the camera ready. Gunner Jim Basserman got his turret cleared away and operative. He first sighted the sub over the port wing as they dived on it.

Both D.C.s splashed in off the sub's starboard quarter. As they banked, Blazer clicked his shutter, Basserman opened up with the turret gun. Forney saw the charges explode just aft of the U-boat's stern, about twenty feet away, then he was busy getting out of the way of the two eager Wildcats, which were strafing the target again.

He heard Hodson call, 'The sub's going down!'

The U-boat was turning to starboard, her stern settling beneath the waves. When she had disappeared completely, Forney, who was closest to the spot, lowered his flaps and wheels ready to drop his Fido, but while he was losing speed the submarine came up again, levelling off with the conning tower out of the water and the fore deck just awash. Seeing this, Forney pulled up his wheels and flaps, and turned away.

Stapler too was coming in to drop his torpedo. He saw the U-boat struggling to surface, moving very slowly, then slip back again and begin to settle. Her bow came up slightly, the conning tower disappeared, and finally the bow went under. Stapler dropped his Fido about 200 feet ahead of the big oil slick which the sub had left, a hundred yards to starboard of her last track. Ten seconds later Forney dropped his torpedo on the port side.

He circled the spot very slowly, and after about five minutes Blazer called his attention to a big shock wave on the water forward and to starboard of the place where the submarine had gone down. A few minutes later he saw air bubbling to the surface inside a big circle of light blue water. When they left the scene Basserman watched the pattern of snake-like tracks left on the water by the submarine until

101

they were out of sight. This was the last sign anyone ever saw of U-117.

The next day was Sunday, August 8th. Sallenger and his crew in T.B.F.9 and Ensign John F. Sprague in a Wildcat were on morning patrol together. The previous day's good weather had not lasted. There was a solid overcast with occasional rain squalls and poor visibility, so they were constantly ducking in and out of the cloud base. Just after eight o'clock they came out of cloud at 800 feet, and on his port bow Sallenger saw two U-boats about a mile away, close together on slightly different courses, as if they had just parted company, both heading in a northerly direction. Their decks were awash but they were going very slowly, and there was no bow wave or wake.

It all happened so fast that he did not report the contact before attacking, but turned on his transmitter to warm it up, figuring on reporting immediately after his first run.

He signalled the F.4F. to attack. Sprague's fighter slid under the belly of the Avenger and they made a split attack on the nearer of the two submarines, coming in from bow to stern, the Wildcat from port, the Avenger from starboard.

The F.4F. made a classic strafing attack, working over the U-boat's deck and conning tower methodically. But the crews of these two subs, U-262 and U-664, were fit and fresh from leave, and in a belligerent mood after beating off aircraft attacks in the Bay of Biscay.

They concentrated on the slower, bulkier T.B.F. When Sallenger was little more than half way to the target, with about 1,000 yards to go, he suddenly felt the whole plane jolt with the force of a hit in the belly, and he noticed the bomb bay light go out. A twenty-mm explosive shell had smashed up through the bomb bay into the tunnel compartment, knocking out the radio, inter-com and other electrics. Another shell hit the fin and rudder. The T.B.F. took several more hits in the tunnel, and one of these killed John O'Hagan.

Something started to burn in the bomb bay, and Sallenger knew they were seriously damaged, but he carried on and pressed the depth-charge release. Nothing happened. With the damage to the electrical system, the D.C.s would not drop. He turned for a second run.

As he came in from the starboard quarter his engine was popping and cutting out, and he could not get up enough speed. This time the flak seemed even heavier, and the F.4F. was busy working over the other submarine. The T.B.F. was hit in the port main gas tank at the wing root. The tank only had about thirty gallons left in it at the time, but the shell tore a hole in it about a foot wide, and it burst into flames. They could feel the plane shudder from other hits.

Sallenger held on and detached the D.C.s with the manual emergency release. He looked back to make sure they had gone, and saw them explode close aboard the enemy.

By now his wing tank was burning badly, so about a mile ahead of the course of the U-boat he turned directly into wind, reduced speed, held off and sank towards the water. His flaps and bomb bay doors were hanging open. He tried to close them but the hydraulic system had been punctured and they would not budge. They churned the water as the plane came in, then the whole big machine flopped in with a jarring crash.

The water doused the fire in the wing. Sallenger was unhurt, Downes popped out of the turret and together they got the rubber boat out. Then Sallenger realised that O'Hagan was missing. He swam to the other side of the plane, dived under, and opened the tunnel door. He was half-way into the tunnel when the plane started to settle and he had to get clear in a hurry. In a few seconds it was gone.

As he and Downes were inflating the rubber boat they saw Sprague's F.4F. going in for another strafing attack. Then quite suddenly the plane had vanished and its engine was silent.

Sallenger and Downes paddled as fast as they could down-wind, thinking one of the U-boats might surface near them. This, though they did not realise it at the time, took them right back over the scene of the action. They actually paddled through a big oil slick that must have been left by the attacked submarine as it submerged. It was so new that they could smell the fresh oil.

When neither the T.B.F. nor the Wildcat returned from patrol and all efforts to contact them by radio failed, Isbell turned the task group towards the centre of their patrol area. There the destroyer *Barry* found Sallenger and Downes sitting in their rubber boat. A little later they were told that Sprague was missing. No trace of him could be found, and it was learned some time later that he had, as presumed, been shot down by flak from the U-boats.

But *Card* was not finished with these predators. About eight o'clock that evening the watch officer of U-664, continuing on her passage to far-flung hunting grounds, saw the shape of a large ship in the dusk.

'Big tanker ahead.'

The Commanding Officer of U-664, Kapitänleutnant Adolf Graef, who had been playing chess at the time, decided that this was a prime target, but his marksmanship was about as good as his subordinate's ship recognition, and he missed with three torpedoes. *Card* steamed on in complete ignorance of her escape.

Graef was an officer who tried to make up for his own inefficiency by harsh discipline. At midday the next day, August 9th, he foolishly surfaced to recharge batteries.

Lieutenant (jg) G.G. Hogan U.S.N.R. in *Card*'s T.B.F.12 broke cloud cover and saw U-664 as an 'object on the water with a short, bright, white wake,' on the port bow not more than two miles away.

Captain Isbell and Compo 1's C.O. Carl Jones, had passed the night watches working out a new tactic which they hoped would cope with a U-boat fighting it out on the surface. They could not afford to lose any more aircraft and crews. They decided to try an attack team composed of one fighter and two T.B.F.s, one of the latter armed as before with two depth-charges and a Fido, the other with two 500-pounder instant-fuzed bombs. If a U-boat fought it out on the surface, the bombs were to be used first, either to deal her a mortal blow or force her down. If she did dive, in went the other T.B.F. with D.C.s and Fido. Hogan's team, with Forney in the other T.B.F. and Norman Hodson in the fighter, was one of the first of these guinea-pig units.

Hogan was carrying the bombs, Forney the Fido and D.C.s. The first Hogan's radioman Casper Pfeifer and turret gunner Leslie Miles knew of the submarine was when the pilot shouted 'Contact! Contact.' over the inter-com. Then they were climbing at full power towards the target, and Hogan was making his contact report to the ship. Pfeifer checked his switches, broke out his camera and got down in the tunnel. Hogan levelled off at 2,000 feet and dived. By this time the sub was diving too, and only her conning tower and part of her stern were still visible.

Hogan dropped one bomb from 750 feet. It screamed down and exploded off the submerged port bow of the target. The blast rocked Forney's T.B.F., close behind. Hogan pulled up sharply just in time to see Forney's D.C.s explode almost under the sub.

Below, in U-664, men were thrown off their feet as the whole boat was lifted in the water. Lighting failed, the switchboard for the electric motor short-circuited, fuses blew, and there was a lot of minor damage. The switchboard was quickly repaired, and the boat might have escaped by going deeper, but Graef ordered her brought up.

As she broke surface, Hodson's Wildcat dived and raked her from stern to bow, and flames shot up just abaft of the conning tower, followed by heavy clouds of black smoke, where he had hit an ammunition locker.

The Wildcat made several more strafing runs, and about ten men came up on deck and started to break out life rafts. They either jumped into the sea or were hit by Hodson's bullets. Then the submarine got under way and seemed to be diving, so Hogan told the other planes to stand clear, and pushed over from 3,500 feet to drop his other bomb. The big 500-pounder left the bomb bay at 650 feet and hit the sea fifty feet off the U-boat's port quarter. The explosion seemed to slow her down but she continued her dive and in about half a minute was completely under.

Now Graef decided to try to go deeper to escape. He got the boat down to fifty feet, but severe leaks were reported, one in the radio room, one in an after compartment. The boat was filling rapidly, and the trim could not be maintained. The main lighting system was still out of action, and cracked battery cells were filling with water, though the electric motors were still working. After ten minutes of this Graef ordered the tanks blown.

The entire attack area was covered with oil patches and bomb scum. Forney said, 'Get ready for attack,' and prepared to drop his Fido, but looked at the men in the water, some on life rafts, some floating helpless or dead, and decided it was superfluous, though it was against doctrine not to complete the attack. Then the submarine suddenly surfaced again in the midst of the foul scummy slick. She moved slowly, stern-down, circling to port.

As she drifted round, her bows rising inexorably higher and higher in the air, three relief T.B.F.s arrived from *Card*, with attendant fighters.

The Avengers of Lieutenant (jg) C.C. Hewitt and J.B. Thompson were the first on the scene. Although the submarine appeared to be in her death throes, they had all been firmly ordered en route to attack the U-boat until she sank, and the two T.B.F.s prepared to dive.

Hewitt came in first, but he could not get his bomb bay doors to open fully and had to go round again. Thompson made an attack thirty seconds later and released one 500-pound bomb which fell some thirty feet astern of the U-boat and set the trailing oil on fire. The sub continued to turn to starboard, and Hewitt dived for a second attempt. Again, lack of hydraulic pressure prevented the bomb bay doors from opening fully, and he had to turn away once more without dropping. He turned sharply and made a third-time-lucky approach. By this time he knew what the fault was and managed to get the doors open with the hand pump. He dropped both his 500-pounders in salvo and they hit the water about seventy-five feet ahead of the U-boat's tilting bows. About five minutes later Ensign P.J. Carter in T.B.F. No. 6, in company with an F.4F., joined the others. There were already men abandoning ship, but Carter followed orders, signalled the Wildcat to make a strafing attack, then began his bombing run. As he approached he saw men on the conning tower. To be on the safe side he decided to give them a burst with his front gun, but in reaching for the trigger he accidentally pressed the bomb release as well, and two depth-charges hit the water some 200 yards ahead of the much harassed submarine. There were no more attacks after that, as the entire crew was obviously leaving the boat, breaking out and inflating life rafts, throwing them overboard and leaping in after them. Shortly after the last able-bodied man had come out of the stricken submarine, at nine minutes past three, she raised her bows vertically in the air and sank. The Group cartoon swordfish painted on the conning tower made its last plunge. After seven hours in the water, the U.S.S. *Borie* came up and began taking the men aboard. She had reached forty-four when another U-boat fired five torpedoes at her. They all missed, but she had to abandon the rescue.

The area south of the Azores, so well policed by the American C.V.E.s, was too hot for U-boats. A stream of signals showed that boats on transit were being routed north of the islands, and after she had taken U-664's survivors on board, *Card* was ordered to hunt in that area.

In the afternoon of August 11th, a fine, clear afternoon except for a slight haze on the sea, Ensign Jack Stewart in F.4F4. No. 18 was flying wing on Hewitt's T.B.F. 370 miles west-nor'-west of Corvo when he saw a long white streak below on the sea, about fifteen miles away on his port bow.

He zoomed ahead, pointing at the white patch. Hewitt followed him and they went in at full throttle for an attack. At the end of the white water, not showing up at first against the sea, was the long grey shape of a U-boat.

Stewart held his fire, as there was nothing coming up

from below, until he was some 400 yards away. There was no one on deck, and U-525, a 740-ton supply boat, was not expecting company. Stewart's bullets sprayed the conning tower and produced some big red flashes followed by dense black smoke.

The T.B.F. came in behind him on the same course, and dropped two depth-charges which exploded about twenty-five feet off the U-boat's port beam. Stewart made a strafing run from the starboard quarter. There were more red flashes, and he noticed the bow going under water. He climbed and circled the scene of action.

This gave him a grandstand view of a Fido in action. He could see the submarine quite clearly, about twenty feet beneath the surface, and he watched the torpedo hit the water about twenty feet to starboard of her. Then he saw the underwater track of the missile as it swung round towards the sub, striking her on the starboard side about half-way between the conning tower and the stern. Then came the explosion, with a surge of dirty brownish water rising in the air, followed by a gusher of oil which spread over a circular area. From the midst of this a huge bubble erupted like the last breath of the dying boat and her doomed crew. Hewitt dropped dye markers, and they returned to the ship after about half an hour.

Card was now due to go Stateside for an overhaul, and she left Azorean waters for Casablanca, where she was to pick up a G.U.S. convoy and escort it back to Norfolk, while *Core* and her group patrolled the Azores in her place.

By August only three of Dönitz's twelve milch cow submarines were left, and he was having to curtail the patrols of his boats in the Caribbean and South American waters. 'There are no more reserve tankers available,' he recorded in his War Diary for August 5th, 'only the most essential supply operations can be carried out, and then only on an outward passage.'

U-84 had had an unsuccessful patrol off Cuba, and on August 23rd was homeward bound 750 miles south-west of Fayal in urgent need of fuel when a *Core* T.B.F. team, patrolling ahead of Convoy U.G.S.15 in an area where Intelligence had reported a concentration of U-boats, sighted her. They attacked, but U-84 got away this time.

U-604 and U-185 had both been patrolling off the coast of Brazil. When U-604 was sunk, Kapitänleutnant Maus' U-185 rescued survivors, including U-604's commander, Kapitänleutnant Holtring. U-185 was now also on her way home and looking for a milch cow in the same area.

Two patrol teams were launched from *Core* just after six o'clock on the morning of the 24th to search this area, with particular attention to the spot where the previous day's attack had been made.

It was a clear day, with some useful cloud cover between 1,500 and 3,000 feet. Lieutenant Williams, who had made three previous attacks on U-boats, with his usual crew of Radioman Grinstead and turret gunner Paden, was flying at 7,000 feet, above the clouds, in company with Lieutenant M.G. O'Neill's F.4F. They were about a hundred miles away from the ship when the alert Grinstead's attention was attracted by the sun glinting off a fully surfaced light-grey submarine about four miles on their starboard bow. It was U-185, cruising at twelve knots.

The two planes dived for cloud and turned to starboard to approach the enemy from astern. They burst out of the cloud and O'Neill immediately made a strafing attack, while Williams called up *Core* to make his report. There was no acknowledgement, so he gave up talking to himself and dived towards the sub's starboard quarter. Checking the bomb bay door light, Grinstead saw that the pilot had forgotten to open the doors. He quickly operated the release himself and got back just in time to take pictures. Williams dropped two D.C.s which straddled the enemy, the first exploding underneath her, the second off her port bow. White water completely enveloped the U-boat except for a few feet of her bow. She turned sharply to port with dense smoke pouring from the conning tower, and began to settle by the stern. O'Neill turned tightly to port and made a second strafing run from the sub's starboard quarter.

Below in the submarine the pressure hull had been ruptured under the battery compartment, and water was pouring in, flooding the batteries and releasing choking chlorine gas. Holtring, the passenger, grabbed his Luger and ran to the for'ard torpedo room where two badly wounded members of his crew were lying. He knew that the would never be able to get out if the boat sank, and in fact when they saw him they both begged him to shoot them rather than let them die by drowning. Holtring raised the gun and did so, then shot himself.

Meanwhile the other patrol team from *Core,* Lieutenant R.F. Neely in the T.B.F. and VC13's C.O. Charles Brewer in the Wildcat, had intercepted Williams' call to *Core.* Their communications were in order and they relayed the message to the ship, being immediately told to go to the assistance of the other pair.

After about four minutes' flying Neely sighted the U-boat about ten miles off their starboard bow. Brewer made a strafing run on the target from astern. The T.B.F. followed him down fifteen seconds later but the circuit breaker was out, and its D.C.s would not release. Neely flew very low over the submarine and his turret gunner raked her with a burst. Brewer saw his failure and told him to make another run. He himself dived and strafed again from astern. As he passed over the U-boat he saw survivors jumping overboard, and called to Neely, 'Hold your bombs, she's finished.' Soon after he had spoken the submarine sank swiftly by the stern.

Neely's T.B.F. stayed in the vicinity of the sinking for four hours until relieved by another T.B.F. from *Core* which had been sent to guide the destroyer *Barker* to pick up survivors and give cover while the rescue was going on. Of the thirty-six men taken aboard, many were suffering acutely from inhaling chlorine gas.

As these wretched men were being hauled into *Barker*'s boat, Lieutenant (jg) William A. Felter in his Avenger saw U-84, which had escaped the day before, poke her grey bows out of a rain squall ten miles away from the scene. As

Felter began his attack the submarine dived. The T.B.F. dropped her Fido, which made sure that U-84 would never need a milch cow.

Core's engines now needed attention and she was forced to break off the cruise and return home for repairs. *Card*, waiting at Casablanca for her G.U.S. convoy to assemble, was ordered to take her place and investigate a reported concentration of U-boats north-east of the Azores. On August 27th Hogan, with Fido in the kennel and a 500lb bomb, attacked U-508, which evaded the bomb and dived too smartly for the dog to find his bone. Half an hour later Lieutenant Ralph Long found the 740-ton supply submarine U-847, which had already provided five other U-boats with fuel and stores since August 19th. The milch cow was not so lively. Two F.4F.s drove her under, and Fido got her.

In a hundred days of action in the Central Atlantic, the aircraft from four small carriers had sunk sixteen U-boats, for the loss of three planes from their squadrons and only one ship from the convoys they had protected.

Aircraft from Royal Navy escort carriers had not sunk a U-boat since *Archer*'s kill on May 23rd, and Washington again accused the R.N. of unjustified delays in making C.V.F.s operational. On August 27th, with the British adding further modifications to some ships for 'fighter' and 'assault' roles, the Anti-Submarine Survey Board recommended that the U.S. Navy should man five of the next seven carriers allocated to the R.N. The situation afterwards improved, especially when the anglicising modifications were taken over by a Canadian yard.

[1] All U.S. auxiliary carriers were re-classified for the second time, from A.C.V. to C.V.E., on 15th July 1943, with 'E' standing for 'escort.' All former 'auxiliary' carriers became henceforth 'escort' carriers in U.S. terminology, whereas the British Admiralty, unlike the U.S. Navy, refitted their American-built auxiliary carriers as specialist ships, and listed them in accordance with these functions, e.g. 'escort' (meaning just that), 'assault' (for combined operations), and 'fighter' carriers, though these ships were often referred to as C.V.E.s, American style.
[2] Later the Fourth Fleet.
[3] Named after a sound off the North Carolina coast.
[4] A version of the F.4F.4 with the outer pair of guns eliminated but the number of rounds increased from 1,440 to 1,720, built by the Eastern Aircraft Division of General Motors at Linden, New Jersey.

7. 'Scratch one pig boat . . . Am searching for more!'

On the evening of October 3rd 1943 a strange little convoy steamed out of the river Clyde, Scotland. Rounding the Mull of Kintyre, the ships entered the North Channel and were soon out in the Atlantic, where they found winter and rough weather.

Had there been U-boats on station off the west coast of Ireland any skipper raising his periscope and picking up this oddly assorted squadron would have studied the grey-painted liner and concluded that she must be a V.I.P. to be escorted by three destoyers, anti-submarine trawlers and her own escort carrier. A spread of torpedoes would have followed, and Operation Alacrity, two frustrating years in the making, might have foundered in two minutes.

'Alacrity' was the implementation of the Salazar agreement to give British aircraft the use of airfields in the Azores. Aboard the liner *Franconia* were Air Vice-Marshal Geoffrey Bromet, Senior British Officer, Azores, his headquarters staff and other units of the British Army, Navy and Air Force, including R.A.F. personnel to run the airfields, and ground crews for Numbers 206, 220 and 233 Squadrons, which were to be the first Coastal Command Squadrons to operate from Lagens airfield on Terceira against submarines. The destroyers were the British H.M.S. *Inconstant* and the Polish O.R.P. *Burza* and *Garland*. The escort carrier was the *Bogue*-class, R.N.-manned H.M.S. *Fencer*, built by Western Pipe and Steel Corporation in San Francisco. Aboard her was Number 842 Composite Squadron, Fleet Air Arm, with nine Swordfish and six Seafire fighters, the navalized version of the famous Spitfire, and one Walrus amphibian.

It was much too rough to fly. Captain Anstice mustered the ship's company and briefed them on the object of the expedition. 'Resistance by the inhabitants of the Azores is not expected but you should be on your guard, as German agents are known to be working in the Islands,' he cautioned. U-boats were also thought to be using the bays and creeks of the Azores to make repairs, charge batteries and load fresh stores.

Thankfully there had been no U-boats off the Irish coast since 1940, though a big pack of them was attacking the convoys in the north-western Atlantic with their new acoustic torpedoes. They had sunk six merchantmen and three escorts from O.N.S.18 but lost three boats out of the twenty that had been gathered. The first M.A.C.-ship *Empire MacAlpine* and the Lend-Lease carrier H.M.S. *Tracker* were doing well up there, and planes from Iceland had sunk three more U-boats. The first tanker M.A.C. *Rapana* was coming over from Halifax with SC143.

The *Fencer* group headed south-west, pitching and rolling fiercely, towards the central Atlantic and out of range of German bombers from France.

Coming up from Bermuda, almost on a reciprocal course to theirs and crossing the Halifax-Finisterre parallel, was Buster Isbell with *Card* and her group. *Card* had left Hampton Roads on September 25th as guide to Task Group 21.14, with the old four-stackers *Borie*, *Barry* and *Goff*.

She had lost her old Composite Squadron 1, but gained *Bogue*'s veteran VC9, now commanded by Lieutenant-Commander H.M. Avery, with their new T.B.F.1Cs, a model in which two 0.5-inch cowl guns replaced the T.B.F.1B's single 0.3-inch. During her overhaul at Norfolk she had had the forward part of her flying bridge completely enclosed for protection in the forthcoming winter weather. Also fitted was a Foxer, a noise-making device trailed in the water to detonate an acoustic torpedo. The Foxer was noisy enough but also drowned out the ship's sonar at ten knots plus. *Card* reached Bermuda on the 27th, refuelled her escorts, and left again next day, heading due east. On the morning of the 30th young Ensign Jones, on refresher deck landings, gave his Wildcat the deep six when his engine cut

113

out, though *Goff* hauled him out of the drink none the worse, and in the afternoon Lieutenant Harwood dived his fighter into the deck, smashed his prop and landing gear, damaged the engine, badly wrinkled the fuselage, and severed wing fittings. The plane could be repaired on board, but it would take a long time.

Late that night Isbell received a signal reporting a concentration of U-boats north of the Azores. He swung north-east with his vintage D.D.s and steered for the U-boats at *Card*'s best speed of fifteen knots, throwing out T.B.F. patrols and refuelling *Borie, Barry* and *Goff* as he went.

On the afternoon of October 3rd *Card* sighted planes from *Santee* which had come up from Casablanca, and two hours later Isbell saw the other carrier group overhauling them on their starboard quarter.

Card stood on, making for the U-boat line which lay between them and the *Fencer-Franconia* convoy, heading south for the Azores.

At 6.30 a.m. on October 4th *Card* began to catapult four T.B.F.s on anti-submarine patrol. Two hours later one of them sighted a freighter lying dead in the water. She looked like a U-boat's victim.

Challenged, she flashed 'S.S. *Surprise*. Have engine trouble. Request help.'

There was not a lot the T.B.F. could do, except to fly the eighty miles back to the ship and drop a *Surprise* packet with her S.O.S. on the deck.

Isbell ordered another Avenger ranged to go and give the helpless freighter some cover from lurking U-boats.

By now the wind had died, and the accumulator pressure at the catapult had to be increased to get the heavy T.B.F. away. The plane, with Lieutenant (jg) D.E. Weigle at the controls, was poised on the catapult ready to go when, at 11.04 a.m., Isbell heard Bob Stearns' Avenger T.3 calling.

The signal was weak and the message garbled. '. . .sub sighted. . .' was about all that came through, but it was enough for Isbell. *Surprise* would have to wait. The loudspeaker barked.

114

'Launch the T.B.F.'

The Pratt & Whitney roared like thunder, the plane quivered on the catapult, straining at the strop. The pilot chopped his left arm across his chest . . . *Ready to go.*

The Air Officer dropped his flag. The T.B.F. went off like a fat rocket.

The bull horn roared again. 'Scramble two Wildcats.'

The klaxon squawked. A chasm gaped in the deck aft as the lift dropped. In minutes it came up again, bringing two fighters, their wings folded back like giant blue and white moths. Plane handlers in yellow, blue and green grabbed wing tips, deftly flipped them up and around, and two more Grummans were ready to fight. The pressure at the catapult was reduced for the lighter F.4F.s.

'Bong! Bong. Bong!' went the alarm bell. The voice of the Air Officer spluttered from the loudspeaker.

'Pilots, man your planes!'

The two young Wildcat jockeys, Lieutenants (jg) Heim and Puckett, in their khakis, yellow life jackets and helmets, jumped up out of The Goofers, ran across to their planes and climbed in, plane captains helping them strap in.

'Stand by to start engines.' The pilots eased throttles open, set mixtures, activated fuel pumps.

'Stand clear of propellers.' Plane handlers ran for The Goofers.

'Start engines!' One motor coughed, spluttered, roared into life, then the other, blue smoke wreathed the blunt rounded noses of the two fighters. The noise was too great now for speech. The flight deck officer switched to visual signals. He lowered his hands and fanned them outwards as if for the Charleston. Two crouching plane handlers, the gale from the slipstream trying to tear their clothes from their bodies, the hair from their heads, jerked the chocks from under the wheels and scrambled clear of the whirling prop. The F.D.O. raised his arms and waved the first plane forward, guiding it up the deck to the catapult, then turned to the second aircraft. One after the other the two were boosted into the blue. A few minutes after they had gone three other T.B.F.s which had been out on the dawn patrol and were circling the ship were vectored to the scene of Stearns' contact.

Meanwhile, below Stearns' still circling T3 four U-boats were having a fuelling party. The big 1,600-ton milch cow U-460 was about to cast off its nose from the smaller 740-ton U-264, into which she had just pumped sixty tons of diesel oil, and was preparing to launch balloons on which to float it across to the 1,600-ton U-422, waiting to port for her turn at the tit, while U-455 stood by in the queue to starboard. The fueller was towing a small boat with a man in it. Some seven or eight miles ahead were several more shapes which could be another group.

Weigle's T.B.F., Heim's and Puckett's Wildcats and the three T.B.F.s off the dawn patrol were on their way, but Stearns was not going to give this prize bag any more time to get away.

The four submarines were shifting their formation. The two big 1,600-ton flankers pulled out wider, and the smaller U-264 and the milch cow U-460 fell in behind the port hand 1,600-tonner, with U-264 pulling slightly ahead of the fueller.

Stearns attacked in spite of having no fighter support against the combined A.A. fire of four U-boats, which had made no attempt to dive, quite confident of being able to deal with one solitary bomber. He was aiming for the small triangle formed by the small sub, the fueller and the 1,600-tonner to port of them, but the blazing barrage put him slightly off his stroke, and his 500-pounder fell between U-264 and the fueller. The precious milch cows were under orders to dive if attacked but this one stayed where she was as if proving that the courage of a fighting bull comes from its mother. The skipper of U-264 shouted against the racket of his twenty-millimetres 'Dive. Dive!'

Stearns still had a homing torpedo in his bomb bay but doctrine forbade letting Fido loose while there were still subs on the surface. Beside, to lay a Mark 24 meant releasing from 200 feet and at 120 knots, and he would have been shot down long before he had reached release point.

He circled out of range of the U-boats' guns, waiting for reinforcements. After his bomb attack the submarines closed in again and began weaving about on radical zig-zag courses independently of each other but always staying as close together as they could without hitting each other. It looked to Stearns like a well-planned thoroughly rehearsed manoeuvre.

At 11.30 Weigle's T.B.F. arrived to join him and while the newcomer circled to await the fighters he made a report to the ship which was the first indication Isbell had had that there were four targets. He at once sent off every available plane, and it 11.35 began launching five more T.B.F.s and two F.4F.s. There was then a total of ten T.B.F.s and four F.4F.s in the air.

On the appearance of the second bomber the U-boat skippers, realizing that the Americans were getting help and that they would eventually be overwhelmed if they stayed on the surface, began circling so that they would be in a position to cover each other's dive.

At 11.34 U-264 pulled out of the circle and began to dive. Neither Stearns nor Weigle made any attempt to attack this boat as it was the smallest of the four and the least important target, and all *Card*'s T.B.F. pilots had been instructed to await fighter support before attacking a U-boat.

About a minute after U-264 had started to dive Heim and Puckett arrived. After exchanging signals with the T.B.F. pilots, Heim's Wildcat, followed closely by Puckett's, dived to attack the 1,600-tonner which had been on the port side of the formation to start with. The attacking team figured that as this boat was putting up the most lethal barrage, to silence it would give them a better chance of sinking the fueller. Heim pushed over at 1,500 feet, Puckett behind him. They seemed to be flying through a solid curtain of fire 150 feet high, some 300 feet wide and twenty-five feet thick, filled with black and white bursts of smoke.

Heim passed over the U-boat's stern and pulled out fifty feet from the water. David Puckett was following him down

117

into the fire, his six fifties blazing away. Heim's guns did not seem to have cut down the barrage at all, and Puckett's Wildcat lurched several times as it was hit. Shrapnel struck the fuselage just below the cockpit, and another piece knocked his port outboard gun off its trunnion.

Heim came in for another strafing run. At first the barrage seemed as heavy as ever, but as the sub loomed large over the nose its guns fell silent until there was only one firing at him. When he was about 500 feet from the target this one stopped. As he flashed across the submarine he caught sight of a man stretched out face-down on the deck well aft of the conning tower.

This boat, U-455, then dived before Puckett could get in another run, so he joined up with Weigle, who was preparing to make a bombing run on what he thought was the fueller.

When Puckett strafed this boat the flak was moderately heavy to begin with, but had died out almost completely before the end of his dive, so Weigle was hardly fired on at all when he made his attack.

He came in up the U-boat's stern fine on her starboard quarter. On his way he started to strafe with his own two fifty-calibre cowl guns. In doing so he inadvertently pressed the bomb release button, and all his four D.C.s fell and exploded, the nearest a good 750 feet short. He vented his anger by strafing the whole length of the boat, then just had time to make a second strafing run from the sub's starboard beam before it submerged, at 11.41, in a very steep crash-dive, with at least a quarter of the hull out of the water as it went down.

Now there were two – two submarines, two T.B.F.s with two torpedoes, two fighters. Stearns, seeing Weigle starting to attack, had manoeuvred so that he could drop his Fido on the last submarine as soon as it dived, but when he saw that the other boat was undamaged he flipped his plane round in a tight turn and started a run on this one, as a fueller was by far the most important target. But by the time he got to the spot there was no clear sign of where she might now be, so he saved his torpedo for the last U-boat left on the surface, which was actually the fueller, U-460.

Heim strafed her from the starboard beam, Puckett from abaft the beam. Heim came in again from the starboard quarter. The sub was not fighting back. As Puckett dived on her again she started to dive, making a violent turn to port.

As the sub began to dive Stearns, flying slightly out on its starboard side, lowered his wheels and prepared to make his run up the U-boat's track from fine on its starboard quarter. The U-boat suddenly put on left rudder but Stearns turned with her and his Fido splashed fifty feet in front of the point where she submerged. The torpedo travelled a short distance straight ahead, turned sharply to port towards the quarry and exploded about 250 feet further on. There was no plume of foam, but the water erupted in an unmistakeable shock wave. A brown slick formed, and about a minute later a mass of debris began to rise to the surface in the middle of it, evidence that the target was breaking up.

This was all there was to see when the second killer group of five T.B.F.s and two F.4F.s arrived to assist the seven planes already on the scene. They patrolled the area and attacked four whales which happened to pass through this patch and broached at the wrong time. A second quartet which came up to breathe in the afternoon was also strafed by *Card* planes, and when Stewart Holt in T.B.F.7 reported a surfaced sub three miles from the scene of the earlier U-boat battle Isbell was sceptical.

But this was the real thing. The eistacean patrol had found the damaged U-422. Holt was at 4,000 feet when he sighted her, with Ensign Horn in a Wildcat flying wing on him. He waggled his wings and pointed to the target, about two miles ahead on their starboard bow. Horn saw it and broke away to strafe. Holt reported the contact by radio.

Horn dived and beat up the sub, which crash-dived. Holt, coming in from astern, lowered his wheels and throttled back just as the sub's conning tower dipped below the sea. He dropped Fido ahead of the swirl and slightly to star-

119

board, pulled up his wheels and closed his bomb bay doors, while his radioman Don Allen took pictures as the torpedo splashed. Frank Kuczinski was taking photographs too with his turret gun camera, and saw the shock wave as the Fido exploded. As they circled the spot they saw oil and debris and a dark-coloured life raft come to the surface. An oily, scummy, stationary slick mushroomed up and grew steadily in size. It was *Card*'s sixth kill.

Isbell broke radio silence to report the S.S. *Surprise*'s predicament to Commander Tenth Fleet, then steamed on north. As his planes fanned out looking for more U-boats, a report came in that U.G.S.19 was being menaced by another pack on its passage eastward, and Isbell turned his group round and went south again to head off the wolves from his sheep. On the way, being a good shepherd, he sent off a T.B.F. to find the *Surprise*, and check on her condition, and started to top off *Borie* to go and stand by the vulnerable merchantman, but Com.in.Ch. reported the freighter under way, and *Borie* was unceremoniously cast off again without refreshment. At 10.30 Isbell was told that *Bogue* was going to the help of U.G.S.19, so he reversed course once more to head for the more northern concentration. *Bogue* had begun another cruise on September 7th with Composite Squadron (VC)19, a unit new to anti-submarine warfare, commanded by Lieutenant-Commander Claude Weaver Stewart U.S.N. of Seattle, Washington.

The weather now was fierce and foul, the Atlantic at its worst, and really unfit for flying, but H.M.S. *Fencer* and the Alacrity group were passing through a U-boat danger area as they steered for the Azores, and *Fencer* got off a patrol on October 6th, though the carrier was pitching heavily. On recovery the first Swordfish to land on missed all the wires, but *Fencer* was following a recommendation made by *Biter* to keep both barriers flat so that aircraft could go round again rather than incur certain damage. The Stringbag just managed to claw her way into the air again, removing one wing tip on the H.F./D.F. mast on the way, and landed safely on its second pass. After this experience *Fencer* used her for'ard barrier, but kept the after one down and wedged wood blocks under it to make an additional 'Jesus Christ!' wire.

Card and her old D.D.s were fighting the same wild weather. At dusk on October 7th Avenger T5 was caught in a bad squall attempting to land on, and spun in on its approach at the end of the down-wind leg. *Barry* picked up turret gunner H.M. Sams, but the pilot, Ensign C.H. Goodchild, and radioman P.E. Bartoszek could not get out in time and were drowned.

The two sister carriers had now passed each other, *Card* still butting her way through the Atlantic rollers, *Fencer* nearing the Azores and the end of her mission, but they were still close enough for the American T.B.F.s, searching for some sign that Goodchild and Bartoszek were still alive in that grim grey waste of ocean, to be diverted to look for a Swordfish from the British carrier which had also gone down there. Both searches proved to be hopeless.

On October 8th the *Fencer* group passed between Terceira and San Miguel Islands. The weather was milder here, and the carrier flew off patrols all day. In the evening she parted company with *Franconia,* which anchored off Angra Island.

Fencer continued to fly off patrols throughout the 9th and most of the 10th, when the R.A.F. Coastal Command Hudsons and Fortresses which were to operate from the Islands were expected at Lagens on Terceira.

But the bad weather had delayed them, and it was decided to put *Fencer*'s squadron ashore for temporary duty in their place. The Walrus was flown off to Lagens on the 10th and on the following morning *Fencer* flew off most of her Swordfish, one of which crashed in the sea, and her six Seafire fighters to Lagens, then anchored off Angra to act as controller for her shore-based aircraft, under the command of the new Azores Number 27 R.A.F. Group Headquarters.

Card continued to head north, flying off patrols, refuelling her short-winded old destroyers. Weather had improved, but by noon on October 11th it had worsened again, and all planes in the air were recalled to the ship.

Wind and sea had abated sufficiently by dawn on the 12th, Columbus Day, for four T.B.F.s to leave the catapult and carry out *Card*'s anti-submarine patrol plan 1A, the set-up normally used for the first patrol of the day. The four planes divided up the compass card between them into quadrants – forward port, forward starboard, after port, after starboard, each plane making three long triangular sector searches, with the apex at the ship, to cover each quadrant as thoroughly as possible. The two aircraft on the forward sectors first flew a short search out to forty miles from the ship and back, then each covered two larger sectors in their quadrant, with the planes on the after patrols each covering three large sectors in their quadrant. Plan 1, used on later patrols, was very similar, but the two initial small-sector patrols were not flown. Deepest patrols were those off the bow and just aft of the beam, which extended to some 450 miles. The two stern patrols went out as far as a hundred miles. The other patrols were pushed out to more than 200 miles.

At 10.20 a.m. four more Avengers started to leave the deck to relieve the dawn patrol and carry out Plan 1. The four tired early birds landed on as the last of the four fresh ones climbed away from the catapult.

Balliett, out on a port sector forward search, about 600 miles north of Flores and in mid-ocean directly between Newfoundland and Ireland, sighted a U-boat heading west-nor'-west in the direction of the northern convoy lanes.

The milch cow U-488 had been ordered to refuel several boats of the *Rossbach* group, which had been suffering such heavy losses at the hands of aircraft from Iceland, and was making for a rendezvous after dark.

Isbell ordered Weigle to assist Balliett, who almost immediately afterwards reported that he had attacked, and almost certainly sunk, the submarine with his Fido.

122

Balliett landed at 12.15. At 1.40 Bill Fowler reported another sub contact, and shortly afterwards another Fido kill.

At 3.46 p.m. Stewart Doty reported a fully surfaced U-boat, but missed with his 500-pounder and lost the contact. Three other T.B.F.s on patrol were vectored to the scene. One missed with a 500-pounder. Hodgson dived through intense flak, a piece of which put a one and a half-inch hole in one of his prop blades, and shook the sub with four D.C.s, but she stayed firmly on the surface, more confident in her gunners than in her ability to shake off a Fido dog. At 4.50 she did dive. Doty immediately dropped his homer on her, and believed he had destroyed her.

These boats had been heading for the rendezvous with U-488 after dusk, and there were other *Rossbach* subs going dry. But they would have to eke out what fuel they had, because the milch cow, critically damaged, was crawling out of the area, and she would only just make it home.

By dawn the next day, October 13th, Isbell had turned south again looking for better weather. The first patrol of the day was delayed by high winds and sea, but got off just before seven o'clock.

An hour later Fowler again reported a contact, and Howard Avery was catapulted to assist him. Avery flew the twenty-five miles in just over ten minutes, and Fowler dropped his Fido on the now submerged sub. No explosion was seen, but pictures taken by Avery's radioman suggested that the U-boat had probably been sunk.

U-402 was one of the boats looking rather urgently, and in vain, for a milch cow. At 10.45 a.m. Avery spotted her, heading south. Ensign Barton C. Sheela dropped his 500-pounder too far away to damage her, but close enough to frighten her into diving. Avery then unleashed his Fido. The crew of Sheela's T.B.F. had a very good view of the explosion and the oil and debris which came up.

For the rest of the morning and early afternoon Avery's crews combed the area of the earlier attacks and pushed further out to follow up contacts signalled to *Card* by CominCh.

At 4.45 p.m. Harry Fryatt in Avenger T9 found U-378 forty-four miles from the ship. He dived, and the U-boat fought back with all her guns. T9 was hit several times. One shell struck the starboard landing gear, and shrapnel cut both the hydraulic lines for lowering the gear, as well as the manual emergency release cable. Fryatt dropped his 500lb. bomb, the sub began a crash-dive, and Fryatt followed up with his Fido before the periscope had disappeared.

U-378 was damaged, but survived. Fryatt, heading back for the ship in rapidly worsening weather, with the high wind and heavy seas of a Force 10 gale blowing, knew the plane was hit, but did not know the extent of the damage.

He arrived over *Card* to find the carrier pitching and rolling heavily in the darkness. As he flew down-wind past the ship he tried to lower his undercarriage, but could not get his starboard wheel down.

All efforts to dislodge it failed. By then four more T.B.F.s were in the circuit. With darkness increasing rapidly and the weather getting worse all the time, Isbell acted decisively to save his aviators. Having recovered the four undamaged aircraft, not without difficulty, he took a calculated risk, ordered the flight deck lights turned fully on, and signalled Fryatt to come in.

The T.B.F. sank towards the round-down. Fryatt got his port undercarriage down, but the starboard wheel was uselessly jammed up and because of the loss of hydraulic fluid he could not get his landing flaps to extend fully.

He made a fair approach, slightly fast. Ahead of him the flight deck was clear, except for T.B.F.12, which had been pushed for'ard to the extreme starboard of the deck as there was no more room on the hangar deck.

The batsman whipped his paddle across his chest. Fryatt shut his throttle. But he was going too fast. Hook trailing, roaring through the darkness across the dim footlights of this grim floating stage, the big plane missed all the wires, ballooned over the barrier, hit the bridge island just above

124

Flying Control with its starboard wing and lost a wing tip, careered on, smashed into the T.B.F. parked for'ard, and screeched to rest fifteen feet from the edge of the flight deck. The parked plane fell off the deck, and as it did so swept pilot Roger Kuhn, who had been standing alongside it, into the sea.

Instinctively, or luckily, Kuhn kept a tight grip on the flash-light he was carrying. When he bobbed up in the water he switched it on. In a few minutes *Barry* came up out of the darkness and hauled him aboard, with nothing worse then a minor leg injury. Fryatt's plane was inevitably badly damaged, but it was repaired on board and, although not used again for operations on this cruise, was ready to be flown ashore on November 9th. Fryatt and his crew were shaken but unhurt.

As *Card* began to swing south-east, en route for Casablanca to contact and support west-bound convoy G.U.S.18, away south-west in the Azores the shore-based aircraft from an American-built carrier flying the White Ensign of the Royal Navy were still providing their rather restricted stop-gap cover over an area of American responsibility from a neutral Portuguese base the sovereignty over which was in the hands of a reactionary Catholic moralist who hated and feared the influence of America and the American way of life, and would not allow a single American airman to set foot on the islands, though he could not stop the American-built Flying Fortresses with R.A.F. crews which were due to fly in to Lagens as soon as the foul weather allowed.

Fencer's Seafires flew from their primitive grass field on anti-submarine patrols round the islands, watching bays and inlets for the U-boats which were said to come in for succour there. For eight days the British fighters swept round Terceira, Graciosa, San Jorge, Pico, and Fayal, and saw only fishing smacks. They began to doubt the stories about enemy subs lurking in sea caves, the sort of rumours which were also currently rife about U-boats using the coves and creeks of Eire and the remoter anchorages of Spain.

125

With some ancient oil lamps lining the flight path, they flew a few dusk patrols to try to catch conning towers rising at night, but had no better luck.

The aircrews lived in a one-roomed stone building or in tents, with no toilet facilities. Water was short and had to be treated before drinking. They were glad of a run ashore in Angra to drown the vile taste of chlorinated tea in muscatel or aniz. They could not cook anything, and dined mainly out of tins from *Fencer* or on ship's biscuit, flown in by a Swordfish from the anchored carrier, which also donated some canned beer. In fact Mother *Fencer* supported the entire expedition for twelve days. The aircraft were maintained with difficulty by R.A.F. mechanics and the naval Walrus ground crew. Sand was a real plague, and filters had to be inspected regularly. Truth to tell, though, the Seafires were happier flying from terra firma. The undercarriage legs of a Seafire approaching the deck looked like matchsticks, and if the deck was heaving or the wind had dropped, the matchsticks too easily snapped, whereas the underpins of the slower but sturdier Wildcat-Martlet would absorb most of the shocks which deck-landers were heir to.

As *Card* dropped the hook in Casablanca harbour on the morning of October 18th the first of the Coastal Command Flying Fortresses arrived at Lagens. From now on land-based air protection would be available to Allied ships over the whole North Atlantic north of 30° North, the latitude of the Canary Islands, with patrols from the Azores overlapping those from Newfoundland, Great Britain, Gibraltar and Morocco. Allied convoys from Britain to the Mediterranean, recently rerouted further west to avoid renewed surveillance and attacks by Luftwaffe maritime bombers from France, would benefit, as well as the U.G.S. convoys from the U.S.A. Already more than a week overdue, the new Azorean Fortress now lost no time in starting work, and was out on patrol the day after it had flown in. When *Card* left Casablanca on October 20th to escort G.U.S.18 through U-boat waters, first aircraft from Gibraltar gave them its protection, then the Lagens Fortress took over, and tired men and machines of VC9 got a three-day rest before they had to take over patrols, though four fighters were kept standing by on the flight deck to deal with Condors.

There was still a big job to be done by escort carriers in the Central and North Atlantic. Land based planes could not cover every square league of ocean. Communications between aircraft and base were frequently bad, and even Long Range Aircraft had a strictly limited loiter time over a contact. The quick response and extra fire power which a carrier could provide, and her availability as local radio and radar controller of both her own and land based aircraft in a combined attack, were important factors in the anti-submarine war. While *Card* was steaming west under the new Azorean umbrella, *Core,* now commanded by Captain James R. Dudley, with *Greene, Belknap* and *Goldsborough,* had taken her place north of the Azores, having left Hampton Roads on October 5th.

On the afternoon of October 19th Charles Brewer, C.O. of *Core*'s VC13 Composite squadron, in a Wildcat, and Lieutenant R.W. Hayman in a T.B.F. sighted U-378. This submarine's torpedoes had just sunk the Polish destroyer *Orkan,* and on her 'bandstands', which the German matelots called *wintergarten,* were the two single twenty-millimetre cannon and the fearsome quadruple twenty-mm which had almost terminated the young lives of Harry Fryatt and his crew on October 13th. Hayman was luckier than Fryatt, with a fighter to block for him. Brewer braved the awesome flak, chased the gunners out of the *wintergarten,* and exploded ammo in the conning tower, which was like a lethal Fourth of July for some wild moments. While everyone on the bridge was diving for cover, Hayman dropped his bomb, which blew U-378's pressure hull apart and sank her.

On October 21st a T.B.F. on dawn patrol sighted U-271 about thirty-five miles south-west of the carrier and called in help from Lagens. The carrier plane could not wait for Coastal Command, dived and damaged the submarine, which submerged and was hunted unsuccessfully by *Belknap*.

Several hundred miles further south in *Card*, six fighters were kept on deck all day and throughout the 22nd, as the Group and the convoy were still within range of long-reaching bombers from Biscay. At dawn on the 23rd they had reached a no man's land on the border between air patrols from Gibraltar and Terceira and submarines were reported in the vicinity. *Card* closed the convoy and launched four T.B.F.s on a 1A all-round search pattern. Bad weather blew up, and all planes were recalled at 9.40 a.m. The weather had cleared by half-past one in the afternoon and four Avengers went off again. Compo 1's reduced aircraft strength was now showing signs of combat fatigue. Of three T.B.F.s launched early on the afternoon of the 24th, T3 was back in twenty minutes with a faltering engine, and T6 returned later with hydraulic leaks.

On the 24th H.M.S. *Fencer* and her screen of mixed British and Polish destroyers put to sea from Angra, her Azores mission completed. She re-embarked her squadron, and later joined Convoy SC145 to give it support to the U.K. The Seafires were at readiness from dawn to dusk, with two pilots manning their aircraft, engines warmed up ready for an immediate scramble. The Swordfish began flying L-shaped or U-shaped patrols ahead of the convoy almost continuously round the clock. The slow Stringbags, as *Bogue*'s Giles Short had predicted, found it practicable to operate from the deck by night, and their hooded exhausts did not betray them to the enemy. The Americans had also begun night flying, badly needed to counter the U-boats' practice of surfacing in the dark to recharge batteries and radio their base. *Croatan* had initiated this in U.S. home waters on September 5th, and the *Bogue*-class U.S.S. *Block Island*, commissioned on March 8th but hitherto used to transport Army fighters from New York to Belfast, was now hunting U-boats north of the Azores using 'night owl' Avengers, which had had guns and bomb racks removed to allow extra gasoline tanks to be fitted, giving them the stamina to stay airborne for as long as fourteen hours.

At dawn on October 25th the *Card* group was still covering G.U.S.18, though it was now in an area south-west of the Azores which the C.V.E.s had cleared of U-boats, and Isbell had drawn off to visual distance again. He felt fairly certain that G.U.S.18 was out of the danger zone now, and wanted to break off to hunt U-boats. He took his ships into the convoy once more so that his D.D.s could refuel from convoy tankers, then left in the early afternoon for flight operations. At noon on October 26th he was heading east, with patrols up, when he received a report of a U-boat refuelling concentration to the south-east, off the Canaries. Breaking radio silence to recall his planes, he altered course in that direction. By dawn, sonar, radar, Huff-Duff alike had found no contacts, and the long night chase at full speed had depleted his D.D.s' fuel once more, so he secured flight operations and turned north, topping up the destroyers as he went. At dawn on October 28th *Card* was a hundred miles east of the Azores, steaming hard for a reported U-boat refuelling area north-east of Newfoundland and some 500 miles north of Flores, where both the *Fencer* and *Block Island* groups were at this very time getting involved with the enemy. The operation of Very Long Range aircraft from the Azores was now pushing U-boat refuelling areas away from these sheltered waters to the north, south and west.

Fencer's Swordfish C had sighted a U-boat twenty-eight miles on Convoy SC145's port bow. This boat stayed surfaced and opened fire on the Stringbag, which prudently retired out of range and stayed clear until an attack team arrived from *Fencer* comprising one Swordfish with eight R.P.s, another with depth-charges, and a Seafire. The U-boat dived before they could mount a full-scale attack, but Swordfish C depth-charged her. There was no apparent result, though the other D.C. Swordfish circled the spot for half an hour. By now the weather had worsened, and *Fencer* was pitching badly. Two of the returning aircraft were damaged landing on.

Meanwhile *Block Island*'s planes had spotted and broken up the refuelling party. U-220 had been sewing mines off St John's, Newfoundland, and was making for a rendezvous with the milch cow when the C.V.E.'s aircraft attacked and sank her.

Card was over 500 miles from the scene of this attack but heading that way at her best speed of fifteen knots at dawn on the 29th. Isbell had altered course twenty degrees to port to come into the U-boat area from further south in the hope of intercepting replenished subs heading his way. Four T.B.F.s were launched on an all-round search, and *Goff* came alongside for a drink. At 10.36 a.m. two Avengers left the catapult to cover the sectors forward of the beam, and the first patrol was recovered.

One of these machines broke a wheel on touch-down. There had been fourteen previous cases of broken wheels, caused by hard landings in heavy weather. *Card* had only been allowed a quota of eight spare wheels, all of which had been used up before her last call to Casablanca, so this otherwise minor crash put one more aircraft out of commission. The Squadron was already reduced in strength, and other T.B.F.s had been giving trouble. T6 had aborted again with engine trouble, T10 had returned prematurely on the 28th with an oil leak. In fact the squadron ground crews were wishing they had their old T.B.F.1s back. All the brand-new 1Cs showed signs of failure at certain of the fuselage horizontal bulkheads. Two aircraft which failed were repaired completely by *Card*'s fitters and operated with no further trouble. A plague of hydraulic leaks in flight was temporarily overcome by putting a gallon can of hydraulic fluid in the radioman's compartment to fill the reservoir as needed. To a grumbling A.R.M.2c one mechanic was heard to say, 'Hell, it'll give you something to do up there.' For some defects there was no permanent solution this side of a Navy yard. One of the worst of these was the persistent failure of the generator gear box oil seal, which brought eight T.B.F.s in for deferred forced landings. One machine had to have an engine change, a very unpopular exercise in an already overcrowded hangar, with aircraft constantly coming in and out on and off patrol, and the imminent possibility of a rapid turn-over in a U-boat danger area, and three others were removed from the flying schedule suffering from this fault plus the wheel shortage.

To preserve his aircraft, therefore, against the passage through heavily infested U-boat waters in the days ahead, Isbell secured all flight operations when the second patrol of the day had been recovered. The dropping of a message from a T.B.F. reporting the remains of some torpedoed freighter's deckload of timber had helped him make the decision.

At first light on October 30th *Card*, with faithful flush-deckers *Borie*, *Barry* and *Goff*, was some 225 miles south of the point where *Block Island*'s planes had sunk U-220, making fifteen knots. Avenger T11 on the dawn patrol reported an oil slick ninety miles ahead of the ship, drifting north. As the first patrol was returning to the ship, two T.B.F.s were launched to cover the forward sectors. Both of these returned after about two hours on patrol with engine trouble. Scraping the barrel, Isbell's Air Officer found five T.B.F.s to launch on another patrol, one of them, T11, to fly an expanding square search round the area where the same plane had found the oil slick earlier.

At 1.52 p.m. Harry Fryatt, who had the Squadron record for sighting subs, found another one in the refuelling area, fifty-seven miles from the ship. This boat followed Dönitz's new orders belaying the 'fight back' tactics, and dived as Fryatt came in with his 500-pounder. He held back the bomb and dropped his Fido. There was no oil or debris, nor even any spoiler fragments from the Mark 24, but photographs taken convinced Isbell and his staff that the sub had been sunk. The usual flotsam had probably been hidden by the rising sea. The weather, in fact, got so bad that Isbell recalled all aircraft at half-past three and shut down flight operations.

The foul weather persisted through the night and prevented all flying until shortly after noon on October 31st.

131

At eight minutes past four Bill Fowler in T7 reported one U-boat refuelling another twenty-seven miles astern of *Card*. The other four planes on patrol were immediately vectored to the scene, two with bad compasses being given sun bearings.

Both boats opened fire on Fowler, with the suckling sub, U-91, frantically casting off the hose, then crash-diving. When Balliett's and McAuslan's T.B.F.s arrived twelve minutes later, the milch cow submerged and was immediately attacked with Fidos by Fowler and Balliett at fifteen-second intervals. Two explosions were heard, and oil and debris came to the surface to mark the end of U-584.

Isbell mistakenly thought he had killed the calf and lost the cow. It was too late for a further air search, but he sent the keen young Charles Hutchins in *Borie* to chase the escaping sub.

U.S.S. *Borie* D.D.215, was a typical old four-piper, with a record of long and faithful service. She was launched on October 4th, 1919, from the yard of William Cramp & Son, Ship and Engine Building Company, of Philadelphia, by Miss Patty Borie, great-grandniece of Adolph Edward Borie, Secretary of the Navy under President Ulysses S. Grant, and first saw service in Turkish waters in the Black Sea in 1920. She then served for three years in the U.S. Asiatic Fleet, spending her summers based at Shanghai, her winters in the Philippines. Two years in home and Caribbean waters were followed by a cruise to Europe with the Atlantic Fleet, then three more years in the Far East. Through 1932 and 1933 *Borie* led Destroyer Squadron 2, Battle Fleet, sailed the Pacific until 1939, and returned through the Panama Canal to join the Neutrality Patrol and Inshore Patrol off the Americas. She left the sunny Caribbean on June 26th, 1943, for Norfolk, Virginia, and service in the Atlantic with *Card*. Unlike many of her class, she had been on active service all her life, and could still raise twenty-plus knots when asked.

The old destroyer plunged through the rolling seas, her hull creaking and groaning, spray hitting her bridge screens, wake gleaming in the darkness, radar and sonar probing through the night. A little after midnight radar got a small contact, which the operator thought must be a surfaced submarine. As *Borie* approached, the sub dived. The destroyer fired a pattern of D.C.s and there was a rumbling underwater explosion. She came in for a second attack. This time the submarine surfaced, only to dive again stern-First. After a third run with D.C.s, sonar ceased pinging and all traces of the enemy vanished. Optimistically Hutchins signalled to *Card*,

'Scratch one pig boat. . .Am searching for more!'

Forty-five minutes after he had sent this signal Hutchins found his second 'pig boat', which showed itself on radar. *Borie* closed to 2,800 yards, and the sub dived, transferring her image from a green blip on the radar to a musical ping on sonar. Hutchins closed to within a quarter of a mile and fired depth-charges. Through a defect in the firing mechanism all the D.C.s on the racks ran down the rails. There was a series of crumping explosions and U-405 reared to the surface, eerily white, like Moby Dick come to Ahab.

Hutchins turned a blazing white searchlight full on her and ordered 'All guns open fire!'

The U-boat, damaged and unable to submerge, tried to run. Hutchins increased revolutions, and *Borie* gave chase, four-inch, twenty-millimetre and machine-guns all firing on the enemy. As she closed the range men came up out of the U-boat's hatches, looking like Long John Silver's crew, long-haired, with coloured shirts and bandannas round their heads, manned their guns, and a furious gun battle began.

The U-boat's shells hit *Borie* in her for'ard engine room and bridge. From her starboard quarter *Borie*'s cannon raked the sub's decks, and a four-inch shell from the destroyer knocked out her big gun. As *Borie*'s bows drew abreast the U-boat's starboard quarter Hutchins ordered,

'Hard-a-port. Stand by to ram!'

Seeing the destroyer's bows keel over, Korvettenkapitän Hopman turned the sub to port to comb *Borie*'s track. As a result, the destroyer's sharp stem smashed into her about thirty feet abaft the U-boat's bows, riding right up over the submarine's hull and coming to rest there with a screeching, grinding crash.

The two vessels, locked together, rose and fell in the twenty-foot waves, screws racing, sawing at each other. Water poured into *Borie*'s engine room as her worn-out old plates, held together by rust, collapsed. Soon her Engineer Officer, Lieutenant Morrison R. Brown, was deep in water at the throttles. Up above, *Borie*'s guns poured a point-blank fire into the after part of the submarine, still above the surface. A four-inch shell completely demolished the conning tower, and *Borie*'s men grabbed any weapon they could find to fire or hurl at the U-boat pirates in their raffish rags. Revolvers, rifles and shotguns poured bullets across the narrow gap, and the thump-thump-thump of the twenty-millimetres kept up a steady beat. Lieutenant Phil Brown, *Borie*'s Exec., poked a tommy gun over the bridge rail and opened up Chicago-style. A German running to man a gun collapsed with a Bowie knife in his stomach. Chief Bosun's Mate Wally Kruz knocked another man down with a four-inch shell case still hot from the gun

This feverish action lasted only ten minutes, though it was to seem much longer in memory. Then with a grinding screech the U-boat backed off, and left the badly holed *Borie* taking water.

As the two vessels circled one another like battered boxers, the old D.D. still had enough fight in her to try and ram the sub again, and four of her four-inch shells burst in the U-boat's after torpedo room. Then both vessels tried to torpedo each other. Hutchins saw *Borie*'s tinfish miss, then the U-boat's stern tubes swung round and pointed at them. Hutchins shouted 'Off searchlight!' and in the sudden blackness U-405 tried to escape.

Hutchins was just not going to let that happen. On went the big searchlight, up went the speed to twenty-seven knots, never mind the holes in the bottom, and *Borie* closed to ram again.

The U-boat turned on her attacker and tried the same

tactics, heading for her starboard quarter. Hutchins slewed his stern round to port and fired three depth-charges. He saw them fall across the sub, straddling the remains of her conning tower. There was a pause, then the explosions, lifting the U-boat in the air. Its stem stopped dead six feet from *Borie*'s fantail.

But Hopman was not yet beaten. Getting way on his boat again he swung clear and tried to run for it. Hutchins went after him, the gallant *Borie* making one last effort for her young captain. A four-inch shell exploded on the already wrecked conning tower and killed everyone left there, including Hopman. Another hit abreast the engine room. Without power or guidance the U-boat slowed to a stop.

The conning tower hatch opened and men started to climb out. Some put their hands up, one raised a pistol and fired. A white Very light burst in the darkness. Others were running to the guns, and *Borie* kept on firing. Hutchins saw that at last all resistance in the sub had ceased. As he ordered 'Cease firing,' shouts of 'Kamerad!' floated across the heaving black water. Then the submarine began to settle. At a few minutes before three o'clock in the black graveyard watch U-405 raised her streaming bows and took her last plunge. At five minutes past three *Card* picked up a very weak and mutilated signal of which it was just possible to catch the words 'Just sank number two in depth-charge attack, gun battle and . . .' Details of *Borie*'s own condition were lost in the gusting wind and darkness.

At the scene of the battle, U-405, though gone forever into a 2,000-fathom deep, was still giving trouble. *Borie*'s searchlight picked out about fifteen men in the surging waves. When the crippled old D.D. tried to rescue them some of these men fired coloured Very lights from the water. Whatever their intentions, these fireworks attracted the attention of another U-boat, which fired at least one torpedo at *Borie*. The tinfish missed, and the ship was forced to abandon the rescue and leave the scene as fast as her battered engines would allow. As she did so some of the survivors in the water were run under.

The first Isbell knew of *Borie*'s own critical condition was from a weak signal which came in at 4.52 a.m. reporting her position and the sobering news 'May have to abandon . . .'

At 6.50, as soon as there was enough light in the sky, Avengers T6, the rogue aircraft, and T8 were launched from *Card* to search for *Borie*, as well as four T.B.F.s for the usual dawn patrol round the group. When nothing had been seen of *Borie* by ten o'clock all three planes then in the air were ordered to look for her, but they found flying conditions so bad that they had to be recalled almost immediately.

With growing anxiety Isbell's three ships continued to search for their missing partner, radar turning, the radio watch listening closely.

At 11.10 a.m. *Card*'s operator picked the ominous words '. . . commenced sinking . . .' out of the crackling static. Isbell at one directed Hill in *Barry* and Smith in *Goff* to light off all boilers and prepare for any emergency, and ordered two T.B.F.s launched to search for *Borie* between the bearings provided by Huff-Duff from her last signal.

An Avenger found her ten minutes later, fourteen miles from the ship. *Card* changed course towards her and went to eighteen knots, the fastest speed she had ever achieved. In eighteen minutes the carrier's masthead lookout reported *Borie*, about eight miles off.

Isbell closed the destroyer, which was making headway very slowly in the heavy seas, and Hutchins reported salt water in the boilers, the remaining undamaged condenser beginning to give out and the blades of their surviving turbine locked with salt. But everything possible had been jettisoned to try and keep her afloat, including anchors and cable, guns and torpedo tubes, and the ship was now 'in no immediate danger of sinking', Hutchins said. Soon, however, she lost all power and fell off helpless into the trough of the heavy sea.

At noon *Card* flew off four T.B.F.s to patrol round the group while they tried to salvage *Borie*. The main tasks were to try to prevent further flooding, and to get steam on her boilers again. She could not be towed, as she had jettisoned her anchor chains, and *Card* had no towing engine, and Isbell could not afford to leave one of his two remaining destoyers with her until a tug could be sent. He had Handy Billy pumps and 130 feet of suction hose passed to *Goff* for transfer to *Borie* but Hutchins said he had no use for it as the water in *Borie*'s cofferdam was heavily contaminated with oil and she had no other fresh water available for her boilers. With *Borie* wallowing so heavily in the trough it was impossible for any of the other ships to pass fresh water across to her.

At half-past four in the afternoon, with bad weather and darkness closing in and no prospect of improving his situation during the night, Hutchins finally decided to abandon ship lest she capsize before dawn.

The departure was orderly. The men climbed over the windward rail and the fantail, and down into floats and nets. But many men who tried to swim to *Goff* or *Barry* when they were close aboard them were drowned in the rough seas, and others were knocked off their rafts by the propeller guards of the rescue ships, pitching heavily. Three officers and twenty-four enlisted men died in this way.

Goff and *Barry* picked up survivors from rafts and nets, and eventually managed to rescue eight officers and 122 men out of *Borie*'s original eleven officers and 146 men. Many rescues were made in the darkness, with rafts spotted by their flares and various lamps and torches. Many men were picked up floating singly and alone in the heaving water. Choking on oil and salt water, unable to see the rescue ships over the towering wave crests, most of these had given up hope and had become helpless human flotsam. The last raft was found at a little before eleven o'clock that night. On it were three living and one dead, the latter secured to the raft but unfortunately face-down in the sea. The three survivors were transferred with difficulty, and the rough water left no alternative then but to abandon the raft with its unidentified dead. The search was continued throughout the night for any other surviving individuals

137

who had either slipped off or been knocked from the rafts, and might be trying to swim to *Goff* or *Barry*.

During these rescue operations *Card* steamed round the destroyers in a circle of ten miles radius. Her speed was limited to ten knots by the high seas, and with no screen she was very vulnerable to any determined U-boat.

About four o'clock, at the beginning of the morning watch, she picked up a radar blip on the port quarter and at once turned away from it. Shortly after this another blip was picked up close aboard on the starboard beam. Again *Card* turned away and managed to work up to fifteen knots, down-wind. The bogey followed and closed to 2,800 yards astern.

Isbell signalled to *Goff* and *Barry*, 'Submarine on our tail. Pick it off.'

The destroyers gave chase. The contact opened to 3,200 yards. Isbell got on the microphone and coached *Barry* and *Goff* in for an interception. *Barry* picked up a blip at 6,000 yards on the starboard beam. The bogey then faded from the screens of both ships, and they rejoined *Card* at dawn. A last search for survivors upwind from *Borie* was begun. Numerous rafts and nets were sighted, but all were empty, and several bodies seen were all too obviously dead.

By the time Isbell called off the search at eight o'clock, *Borie*, deserted and helpless in the ocean vastness, was nine miles away. She was still afloat, though down by the stern, but the heavy seas had not abated and she was still rolling wildly in the trough.

As he came up with her again Isbell had to decide what to do about her. She was holed, all fuel and water tanks ruptured, forward engine room flooded, main deck cracked athwartships over Number 2 fireroom, no radio, no electrical power, no feed water or fresh water, boilers and turbines bad from salt water, no anchor chain for towing, the seas too rough to transfer men to man her, or for her to be brought alongside for fresh water even if it had been possible to get steam on her boilers. . .

Added to all this was the knowledge that the scene of the

action was approximately the centre of and touching several reported heavy submarine concentrations. CominCh. had reported a refuelling group eighty-six miles to the south-sou'-west, at least twenty boats patrolling some 200 miles to the westward, and another concentration to the south-west. The Admiralty reported a concentration only fifteen miles away to the south-west, some five boats patrolling a hundred miles to the north, and several approaching from the south-east. The nearest port was Horta in the Azores, and that was nearly 700 miles away. Ireland, Iceland and Newfoundland were all a hundred to 200 miles further off than that. Any salvage tug would have to be escorted, and a salvage group would have to operate in heavy seas and very dangerous waters. The weather was bad, with a new front approaching and no sign of improvement thereafter. *Goff* and *Barry* were getting low on fuel. Radio silence had been completely broken on several frequencies during the past twenty-four hours, and several radar and sonar contacts had been reported during the night. The men were jittery and without sleep. The cold water, heavy seas, overcrowded destroyers, and the distances to the nearest land all warned Isbell that his entire task group might be wiped out if one of the remaining ships were torpedoed. A small tragedy could become a disaster.

He decided that no further attempts to salvage *Borie* could be made. At nine o'clock *Barry* was ordered to sink her sister ship with gunfire and torpedoes. But the heavy seas made all her attempts useless, and at 9.40 *Barry* gave up, after she had scored several shell hits which did no major damage and fired three torpedoes which missed, and Lieutenant Connley in the T.B.F. which was circling the area was ordered to do the job with his four D.C.s, dropped one at a time. Just before ten o'clock, after receiving a third depth-charge close aboard, *Borie* sank swiftly by the stern.

The depleted task group then resumed its mission, heading south-west through an area of reported submarine concentration. *Goff* reported a 'periscope-like object' at 2.15 in the afternoon on her starboard beam, and got a surface contact at 1.25 in the small hours of November 3rd, but both disappeared. Bad weather delayed the dawn patrol until 12.30. The four T.B.F.s were up for an hour, then the winter Atlantic closed in on them and they had to return. At three o'clock *Card* pushed them out again to cover the angry ocean ahead for eighty miles and around from beam to beam. Men and machines of T.G.21.14 were tired and twitchy now. Aviators were living on their nerves. *Goff*'s sonar man reported a contact at 8.53 but it faded when the D.D. tried to pin it down. T4 coming off the dawn patrol next morning broke a tail wheel. T1 caught Number 7 wire with its hook, thundered on into the barrier and fractured its prop.

Now they were 200 miles off Newfoundland, heading west for home. Foul weather slowed them down on November 5th, first light for the dawn patrol was at one o'clock in the afternoon. First *Barry*, then *Goff,* came alongside the carrier, fighting the swell to hold station and transfer survivors from their crowded messdecks. When they had cast off, Isbell found himself waiting for *Borie* to come up and take her turn.

Radar found a blip at 8.30, but it turned into a friendly ship out of St John's. At dawn on November 7th they were off Halifax. A T.B.F from the dawn patrol returned after half an hour with an oil leak, another had hydraulic trouble in the afternoon. T11 came back early off a morning patrol on the 8th.

With the sunrise on November 9th *Card* went to eighteen knots, her top speed, and soon they smelled the flowers of land. The ten planes that could fly, four T.B.F.s and six fighters, left the ship for N.A.S., Norfolk, Virginia. *Card,* after forty-five days and nights of storm and battle, sighted the Capes of Chesapeake that afternoon, passed through Hampton Roads at dusk and at half-past nine had her wires ashore at the Navy Yard, so that a thousand men and three tired ships could get some rest.

8. 'The presence of the aircraft carrier'

'The worst feature was the presence of the aircraft carrier. . .' He had said it in December 1941 after the short-lived *Audacity* had foreshadowed the future, and by mid-November 1943 Grand Admiral Dönitz was seeing the warning come true. American C.V.E.s had beaten him in the Central Atlantic and decimated his milch cows in the Azores refuelling areas, now policed by the shore-based Coastal Command patrols which H.M.S. *Fencer* had done so much to establish. On the northern U.S.–U.K. convoy routes Walker's Second Support Group and other hunter-killer squadrons had defeated the autumn U-boat offensive, bravely assisted by *Block Island* and *Card,* which had sunk U-boats in their new refuelling area mid-way between Newfoundland and Ireland, and by the older B.A.V.G.s H.M.S. *Biter* and *Tracker,* although *Biter* was in dock with damage to her rudder caused by a homing torpedo from one of her own crashing Swordfish, a case of '*Biter* bit,' as a Dartmouth wit in one of her escorts could not resist flashing.

Tracker had won the reputation, even among Woolworth carriers, for extreme liveliness in a sea, and in the North Atlantic in the autumn of 1943 the seas were high and frequently mountainous, with seventy-knot gales fierce enough to force the whole group to heave to, on one occasion because *Tracker* was rolling 52°, 'putting more aircraft out of action in five minutes than in two weeks of flying at sea.' Five Swordfish were damaged in the hangar, and her engine and steering gear developed defects. She went down to Norfolk Navy Yard to have her turbine rotors changed, and as she approached the Capes of Chesapeake she passed *Bogue,* outward bound to assist Convoy

U.G.S.24 across to Africa, then resume the Azores offensive.

Dönitz had withdrawn his defeated boats from the North Atlantic and set up a patrol line between the Azores and Finisterre across the paths of the UK–Gibraltar-West Africa convoys. When a Condor from Bordeaux reported the sixty-six ships of the combined UK-bound M.K.S.30/ S.L.139 on November 15th, thirty-one U-boats were deployed for attack. But radio signals gave away the operation. Strong air cover was set up from Gibraltar and the U.K. and from the Azores, where night-flying Leigh-Light Wellingtons were now based, and the surface escort was continuously reinforced until there were nineteen vessels round the convoy. On the 18th a Wellington from the Azores sank U-211, and U-333 was badly damaged. On the 20th three escorts destroyed U-536, and Coastal Command Beaufighters shot down two shadowers off Cape Ortegal, though U-618 shot down a Sunderland and U-648 destroyed a Liberator. After a six-hour hunt in the small hours of the following morning U-538 was sunk.

Germany had no naval air arm, and, with the exception of Kampfgeschwade 40, the Condor unit at Bordeaux-Mérignac, had never received from the Luftwaffe the kind of air support given to Allied shipping by the R.N. and R.A.F., the U.S. Army and Navy. With his U-boats taking such a hammering at sea and in the Bay of Biscay, Dönitz complained personally to Hitler, and Göring was ordered to give the Kreigsmarine more co-operation. Liberators and Sunderlands flying over the Bay began to meet flights of Ju 88s.

On the morning of November 21st, following the loss of U-538, Dönitz called off his wolves from M.K.S.30/ S.L.139. In the afternoon the Luftwaffe stepped into the breech. A wave of twenty-four bombers attacked the convoy, eight of them the new Heinkel He 177s carrying the Henschel Hs293 missiles or 'glider bombs' first used by the Germans against the Salerno landings in Italy. The He 177s dropped sixteen bombs and sank three merchant ships for the loss of three aircraft.

Dönitz gathered sixteen boats on the Azores-Finisterre line to assault the next southbound convoys, OS59 to West Africa and K.M.S.30 to Gibraltar, but they were roughly handled by the Fourth Escort Group, which sank U-648, the Liberator-destroyer, while the convoy escaped to the west, protected by aircraft from the Azores. The frustrated pack switched their attention first to one northbound convoy, then to another, S.L.140/M.K.S.31 and its sixty-eight ships.

On November 25th the Fourth Escort Group sank U-600 and next day severely damaged U-618. On the 27th a Wellington sank U-542, and the little corvette *Dahlia* damaged another. On the 29th U.S.S. *Bogue* took a hand.

Her first cruise with the new VC19, which had ended on October 19th, had been uneventful. On November 14th she embarked the same squadron and left the Chesapeake Capes to support eastbound U.G.S.24. She left the convoy for a fruitless hunt east of Bermuda, but got no solid contact until despatched east of the Azores to assist in the defence of the combined S.L.140/M.K.S.31.

She was 385 miles east of Terceira when Lieutenant (jg) Bernard Volm, U.S.N.R., of St Louis, Missouri, in a T.B.F. sighted a fully surfaced submarine and immediately made a contact report to Captain Dunn in the carrier. Three more T.B.F.s were launched, led by Lieutenant (jg) Harold Bradshaw U.S.N., who had celebrated his twenty-eighth birthday the day before. Harry Bradshaw was a regular, born in Lyman, Wyoming, and educated in Utah, a graduate of the University of Utah who had thrown up a job as Display Advertising Manager for the Standard Oil Company in Northern Utah, Southern Idaho and South-West Wyoming in 1934 to join the Navy as an apprentice seaman. By the time of the Pearl Harbour attack he had advanced to Chief Radioman, became a pilot and was commissioned in March 1942 when in British waters with VT7 aboard the U.S.S. *Wasp*. He was in *Wasp* when she and H.M.S. *Eagle*, operating in the eastern Mediterranean, had between them flown off forty-seven Spitfires to besieged Malta, and was aboard her when she was sunk in the South-West Pacific, having been in the original attack on Guadacanal and all the other *Wasp* operations. He had helped form and train VC19 on the West Coast.

Bradshaw headed straight for the contact point, followed by the T.B.F.s of Ensign Robert McAshan of Houston, Texas, and New Yorker Lieutenant (jg) Elisha Gaylord, found the submarine and made the first attack run. McAshan and Gaylord went in close behind him and two explosions signalled the end of U-86.

Next day, November 30th, Lieutenants (jg) James E. Ogle III, from Johnstown, Pennsylvania, in a T.B.F. and Carter E. Fetsch of Lakeview, Oregon, in the Wildcat, sighted a surfaced U-boat at dusk. They made a concerted attack through a hot and accurate barrage from a nest of twenty-millimetres on the conning tower of veteran Ober-leutnant Horst Hepp's U-238 and damaged the boat so badly that Dönitz ordered her home.

On December 1st another submarine was sighted. Bradshaw and Gaylord tracked it with sonobuoys until it was sunk by destroyers from the task group.

Bogue sailed down to Casablanca, where she spent four days. Her screen, the three veteran Atlantic D.D.s *Clemson, Osmond Ingram* and *George E. Badger,* plus *Dupont,* having refuelled, the group now headed south-west to escort convoy G.U.S.23 on its way past a concentration of U-boats which Huff-Duff had indicated was gathering in one of the new, far-flung refuelling areas, in this case for South Atlantic-bound boats, forced on Dönitz by the establishment of air patrols from the Azores. In this area cruised the 1,600-ton milch cow U-219, like a queen bee in her hive. One of the workers looking for sustenance from her was U-219, bound for the Indian Ocean.

December 12th was a clear, calm, cloudless day, visibility unlimited. *Bogue* and her screen were steaming some 650 miles west-by-south of the Canaries. Claude Stewart's questing Avengers in their grey and white Atlantic camouflage were scattered round the compass.

At 8.22 a.m. Elisha Gaylord in T.B.F. 13 was cruising about thirty-eight miles south of the carrier when he saw a sub four miles away, called up *Bogue,* turned towards the enemy and started a D.C. run.

On receiving Gaylord's contact report loud and clear at 8.25 Dunn sent off Carter Fetsch in Wildcat F2 and Texan Jack Murray in F7, who were circling the ship awaiting orders, to the scene of the sighting, followed by *Dupont* at 8.38, *George E. Badger* five minutes later, and Harry Bradshaw's T.B.F. at 8.45.

Meanwhile Gaylord had had trouble. A broken line in the hydraulic system meant that his bomb bay doors would not open as he headed for the target. Then he saw the sub alter course and begin to dive. Switching bombing stations from D.C. to Fido he began the labour of opening the bomb bay doors by manual pump.

Because the hydraulic system was out he could not use lowered wheels or flaps to cut his speed for torpedo dropping and had to do this by violent turns and man-oeuvres as he came in. Luckily the sub was slow in getting under. He swung round astern and made his approach. He got his bomb bay doors open just in time to drop Fido about half a minute after the conning tower had slipped beneath the surface. It splashed fifteen yards ahead of the swirl. Gaylord's radioman W.H. Burke saw it run about ten yards through the water, then dive.

Gaylord swung the T.B.F. to port, dropped a sonobuoy ahead of the swirl, and saw oil coming up. A few minutes later Gaylord, Burke and turret gunner J.P. Montgomery all saw a shock wave erupt a hundred yards ahead of the swirl, and a circular pattern of air bubbles which rose with a gush, broken in the centre by a small column of spray. Gaylord waited for his sonobuoy to confirm. This compara-tively new anti-submarine device, which the Navy had been getting since June, was supposed to detect a surfaced submarine within a three mile radius, and a submerged one up to two miles, with a broadcast range, picked up by F.M.

receiver in the operating aircraft, of ten miles, but Gaylord's sonobitch was awfully quiet.

It took Fetsch and Murray in their F.M.1s approximately fifteen minutes to reach the attack point. As they began circling to wait for Bradshaw's T.B.F., Gaylord's sonobuoy awoke from its sleep in the deep and started to operate. There was no indication of any submarines. Bradshaw arrived after about twenty minutes and was ordered from the ship to lay a big pattern of sonobuoys. He had finished the job by 9.25, and none of the buoys registered anything.

They must have been either deaf or asleep, because at 9.27 Fetsch and Murray both saw a conning tower rise 400 yards ahead of the existing oil slick. They at once vectored Gaylord and Bradshaw to the spot, but the U-boat had seen not only the bombers coming at them but *Dupont* and *Badger* on the horizon, and went down again in a few seconds. Jack Murray flew over to lead the D.D.s into the hunt.

At 9.36 Fetsch's Wildcat and Gaylord's T.B.F. left to return to the ship, and Avenger 21 joined Bradshaw over the trail. Planes and destroyers searched the area for an hour and a half, with sonars and sonobuoys registering nothing but whales and dancing dolphins. Then *Dupont*, about five miles south of the first sonobuoy, reported a smell of fresh diesel oil and saw a small oil slick. One minute later her sonar got a ping. With the sonobuoys to guide them, the two destroyers made twenty-one Hedgehog and D.C. attacks, then lost the contact. The T.B.F.s too lent a hand, and the tough and determined Bradshaw flew right up to the limit of the fuel before heading back to the carrier. At 7.48 in the evening *Badger* and *Dupont* began a box search.

At 11.23 *Badger*'s radar picked up a small craft heading north at about eight knots, four and a half miles away. It had to be a sub. Higgins went on tracking it for some minutes, then stopped echo ranging and reduced speed from fifteen to twelve knots to take the submarine by surprise, changing course to put the target between him and the moon. They had closed to just over three miles when the plot showed that the sub had stopped. Suspecting that she was about to dive, Higgins tried gunfire, without much hope of a hit at this range.

A spread of four starshells failed to reveal the sub, which the plot now showed to be back on her former course and speed. Higgins increased to seventeen knots, and sighted a conning tower ahead. Two more rounds of starshell lit up the target, and the for'ard three-inch opened fire. The gunners could not see the target, but pitched one shot close aboard her.

The U-boat dived and retaliated with an acoustic torpedo, which missed wide. Creaming through the choppy sea in the moonlight the old destroyer dropped a five-charge pattern. Sonar regained contact, and *Badger* dropped four of her last seven charges. —of course— I didn't think they'd rise!

They sank through the dark ocean. At 150 feet the first one exploded, then a second, a third, and the last one at 200 feet. Down below in U-172 all gauges were shattered, radio and electrical circuits broken, and one of the diesels knocked out of action. She went deep to get away from the pounding.

Up above, *Badger* steamed through a big oil slick and a stink of diesel fuel, but sonar had lost contact.

The two D.D.s were still hunting when light crept into the sky. In the early morning the seemingly tireless Bradshaw, in spite of long hours aloft on the previous day, led the dawn patrol from *Bogue* to carry on the relentless hunt.

About eight o'clock Bradshaw sighted a moving oil slick about seven miles from the scene of the previous attack and called in *Clemson* and *Osmond Ingram*. Coached by the T.B.F., *Clemson* made sonar contact and dropped a nine-charge pattern, set deep. *Badger* came up, got a firm contact and held it. Jim Ogle in T.B.F. 20 relieved Bradshaw, with Lieutenant (jg) Marshall Burstad of Rolfe, Iowa, and Ensign Tom Jenkins from Tennessee in Wildcats circling *Bogue,* Ogle dropping sonobuoys, and keeping track of the oil slick which the wounded sub was trailing, with the two fighters ready to strafe the enemy if she surfaced.

At 11.16 a.m. both Ogle and Burstad saw the bows of a submarine break surface. Damaged and leaking badly, U-172 came up at a very sharp angle, slid back into the sea, rose on an even keel and began a tight turn to starboard. Men could be seen tumbling out of the conning tower hatch and jumping into the sea.

Ogle banked his T.B.F. and began a D.C. run from the submarine's port quarter, but seeing the crew abandoning ship turned it into a strafing attack from abeam, hoping to force some of the men back into the boat and keep her afloat for salvage. Burstad's and Jenkins' Wildcats also strafed the sub.

On *Bogue*'s bridge the voice of *Ingram*'s Lieutenant-Commander Miller came over the T.B.S. 'Permission to ram, sir?'

Joe Dunn remembered what had happened to *Borie*. 'Permission denied.'

He was too late. Anticipating permission, Miller had put on left rudder for a collision course, but the sub turned hard right, and her stern cleared the destroyer's bow by inches.

U-172 had not entirely given up the fight, and Burstad and Ogle had met some A.A. fire when they strafed. Now the three planes swept back and forth across the U-boat, raking it with fifty-calibre fire. They saw *Clemson*, *Ingram* and *Badger* all firing too. The deluge of shells and bullets were making the sub's topsides untenable, but one man got to a gun and killed an *Ingram* sailor. Then, just three minutes after she had surfaced, there was a heavy explosion and a sheet of flame from the U-boat's conning tower. Smoking heavily, the submarine turned slowly to starboard and submerged. Three minutes later there came the deep rumbling roar of an underwater explosion. A gusher of oil and debris came to the surface making the end of U-172. The destroyers rescued the Captain and forty-five men.

After several blank days searching for the milch cow, *Bogue* headed north-west towards the refuelling zone in the

50 calibre in gunnery terms means "the barrel of the gun is 50 times as long as the diameter of the projectile — so! — he tells us nothing of the size of the shot.

he actually means 0.5 inch dia

Central Atlantic to which, decoded Enigma and H.F./D.F. had established, U-boats heading for the Americas had been forced to go by Azorean air patrols.

At five past one on the afternoon of December 20th Lieutenant (jg) Wallace LaFleur of Lafayette, Louisana, was on patrol in his T.B.F. in clear cloudless weather 600 miles south-west of Fayal in the Azores and 170 miles from the carrier when he saw U-850 six miles away.

He made a D.C. run at once, reporting to *Bogue* by radio but getting no acknowledgement. He had caught the submarine by surprise but his bomb release jammed. Only two depth-charges dropped, and he had to fly through thick flak as he pulled away. The sub had now reversed its course. LaFleur turned and overtook her, dropping his other two D.C.s by emergency release from 300 feet. The drop was short, the nearer of the two splashing 200 feet on the U-boat's starboard quarter. Again he escaped heavy ack-ack, and circled the target trying once more to contact *Bogue*. But a short circuit in the cockpit control box prevented him hearing anything, so he remained circling within range of the U-boat so as to be able to use his torpedo.

Bogue had received his original contact report and five minutes later had begun launching relief planes. Harry Bradshaw went off in T.B.F. 18, Ensign Glendon Goodwin from Shawnee, Oklahoma, in 19, and the Squadron Exec., Lieutenant Kenneth Hance, led off Lieutenant (jg) Irving Cockroft, of Oakland, California, both in Wildcat F.M.1s. Hance was another regular Navy pilot, who had served for two years pre-war in the prestigious Scouting Squadron Three in the *Saratoga,* and had afterwards been an instructor in carrier training.

This group sighted the sub at half-past one, firing at the circling LaFleur. Ken Hance pitched straight in, strafing almost down to the deck. The U-boat gunners were so keen to get him that they left Cockroft's F.M. and Goodwin's T.B.F. alone until Hance had gone. Then they faced the barrage, but the fighters raked the decks and stopped the fire of all but two of the sub's guns, and Glen Goodwin made a good drop with four D.C.s from 150 feet. The first exploded ten feet off the starboard bow, the second hit the U-boat's deck near the conning tower, the third burst fifteen feet from the port beam, the fourth forty feet on the port quarter. The sub emerged from the mountain of spray trailing oil. Then Bradshaw dropped two D.C.s off the port bow.

While he was making this run Hance and Cockroft wheeled and began a second strafing attack from the starboard quarter. Cockroft hit the ammunition locker in the after part of the conning tower and it went up with a bright flash of flame. The sub started to crash-dive, and the fighter turned sharply and sent her on her way with an attack on her plunging stern.

This was a job for Fido. Bradshaw and LaFleur opened bomb bays, lowered wheels and flaps and came in low up the track of the submerged U-boat, which had turned to port as it dived. Bradshaw's hit the sea about 200 feet ahead of the swirl and a hundred feet to the right of the track, LaFleur's in the same area but a little wider.

While LaFleur was making his run the submarine started to surface again, and her bows emerged at a sharp angle just as his homer hit the water. As she levelled off, Bradshaw's torpedo struck her stern on the starboard side, and a split second later LaFleur's hit her further for'ard about half-way between stern and conning tower. The two explosions merged into one great blast, which threw the U-boat's stern high in the air scattering debris and dirty water 150 feet above the surface. The whole after part disintegrated and the submarine sank instantly, bow upwards. *Badger* and *Dupont* were ordered to the scene and lowered boats to pick up debris. There were no survivors.

At the debriefing back aboard *Bogue* afterwards some men described a platform abaft the conning tower of the sub which was thought to be a launching pad for a 'Flying Dutchman', a cross between a kite and a helicopter which some U-boats were now carrying. This weird little aircraft came in three main parts, including the pilot's seat and a central column to carry a horizontally rotating three-bladed *Hubschraube* airscrew. When assembled, the machine was attached to 300 metres of cable which was unreeled from a drum in the conning tower. The submarine went to maximum speed, and as the helicopter rose in the wind the pilot started the motor, which operated the airscrew. When aloft, the pilot communicated with the boat below by means of a sort of walky-talky on his back. To return on board, the cable was reeled in, with the pilot steadying the machine using the propeller, and there was a parachute attached to the rear of the central rotor column. If the boat was attacked while the Dutchman was flying, the cable would most likely be cast off and the pilot abandoned.

While *Bogue* was finishing off U-850 east of Bermuda, the action was hotting up a thousand miles to the northeast, on the St John's–Brest line.

Card, at sea again in support of Convoy G.U.S.24 out of Gibraltar bound for the U.S.A., was ordered north to hunt the *Borkum* Group of thirteen new U-boats which had crept out of the North Sea round Scotland to form a patrol line west of Biscay, north of the Azores, near the new mid-ocean refuelling area for North Atlantic U-boats and right across the paths of two convoys, the combined K.M.S.36/ O.S.62 for Gibraltar and West Africa, and fast tanker convoy P.U.5 from Trinidad for Britain. To complicate matters, there was a blockade runner on the loose. Two ships, the *Pietro Orscolo* and *Orsorno,* had reached these latitudes from Kobe, Japan, heading for Bordeaux with tin and rubber. Dönitz ordered his *Borkum* boats to look out for them and give them what protection they could. H.M.S. *Tracker,* the ship that would 'roll on wet grass', battling through blinding snowstorms in support of a U.S.–U.K. convoy, was ordered to use her aircraft to look for the runners. On December 18th she ran into a full sou'-westerly gale and found flying impossible, but a Coastal Command aircraft torpedoed the *Orscolo. Tracker* rolled on, flying off aircraft when the weather would let her. In six hours of flying on the 19th, two Stringbags crashed landing on. There was no flying on the 20th, and on the 21st three more Swordfish were damaged.

The Germans had collected a squadron of destroyers in the Biscay ports to come out and fetch the blockade runners in, and the Luftwaffe was out looking for the surviving *Orsorno*. On December 22nd one of these aircraft sighted *Card*, heading for the *Borkum* line. On receipt of the report Dönitz told *Borkum* to forget about *Orsorno* and hunt down the carrier.

Card's three 1919 four-stackers *Leary*, *Schenck* and *Decatur* were getting low on fuel, and taking a beating from the pounding seas. Isbell was trapped. He could not top them up in this savage weather, neither could he turn south and refuel in sheltered Azorean waters because the wild gale blowing out of the north-west forced him to run before it towards Finisterre.

Borkum's prime targets, K.M.S./36/OB62 and PU5, were close together right on top of the subs. The Gib-West Africa convoy had the protection of the new *Bogue*-class H.M.S. *Striker*, with her nine Swordfish and six Sea Hurricanes, but on the 23rd two U-boats attacked the rich tanker target of PU5.

All the C.V.E.s in the area were fighting the gale and having difficulty operating aircraft. At daybreak *Card* tried to put up a patrol. The flight deck was corkscrewing so wildly that the T.B.F.s could not even be taxied forward to the catapult, but by 9 a.m. the weather had moderated sufficiently for Isbell to think of heading for the Azores. Then a signal from CominCh. told him that the *Borkum* line was eighty-five miles ahead of him. Isbell decided to carry on looking for it.

Just after ten it was possible to fly. A Wildcat pilot sighted a merchantman steaming north. She was flying the British Red Ensign, but did not answer the F.4F.'s challenge correctly, and the pilot reported the suspicious vessel. Isbell checked with Gibraltar and was told that he had found the *Orsorno*. Coastal Command Wellingtons, Halifaxes and Liberators were vectored towards her, and after a running battle she ran aground, saving her cargo.

In the afternoon another German aircraft sighted *Card* and reported her to the *Borkum* boats, which were still looking for her. At 9.20 in the evening *Card*'s Huff-Duff began intercepting U-boat signals, then her radar operator started reporting a maze of blips on the screen. At 10.30 he picked out a clear target six and a half miles away. After that there were too many echoes to separate any of them. Screen Commander Jim Kyes in *Leary* had to turn on his surface search radar to try to pick out friendly ships by their I.F.F. signals.

'The worst feature was the presence of the aircraft carrier. . .' Dönitz was out to get *Card*. With only three old D.D.s and no Night Owls, Isbell felt naked, with the wolves gathering round him. He could not launch planes, he could not fire guns, or the red flashes would be beacons for *Borkum*. Ordering Logsdon in *Schenck* to attack the one clear blip they had identified, he took evasive action with the three remaining ships.

He did not know that U-415 had already found him. From just under two miles astern of *Card* the U-boat fired three torpedoes at her.

It was too far away, and the German skipper was too keen. They all missed and raced off blindly into the night.

On *Card*'s bridge the T.B.S. squawked. 'Large black object astern!'

Logsdon's voice came through. 'Am engaging U-boat.' *Schenck* had dug out U-305.

Isbell, swiftly computing priorities, called up Kyes in *Leary*. 'Join *Schenck* to assist.' To shake off the pursuing sub he ordered 'Left full rudder. Steer two-two-zero. Flank speed.' As *Card* and *Decatur,* her sole remaining screen, took a zigzag path through the *Borkum* hunters, Isbell told Kyes on the T.B.S. 'Keep subs down during the night. Rendezvous at 06.00, forty miles south-west of *Schenck*'s last contact. Good luck.'

In her running fight with U-305, *Schenck* had hit the

U-boat several times, then lost her. *Leary* came up and joined her in a dogged search, and at 1.30 in the morning there were three good contacts on the radar screens to the north, ranging from five to seven miles distant. *Leary* went off after the most distant blip, *Schenck* found another closer in and ran it down, then lost it again after closing to a mile and a half. A lookout shouted 'U-boat diving. . .' *Schenck* swung round and headed for the new contact just in time to comb the track of a torpedo. At 800 yards Logsdon dropped a nine-charge pattern. Half an hour later a blip suddenly appeared on his radar screen two miles from the ship, where the U-boat was coming up. *Schenck* changed course, the sub dived. Radar handed over to sonar, which found her under a mile distant.

Five miles away *Leary* was fighting her battle. At 1.58 Kyes had picked up the sub at three and a half miles range and fired starshell to get a sighting for his guns. But the brilliant fireworks only served to give Oberleutnant Bork a clear view of the destroyer, and he dived to make an attack with his acoustic torpedoes. Through a breakdown in communication one gun in *Leary* went on firing starshell after the order to cease. The noise plus the drumming of the Foxer trailing astern drowned out *Leary*'s sonar, and when the operator tried to report a contact at 750 yards he found the voicepipe to the bridge out of action as well.

Kyes ordered 'Hard right rudder!' but it was too late. At 2.10 one torpedo, brushing aside the Foxer, hit *Leary* in the after engine room, another blew open the after hold. All power knocked out, the destroyer listed rapidly and settled by the stern.

Kyes ordered 'Abandon ship.' Watson, his Exec., last of his crew to leave, went over the side, and Kyes paused for a second, with only the dead in the mangled engine room for company. As he prepared to go, a torpedo from another sub, the U-382, hit the ship in her for'ard engine room, and she went quickly. The survivors clung on to life in the rough seas. Commander Kyes, seeing a black messman trying to keep up with no life jacket, gave him his own, and was never seen again. Sixty men went down with the ship, a hundred got clear.

They were floating not far from the damaged U-645, with *Schenck* closing in on her. As Logsdon passed the survivors and wreckage of *Leary*, he lowered his gig, which saved a good number of the fifty-nine men who survived the icy, choking salt water. Others were helped by the efforts of Lieutenant Watson, who managed to organize some order and discipline among the men, while himself supporting a dying sailor. No-one remembered it was Christmas Eve.

Card, zigzagging fifteen miles away with only *Decatur* as screen, survived the hunt. On Christmas Day, the seas abated. *Card* refuelled her two parched destroyers, and took aboard survivors. On January 2nd 1944 three ships sailed into Hampton Roads, not one man aboard them unaware that they had once been four.

9. 'The tougher the job. . .'

Isbell docked near the new C.V.E. *Guadalcanal,* and he had barely got his wires ashore when her C.O., Captain Daniel V Gallery U.S.N., an old Annapolis classmate of *Card*'s skipper, came up the gangplank at the double to 'sit at Buster's feet, ask a few questions, and listen for a whole afternoon.' Dan Gallery was a restless, energetic sailorman, an Irish-American who looked like a lean Bing Crosby with a dash of Bogart.

He had already read all the reports turned in by Atlantic carrier captains, and two years away from sea duty as commander of the U.S. Fleet Air Base at Reykjavik, Iceland, made him that much keener to cast off. Up there under the midnight sun the mission of his twelve-plane squadron was to give cover to convoys up to a range of 500 miles. To raise the sagging morale of men who had to fly long hours in fog, freezing cold, cloud and darkness, he built them a new camp with proper streets hacked from the frozen ground, mock-ups of American fire hydrants made from practice bombs painted red and palm trees cut from metal pipes covered with burlap bearing painted softballs for coconuts. He called the place Kwitcherbelliakin, which had an Icelandic ring.

He fretted as he listened to B.B.C. accounts of the great battles of Coral Sea and Midway, in which carrier-borne air fleets fought each other for the first time in history. With twenty years as a professional sailor and naval aviator, 'I didn't want to sit out the greatest war in history on the beach. I wanted a ship.' In May 1943 he got his orders to report to the United States to take command of an escort carrier.

U.S.S. *Guadalcanal,* C.V.E.60, was the sixth of the Henry Kaiser 'assembly line' escort carriers, said by the

Jonahs to be structurally unsound and liable to break in two in a seaway.

On June 2nd 1942, while marine architects in the U.S. Bureau of Ships were working urgently on plans to turn new-conversion auxiliary carriers into an improved *Bogue* class, the dynamic new shipbuilder Henry J. Kaiser called unannounced with a drawing of a proposed 'airplane transport vessel' and an offer to build thirty or more of them in six months, provided the Navy gave him a free hand with the design. He proposed building the ships in his new twelve-way Vancouver yard using the new techniques of all-welding and prefabrication which had enabled him to run up Liberty merchant ships and small craft in record time, and he wanted to start as soon as the yard had finished its current quota of thirty tank landing craft.

The Bu.Ships planners listened while he gave them his hard sell. They had to hear him out, but there was no way they were going to finance a private yard with virtually no previous experience of naval work to build a fleet of aircraft carriers entirely to their own design and with these revolutionary construction methods. Politely, they told him so.

Henry J. went straight to the President, who, like the other Naval Person in London, always had time for a maverick, especially if he could help to win the war. Then Vice-Admiral Land, Chairman of the Maritime Commission, and Navy experts put their side to Roosevelt at a conference in the White House on June 8th. They wanted the ships but they did not want Kaiser. Roosevelt wanted both. The Kaiser yard got a contract to build a maximum of fifty-five auxiliary carriers on Maritime Commission P.1 fast transport hulls, with Bu.Ships and BuAer supervising development and building. On Kaiser's assurance, four ships were scheduled for delivery in February 1943, the rest by the end of the year. If they made it, it would be an all-time record – even for Henry J.

George Sharp, Kaiser's design agent, went ahead with working drawings, hull lines were drawn with the help of Bu.Ships' James Bates, and the Navy gave special advice with the design of the flight deck. Turbine and Diesel output had been reserved for other designs, and the Kaiser carriers had Skinner steam engines, developing, it was hoped, a top speed of twenty knots, an improvement over the *Bogue* class, and with two screws instead of one for greater safety and easier manoeuvering in the confined space of a crowded harbour or near a U-boat or torpedo.

But with Bu.Ships looking over Kaiser's shoulder all the time there were bound to be delays, and Henry himself had underestimated the time required in preparation before mass production could begin for a complicated ship like a carrier. With the first four due for delivery in February 1943, the first, U.S.S. *Casablanca*[1], C.V.E.55, was actually handed over on July 8th. Production then began to pick up speed, and the whole contract was completed one year later.

Guadalcanal was launched on June 5th 1943, and her new Captain designate came to Vancouver soon afterwards to have a hand in her fitting out. He was impressed with the vast new yard hacked out of swamp land, and the way 'factories accustomed to building bridges, oil tanks and farm machinery built miscellaneous sections of ships,' which 'poured into Vancouver by rail, and were put on an assembly line as if they were car parts,' and how 'great chunks of ships were welded together in out-of-the-way parts of the yard . . . picked up by huge cranes, carted down to the building ways, and hoisted into place . . .'

Guadalcanal was commissioned at Astoria, Oregon, on September 25th 1943. Gallery got the men lined up on the flight deck in their best blues, read the orders, and had the commission pennant and colours hoisted. The ship's chaplain, Father Weldon, read a prayer, and the new Captain told his mostly raw crew that if the ship did not have the Presidential Citation flying from her foretruck within a year 'we will be unworthy custodians of the great name being entrusted to our care.' He also issued each man with a printed statement of his philosophy . . . 'The motto of the *Guadalcanal* will be "Can DO", meaning that we will take

158

any tough job that is handed to us and run away with it. The tougher the job the better we'll like it.'

One preliminary tough job which Gallery thought vital for everyone in the crew was fire-fighting school. He himself led the men through smoke-filled spaces in blistering heat learning how to put out shipboard-type blazes. The ship put out for shakedown training, carried out pilot qualifications from San Diego, and departed on November 15th for the Panama Canal and Norfolk, Virginia, where she arrived on December 3rd.

One month later, January 3rd 1944, *Core*'s old Composite Squadron (VC) 13, now commanded by Lieutenant-Commander Adrian H. Perry U.S.N. of Pasedena, California, embarked in the ship, with thirty officers, one civilian technician, fifty-two enlisted men, six T.B.F.1cs, six T.B.M.1cs, and nine F.M.1s.

Two days later, January 5th, *Guadalcanal* put to sea as flagship of Task Group 22.3, with four of the new destroyer-escorts[2], *Chatelain, Pillsbury, Flaherty* and *Jenks* forming her screen.

Guadalcanal was the first of the new Kaiser C.V.E.s to work in the Atlantic, Gallery was a new Captain, and both were on trial. 'Operate against enemy submarines,' was Royal Ingersoll's simple directive. This gave him a roving commission, which suited his temperament. He knew that pickings would probably be lean, that the days of the big wolf packs were gone, replaced by a handful of individualists and boats on transit for the Indian Ocean, but he had one idea in mind, one score which no American skipper had yet made, which, if he pulled it off, would explain all that practice towing their destroyer plane-guard with the one and a quarter-inch wire hawser.

Heading for Bermuda the group ran into very heavy weather. Two F.M.1 fighters were so badly damaged that they had to be put ashore. Gallery fell out with the Commandant at Bermuda when the latter made them wait all night before the destroyers could come in to refuel.

Guadalcanal then steered north-east for the U-boats'

Central Atlantic refuelling area. On January 10th Lieutenant (jg) Jim Schoby's T.B.F. crashed over the port side on attempting to land. His turret gunner was rescued but Schoby, who had won the Distinguished Flying Cross when with *Core* for his part in the sinking of the milch cow U-487 on July 13th, and his radioman Almon Martin were lost.

Just before sunset on January 16th a patrol of two T.B.F.s, piloted by Ensigns B.J. Hudson of Coeur D'Alene, Florida, and W.M. McLane from Gainesville, Florida, flying about 300 miles west-by-north of Flores and forty miles from the ship, sighted the supply boat U-544 refuelling a smaller U-boat. Hudson dived and made a run, firing rockets and dropping two D.C.s between the two boats. The smaller boat sank slowly by the stern, and some forty men began to abandon the refueller. McLane then came in for a similar rocket and D.C. attack. The explosions blew men off the deck of the milch cow and she sank stern-first at a sharp angle. This sub was destroyed and the other badly damaged. The *Can DO*'s account swung into the black.

Gallery had eight planes in the air at the time. Those not at first engaged in the action homed on the scene, but saw only wreckage and survivors. By the time they returned to the carrier it was getting dark. VC13 was not trained in night flying, and it was urgent to get them down before darkness closed in altogether.

None of the pilots could see the deck very well, but 'Stretch' Jennings, *Can DO*'s six-footer Landing Signals Officer, guided Bill McLane and three more planes down safely.

The fifth came in too far over to starboard. Jennings' urgent signals with the paddles had no effect and the big plane touched down, slewed round and ended up with both wheels in The Goofers, tail athwartships across the deck fouling the arrester wires.

With three planes in the circuit, tanks emptying, the flight deck crew fell on the stranded bird and heaved. But push, pull, forwards, backwards, sideways, shout, curse, pray, nothing would move it. Gallery ordered flank speed and threw the ship under full rudder, first one way then the other, to jar the plane free, but nothing worked. It was stuck, and night was on them. As fast as possible the whole tail was cut off with blow-torches. Then, in a quick huddle with Air Officer Dick Kane and Air Group Commander Joe Yavorsky, Gallery thought there might be just enough deck space to get the last three down. Kane told them on the T.B.S., 'Make to port a bit and you'll miss it.'

For the next quarter of an hour the three planes made desperate increasingly ragged passes at the deck, with Jennings in some danger to his own life and limb as each machine lurched to port and lunged at the deck. Time after time Jennings waved his bats high in the air, low on the deck or rowed frantically with arms outstretched as a plane came in too high, too low or dangerously slow, or in any attitude except the one most likely to slot it into that narrow lane between the end of the crashed plane and the edge of the flight deck, where the cold black sea loomed. Every time a plane roared over the round-down the tall figure rose on tiptoe, as if willing the tired and anxious pilot down, trying to fly each machine himself, and talking through his throat microphone.

Each plane took several wave-offs, then at last Bert Hudson's T.B.F. approached in a reasonable attitude, but too fast. Jennings waggled his left arm straight out, his left down on the deck. 'Slow down, get your nose up. . .' He whipped his right arm across his body. The pilot cut his throttle. But he was still too fast. The heavy plane slammed into the deck, screeched to port, bounced, rolled over on its back, and skidded over the side into the sea. The plane-guard D.E. came up and hauled the three men out of the water, but the other two planes were still up there, their dark shapes, picked out by pin-point hooded lights, looked increasingly lonely as they circled in the dark.

Gallery watched them. He couldn't risk another wild lunge like that. There was no place for them to go but in the water. But they would have to have help. He took one of those calculated risks which sooner or later figure in every commander's career. 'Switch on the lights!' U-boats or no U-boats, the whole task group was lit up 'like a waterfront saloon on a Saturday night'. Uncle Dan ordered his pilots to ditch, tracked them with searchlights, and the D.E.s picked them up. 'This was one of the times,' he said later, 'when we had to rely on our morning prayer.' But he did not know how far his prayers would stretch. He vowed that next time *Can DO*'s planes came out to hunt U-boats it would be as night fliers. His flight deck crews too were going to be getting so much drill in clearing the deck they'd wish they'd never joined.

Two days after this adventure a plane made a heavy landing and flung its belly tank across the after end of the flight deck. The tank burst and caught fire, emptying blazing petrol all over the deck. Such a huge pillar of smoke and flame rose from the ship that her escorts stood by to pick up survivors. Luckily most of the flaming fuel poured down the scuppers and over the side, though some got into the flushing pipes to the heads just below the flight deck and drove out three sailors who were skiving there.

On January 20th the T.B.F. piloted by Bert Beattie of Salmon Falls, Idaho, failed to return from patrol. Lost, with its radio apparently out, the plane was last seen on the radar screen heading for the Azores. An aircraft was seen to come down off the north-west coast of Flores that evening, and three men were seen struggling in the surf for two hours before being carried out to sea. An uninflated life raft from Beattie's plane was picked up nearby and the body of his radioman Dale Wheaton was recovered. There was no trace of Beattie or his turret gunner Hugh Wilson.

There followed three days in Casablanca and two weeks of operations limited by bad weather and a shortage of serviceable planes.

When the group was out of the U-boat danger zone and heading once more for Bermuda the flight deck Chief brought up the crumpled, tail-less Avenger which had proved such an immovable object, and three or four times a day had his crews push it over into the gun galleries and practise hauling it out again and sending it below. Like true salthorses they rigged sheerlegs, put a sling round the plane's belly, and heaved it up with a four-fold purchase, until they could pull an Avenger out of the walkways in two and a half minutes.

Nearly all *Guadalcanal*'s planes were in need of repair or maintenance by this time. By working watch-and-watch, Kane's sweating mechanics managed to get six Avengers serviceable. They were flying the dawn patrol one morning when the great liner *Queen Mary*, still every inch a monarch even in her drab wartime grey, came over the horizon, packed with G.I.s for Europe. She was just drawing abreast of the carrier to starboard when Gallery's T.B.S. squawked.

'Have sighted periscope. Submarine screw noises on sonobuoy.'

Guadalcanal's few remaining flyable planes were hastily catapulted. Gallery warned the *Queen*. But the T.B.F.s found nothing, and the sonobitch went quiet. 'Between you and me,' said Gallery, 'I think our flier saw a porpoise and heard the *Q.M.*'

Not long after this alarm five of the six planes on morning patrol had been recovered and parked for'ard when the sixth and last came in too fast and too high, bounced clear of all the arrester wires, vaulted the barrier and alighted in the middle of the deck park. 'That was the end of operations for that cruise,' recorded Gallery. When they returned to Norfolk on February 16th only three T.B.F.s and three T.B.M.s could be flown ashore to East Field, the remainder of VC13's original twenty-one aircraft having been unloaded as unserviceable at Bermuda (two F.M.s), lost at sea (six T.B.F.s), or out of commission on board ship (three T.B.F.s and four F.M.s).

But *Can DO* sailed proudly through the Roads with one swastika painted on her bridge. To have scored after only a fortnight of her first cruise was a high battle honour for the first Kaiser U-boat hunter, which had returned from the Atlantic in winter without a crack in her allegedly frail hull, confounding the critics.

The sinking of U-544 was another contribution to the loss

163

was a type IX C 40
U-tankers/"milch-kühen" were type XIV

of milch cows which had forced Dönitz to abandon the wolf pack system, depending as it did on high speed operations requiring high fuel consumption. A small concentration of boats which had been patrolling the U.K.–Gibraltar convoy lanes during December had continued working north-east of the Azores, but constant attacks by C.V.E. groups plus night sweeps by Wellingtons from the Azores thoroughly discouraged them, and by mid-January this group had been broken up and had returned to port. With few refuellers left to keep his boats on far-flung stations the Grand Admiral drew many of them in round the British Isles to positions no U-boat had occupied since the high-riding days of 1940. But those days had gone. Now the boats stayed down during daylight to avoid aircraft attacks. One submarine sighted in the North Channel between Northern Ireland and Scotland was quickly driven out into blue water again. Fear of invasion also kept a large number of U-boats within easy range of the French coast. There were still some twenty boats having a bumps race with each other in an area half-way between Greenland and Ireland, but they were having no success against the convoys.

As *Guadalcanal* approached the Virginia Capes she passed *Block Island* coming out with her screen, the destroyer *Corry* and the new destroyer-escorts *Thomas, Breeman, Bronstein* and *Bostwick,* and Composite Squadron (VC) 6 with their twelve T.B.F.1cs and nine F.M.2s[3], commanded by Lieutenant-Commander R.M. Payne U.S.N.R. The escorts were refuelled off Fayal in the Azores on February 26th, then the Group headed north to give general support to various convoys which were still menaced by the group of submarines lurking north of the refuelling zone midway between Newfoundland and Ireland.

1944 was a leap year. Just after dusk on February 29th *Thomas'* sonar got a ping about 600 miles north of Terceira, and she and *Bostwick* began a hunt. About half-past nine a second contact five miles to the west appeared on *Block Island*'s radar screen, and Sheldon Kinney's *Bronstein* was detached to track this one down. He reached the scene and fired starshell and in its searing light saw *Thomas* and *Bostwick* and a sub heading for them. He opened fire, hit her several times and forced her to crash-dive. Lieutenant-Commander Kellogg in *Thomas* turned on his would-be assassin and began a very determined hunt. Meanwhile the other sub was out to get the carrier, following Dönitz doctrine. She was just getting ready to fire a spread, a few minutes after midnight, when her skipper saw the white curl of a bow wave coming at him, as *Bronstein* put herself between the U-boat and the carrier. He pulled in the asparagus and dived, but an hour later Kinney's D.C.s burst close aboard, and U-603 never returned from patrol.

The Central Atlantic was still fairly quiet when *Guadalcanal* put out from Norfolk again on March 7th, though there were boats bound for the Caribbean, South Atlantic and Indian Ocean passing through the Central and Cape Verde refuelling areas.

Night flying with *Can DO*'s new air group VC58 began as soon as they had stowed their kit. Luckily they were able to start in full moonlight, and by the time the moon had waned and the nights were black they knew their way down on to a deck in the dark and were getting acquainted with the stars.

There were accidents. One T.B.F., approaching in the dark of a moonless night, came in too high, and the pilot opened the throttle to go round again. He was farther over to starboard than he had thought. His wing hit the bridge, and the plane crashed in flames against the island, blocking the only exit door.

The crew got clear of the burning wreck, miraculously unhurt, but smoke and flames enveloped the island, where seven men, including Gallery, Navigator Jan Bikkers and Father Weldon, were trapped. In the plane's bomb bay were four live D.C.s, which, according to the manual, had a life of three minutes in the middle of a petrol fire. The now well trained deck crew, led by asbestos-clad 'hot papas', got the fire out in two and a half minutes. After that ropes were rigged round the bridge for easy escape.

Gallery accepted the risks inherent in night flying from carriers in wartime. The ship was put at risk every time a night recovery was made, as planes could not land entirely without flight deck lights, and there was a limit to the amount lights could be hooded and still be effective. He figured that to show lights in order to have planes in the air at night was a worthwhile trade-off. He accepted too that he would lose planes in the training period. In fact he lost about a third of his effective aircraft in crashes, but reached the U-boat hunting grounds with a well trained unit.

The *Block Island* group was in Casablanca for urgent repairs, but three days there sufficed and they left again on March 11th, the carrier with a new C.O., Captain Francis M. Hughes U.S.N. This time she headed south-west for the area off the Cape Verdes where Brazilian and Indian Ocean U-boats refuelled.

Four days later and 300 miles west of San Antao she got a blip on her radar. The group headed down the bearing but a thick haze of dusk, like a sandstorm on the sea, blown from the Sahara, lay between them and the target, obscuring the view and interfering with radar reception.

Planes came back aboard with clogged filters, having sighted nothing through the shimmering curtain below them, not even a mirage. Then, in the early evening of March 16th the U-boat surfaced, almost beneath a T.B.F./ F.M. pair returning to the ship. The Wildcat strafed and the U-boat lost some men but dived deep and evaded the group's probing sonar.

But her tanks were parched. Just after midnight she radioed U-boat H.Q. and asked for a course to the nearest milch cow. *Block Island*'s Huff-Duff was listening and Hughes sent *Corry* off down the bearing. The D.E. got a radar bearing and tracked it down through the dark hours. As the sun began to shine through the gold dust on the sea they came to the end of the trail, and found a balloon tied to a float bobbing in the water, with strips of tinfoil throwing back their radar beam at them. Aphrodite, as submariners called this device, had beguiled another sea hunter.

166

But for all her cunning U-801 was not going to get away. *Block Island*'s dawn patrol found her in another part of the ocean, the 500-pounder from a T.B.F. started leaks in her engine room, she dived but *Corry* and *Bronstein* finished her off with D.C.s. She surfaced just before noon. It was a crisp, clear morning, with scudding cloud and whitecapped blue sea. *Corry*, *Bronstein* and the other D.E.s formed a battle line and bore down on the sub, firing all weapons, clearly visible to all on *Block Island*'s flight deck. The U-boat's engineer officer scuttled her and went down with his ship. The D.E.s rescued survivors from the U-boat, all young, very fit men. Then the hunters went off to look for the milch cow, to cut off the cold lifeblood from this last pack of killers.

Some of them, having had no success at all, had almost given up trying. When the sun rose on March 19th U-1059 was taking it easy on the surface. Keep-fit fanatics were even having a morning dip in the ocean, and the whole boat was refreshing itself with air and light, when Compo 6's dawn patrol sighted them, and sent Bill Cole on ahead in his F.M.2 to teach them the folly of relaxing in these pastures. The submariners thrashed their way back to the boat, climbed out and manned their cannon just as they were. Some of them got off a few rounds at the Wildcat as it bored in, beating up the conning tower.

Norman Dowty's T.B.F., diving on Cole's tail and strafing with his front fifty-calibre gun, came in for the full broadside. He got his D.C.s away, two of which blew the sub's stern high in the air and sank her, and began a climbing turn, then suddenly fell away into a sliding descent and crashed into the sea. Ensign Fitzgerald, a T.B.F. pilot who had not yet completed carrier landing qualifications and was temporarily manning Dowty's turret, released the turret hatch, climbed on to the port wing and scrambled forward to help the pilot, but the front cockpit was empty and there was no trace of radioman Edgar Burton either. Fitzgerald removed the life raft from its stowage just as the T.B.F. sank. He inflated the raft, and found himself among

167

the survivors from the U-boat. A badly bleeding German seaman approached the raft. Fitzgerald pulled him aboard, applied a rough tourniquet to his wound, and pushed him back into the sea. Other Germans tried to get aboard, but Fitzgerald warned them off with his knife and .38 sidearm. The rescue boat picked him and seven Germans up, including the U-boat captain, but Dowty and Burton were lost. VC6's flight surgeon, Lieutenant Simpson, removed a fifty-calibre slug from the German captain's buttocks. *Block Island* returned to Norfolk with brooms hoisted at her radar masts, indicating a clean sweep.

Guadalcanal had come across from the U.S.A. without making any contacts, which was not unusual these days. On March 30th she and her group left Casablanca in support of westbound G.U.S.37 and drew a blank for a week until, on April 8th, Gallery broke away to track down an H.F./D.F. bearing.

That night Lieutenant-Commander Dick Gould, C.O. of VC58, caught U-515 creaming along in the moonlight sixty miles from the carrier, the German lookouts relaxed after safely negotiating the dangerous waters of Biscay.

Gould dived as low as he dared in the darkness and dropped D.C.s. They shattered a gauge or two and started a small leak, but were not close enough to do any serious damage. Gallery put all available planes in the air and despatched D.E.s *Pope* and *Flaherty* on a hunt.

Several times during the night the U-boat came up to breathe and re-charge. Each time she was depth-charged, Gould's men were not yet proficient enough to do better than near-misses, but each time the submarine surfaced the escorts were able to get radar fixes on her. Meanwhile the charge in her batteries got lower, the air in the boat grew fouler.

First light revealed an oil slick and sonobuoys dropped by the dawn patrol gave her away. At 6.45 a.m. a T.B.F. straddled her with two D.C.s. U-515's men began to curse their ambitious commander. Kapitänleutnant Werner Henke was almost a caricature of the typical clean-cut, arrogant, ruthless Junker, who gloried in war. As such he was no fake. He had sunk some 150,000 tons of Allied shipping. When he sank the line *Ceramic* 400 miles west of the Azores on December 7th 1942 he surfaced, picked up one survivor for information and propaganda purposes, and left the rest to drown. Seven hundred lives were lost. When things went well his crew forgave, even boasted about the unnecessary risks he ran, the promotions he froze to keep a veteran crew together. But it was well known that, although eligible for shore duty, he had volunteered for this extra cruise. Some said he was in love with war, others that he wanted one more chance to add diamonds to the oak leaves with his Knight's Cross of the Iron Cross. Anyway, it began to look now as if this was one cruise too many.

At 10.30 *Pope*'s sonar registered contact two miles from the carrier. Hedgehogs and D.C.s damaged U-515's pressure hull, but Henke took the boat down, trying to get below sonar's probing fingers. Everyone knew too well that one near miss with a charge down here would crack them open like an eggshell.

At ten minutes past two in the afternoon they all thought it had come. A close pattern from *Pope* shook the whole boat from end to end and started bad leaks. Big oil bubbles rose to the surface.

Commander Fred Hall in *Pope* said tersely into the T.B.S. mike to all the D.E. captains, 'We want to get this baby before dark. *Don't miss any bets!*'

Henke ordered all tanks blown, hoping that the pumps could work faster than the cracks in the hull.

At 2.14 Commander Jesse Johnson, *Guadalcanal*'s Exec. shouted 'Thar she blows.' U-515's bow emerged from the sea between *Pope* and *Flaherty* just as two depth-charges from *Chatelain* exploded near her.

Every gun in the group immediately opened fire on the grey hull, a T.B.F. and two Wildcats strafed with rockets and machine-guns, as the rest of the upper deck emerged, streaming white water. Hatches were slammed open and the men came jumping out into the barrage of shells and bullets of all calibres. Some fell, others leapt overboard, as the water poured in unopposed through the cracks in her pressure hull below and she sank, stern-first, 175 miles north-west of Funchal, Madeira.

Gallery rescued forty-four of U-515's men, including Henke, who angrily accused him of killing six of his men 'as they came up to surrender.' The Irish-American was not the man to listen to arrogant Prussian aristocrats, and put him and his men below in the brig, but the German's words made him think again about that scheme in the back of his mind . . . Henke, the fanatic, the U-boat ace, *had* come up to surrender, not to fight, although he had had three enemy destroyers within point-blank torpedo range. For all they knew the U-boat might have been recoverable when she surfaced, but finally destroyed by the barrage. Perhaps next time, if there *was* a next time . . .

Ingersoll signalled, 'Well done!' The ships and planes of the group searched in a slowly expanding circle round the point where U-515 had gone down, though the weather was bad for flying. Shortly after midnight another U-boat surfaced. T.B.F.s attacked and forced her down.

She came up again at dawn, 300 miles from Horta and fifty miles from the carrier. Three T.B.M.s attacked her from the still dark western sector of the sky and the lookouts did not see them until it was too late to submerge. The Avengers strafed with their fifty-calibres and let go rockets and depth-charges, and U-68 sank, leaving just three survivors and oily debris scattered on the sea. The planes dropped life jackets, and a destroyer headed for the spot to pick them up. When she arrived she found only one man left alive, a seaman named Kastrup, who, though badly hurt himself, was clinging on to a life jacket with one hand and supporting a dead shipmate with the other.

With tongue in cheek, Gallery claimed, 'Probably damaged' for the second victim, U-68. 'Exceptionally well done!' radioed Ingersoll.

[1] President Roosevelt was personally interested in the ship naming process and it was he who suggested that the names of battles and famous actions would be more inspirational than those obscure waterways on the coasts of Florida and the Carolinas, as with *Bogue, Card* and *Core*. The new policy conveniently began with the completion of the first Kaiser carriers, hence *Casablanca, Anzio, Corregidor, Guadalcanal,* etc.

[2] Top speed twenty-five knots, cruising radius 5,420 miles at twelve knots, built specifically for convoy escort, with D.C.s and Hedgehogs and one set of triple torpedo tubes. Three hundred and five D.E.s were built. One hundred and sixty one of them carried two 5-inch guns, 144 had three 3-inch. All were equipped with a mix of forty and twenty mm. quick-firing cannon.

[3] The wildcat F.M.2, built by General Motors, was a version of the F.M.1 specially designed for the short decks of escort carriers. Its Pratt & Whitney R-1820-56 engine contributed to a 500lb. reduction in weight, and gave an improved output of 1,350 h.p. at 2,700 r.p.m., compared to the 1,200 h.p. at 2,900 r.p.m. of the F.4F.4's R-1830-86.

171

10 'Ride 'em, cowboy!'

Dönitz now had most of his North Atlantic boats on short leashes, but was still sending single submarines out to the coast of Brazil and the Indian Ocean. To top up these boats in the new refuelling area west of the Cape Verdes cruised the 1,600-ton milch cow U-488. On the 16th and 17th of April she refuelled U-129, en route for Brazil, and U-537, heading for the Indian Ocean.

To close this route for outward-bound U-boats, Ingersoll sent two hunter-killer groups to the area, one built round the new Kaiser carrier *Tripoli,* the other based on the older *Croatan.*

Tripoli planes got between U-543 and her refueller on April 19th, though the submarine got away from them. Another sub looking urgently for milch cow U-488 was U-66, very low on fuel and provisions after a long patrol in the Gulf of Guinea. Dönitz had arranged a rendezvous for her with U-488 on April 26th, but on the night of the 25th Avenger Night Owl pilots from *Croatan* sighted her briefly in the light of the moon. She dodged sonar and sonobuoys, but early the following morning the DE *Frost* got a ping half a mile from the ship. The *Inch* made two Hedgehog attacks and later in the morning DEs *Snowden, Frost* and *Barber* dropped deep-set charges on a target hanging motionless at 560 feet, some 720 miles west of Sao Antao Island, Cape Verdes. No debris or signs of damage came up, but U-488 was never heard from again.

Oberleutnant Sechausen in U-66 saw this hunt going on but did not know it was the supply boat under attack and went on looking for her. His situation grew steadily worse. He was critically short of food and fuel and needed to recharge his batteries, but there were so many planes in the air that he wondered whether he would ever be able to surface. The *Croatan* group had now been relieved by both *Bogue*'s and *Block Island*'s hunter-killers, and they had been put on the scent by a Tenth Fleet Huff-Duff fix when the thirsty U-boat was some 550 miles west of Sao Antao.

By the evening of May 5th the submarine's batteries had almost run down. Planes or no planes, he had to come up. U-66 surfaced about three miles from *Block Island*. The carrier picked her up on radar, sent Brent Abel's D.E. *Buckley* after her, and got out of the way. Sechausen eluded him but early next morning Lieutenant Jimmie J. Sellars in a Night Owl got him on his A.S.V. screen twenty miles due north of him, and alerted *Buckley*.

The D.E. got an echo at seven miles and closed, steering to get the enemy between him and the moon. Abel got within gun range but held out for a close attack. As he had hoped, Sechausen saw what he wanted to see, and thought the shadowy vessel heading for him was his milch cow. He sent up three red flares to guide her, and a few minutes later Abel had the U-boat silhouetted against the moon's image in the mirror of the glassy sea. At just over a mile he opened up with his three-inch guns and scored a direct hit near the conning tower with the first salvo. Then he ran down the submarine at flank speed, with Sellars up aloft in the Night Owl spotting for his guns, dodged a torpedo and overhauled her. Heeling over under hard right rudder, *Buckley* layed her bows right across the U-boat's foc'sle, and the two vessels remained briefly locked together.

The U-boat's crew streamed out of the hatches and started to climb up on to the D.E.'s foc'sle. Some held their hands up but others had hand guns. The *Buckley* men broke out tommy guns, threw shell cases and coffee mugs at them, or used their fists. The Gunner's Mate threatened a group round the capstan with a hammer and they surrendered. One German ran into the wardroom and fled when a steward's mate threw a pot of hot coffee at him.

The *Buckley* went astern and scraped clear. The U-boat got up speed and made off. As *Buckley* overhauled her once more Sechausen threw the helm over and hit the D.E. on her starboard side aft, his bows going under her keel so that a *Buckley* sailor was able to toss a hand grenade down through the open conning tower hatch to feed the fire he could see burning inside the U-boat. Pulling clear, the sub tried to get away, with men leaping out of her flame-filled hatchways, but sank in clouds of hissing steam, leaving thirty-six survivors. One week later, on May 13th, the *Bogue* group added to the bag when the D.E. *Francis M. Robinson* sank the Japanese R.O.501, formerly the U-1224, with a brief D.C. and Hedgehog attack.

Dan Gallery's *Guadalcanal* and her five DEs flashed up their boilers ready to leave Norfolk again on May 15th. At the departure conference Gallery outlined one of his main objectives on this trip.

'The U-515,' he said, 'was one of Hitler's crack subs. She surfaced within point-blank torpedo range of three destroyers. But she didn't fight, she didn't blow herself up. The next time a sub comes up we shall cease firing anything heavy which might damage her hull. We'll just keep them away from their guns with small-calibre fire and drive them into the water so that we can get a boarding party over. They will get below, shut off any scuttling valves, disarm booby traps and try to keep her afloat. Then we'll pass a towline and bring her back to the U.S.A. Each ship will keep a whaleboat ready to lower in a hurry, and have a towline broken out and near to hand.'

Guadalcanal had a new air group, VC8, aboard for this cruise, commanded by Lieutenant Norman Hodson, formerly of *Card*'s veteran Compo 1, and equipped with twelve Avenger T.B.M.1cs and nine Wildcat F.M.2s. The night flying inaugurated on the ship's previous cruise had paid off, with two U-boats sunk and an ace German captain and his veteran crew taken prisoner, and the new squadron began night operations on the first night of the cruise. There were some crashes but no one was hurt. Crews flew with a confidence backed up by knowing that if they went down in the sea Uncle Dan would stop and pick them up.

For three weeks they searched the Cape Verde refuelling

area for milch cows, *Guadalcanal* steaming a mile and a half behind her screen, their sonars keening through the depths, with the carrier keeping four aircraft aloft round the clock sweeping a hundred miles abeam and 160 miles ahead. Zig-zagging back and forth over this big area of apparently empty ocean grew more and more frustrating. Accidents on deck dwindled almost to nil, but aircrew felt that this maximum effort was being wasted. There were no U-boats here.

Then on May 29th, when *Guadalcanal*'s fuel state was indicating a return to port, her radio officer received a message that *Block Island* had been torpedoed.

Block Island had left Casablanca on May 23rd to relieve *Bogue* on patrol round Madeira and the Cape Verdes. On May 28th one of *Block Island*'s Night Owl Avengers sighted two U-boats. The carrier's strike aircraft attacked both on the 28th and again next day, with no apparent results.

Captain Hughes was following the estimated track of one of the U-boats and was about 320 miles west-sou'-west of Funchal, Madeira, in the pale light of a first-quarter moon on the evening of the 29th when, at 8.13, a torpedo from his quarry, which had slipped inside the destroyer-escort screen undetected, struck the carrier, followed by a second.

She immediately lost all way, power gone, rudder jammed. Hughes got all hands up from below, except the damage control parties. As they were assembling a third torpedo smashed the thin unprotected plating of the C.V.E., and she started to settle swiftly by the stern. Look-outs in the DE *Eugene E. Elmore* sighted the enemy's periscope and attacked her. The aggressive U-boat fired an acoustic torpedo which shattered the stern of the escort *Barr*.

At 8.40 Captain Hughes ordered, 'Abandon ship.' While the men were going over the side another torpedo narrowly missed the *Elmore*. Commander Henry Mullins, Screen Commander in the DE *Ahrens,* ordered the two other escorts to hunt the U-boat. As he was taking *Ahrens* to rescue *Block Island*'s men his sonar got a ping from the

U-boat at a range of just under a mile, and he ordered *Elmore* to attack this one. She dropped three Hedgehogs ahead of her, and seconds after the last charge had hit the water and exploded, 'two short booms and one big wham' followed by 'another heavy, crawling explosion' were heard as U-549 broke up. *Ahrens* and *Robert I. Paine* rescued 951 men from *Block Island*'s ship's company, then watched as the dying carrier's bows rose until they were perpendicular and she slowly slid below. Some very efficient damage control saved *Barr* from sinking.

In *Guadalcanal* one officer had been unable to keep the decoded report of the sinking of *Block Island* to himself, and the scuttlebutt had begun to spread around the ship. Gallery felt he had no alternative but to make the truth public and kill the buzz. On the following morning he cleared lower deck, got everyone fallen in on the flight deck, and confirmed the loss of the carrier, which had been engaged on the same duty as themselves.

'Does this news scare us?' he asked.

He could see it on their faces. *You're damn right it does.*

'The answer is "Hell, no."' he said, and hoped he was fooling *somebody*.

That day Task Group 22.3 left the search area and headed north-east for Casablanca to refuel. Their course followed the U-boat route to the Bay of Biscay, and they got a report of a U-boat homeward-bound on this path. She was calculated to be about 300 miles north of them, and Gallery estimated that he would pass directly over her on June 2nd, if the information was correct.

In fact the U-boat was 680 miles away to the north-west of them, roughly half-way between the northern Cape Verde island of Sal and the coast of French West Africa, some 270 miles north-west of Dakar.

The keel of the U-505, one of the large type IX C. boats, was laid on June 12th 1940 in the Deutsche Werft yard in Hamburg. She was ready for launching in a little less than a year, and was commissioned on August 26th 1941 by Kapitänleutnant Loewe. After four months training in the

Baltic the U-505 sailed for Lorient and made her first operational cruise off Freetown from February 11th to May 7th 1942, when she sank the 6,000-ton British freighter *Benmohr*, an 8,000-ton British tanker, the 6,000-ton American freighter *West Irmo* and the 6,000-ton Dutch freighter *Alphacca*. Her next cruise was in the Caribbean, where she sank two American freighters and a sailing ship, a total of 14,700 tons.

Thus far she had been reasonably successful, but now her luck turned. Loewe went sick and U-505 broke off the cruise. On October 4th she was back in service under a new commander, Kapitänleutnant Cszhech, and assigned to Trinidad. She sank a 5,500-ton freighter on November 7th but three days later was hit and so badly damaged by an aircraft bomb that she barely got home. In February 1943 she was bombed again off the mouth of the Orinoco river. Repairs were made, but when Cszhech tried to take her below 180 metres they gave way. Another three or four times she broke down on trials. 'The U-505 had been very successful before the bomb had hit it,' a crewman wrote, 'but now something like a curse lay over the boat.'

They finally left Lorient on patrol again in June 1943, bound for the South Atlantic, but did not get very far. A British destroyer depth-charged them off the Spanish coast, and they limped back to base leaking oil. Morale was now low, and the Captain was particularly depressed and nervy. In October they put out again, managed to get clear of the aggressive Allied air patrols over Biscay, but when they were at 200 feet off the Azores, a ship crossed their course, Cszhech brought the boat up to periscope depth, and six depth-charges shook them 'like peas in a can.' The boat went out of control, but the hunter lost the scent. It was enough for the wretched Cszhech, however, who went into his cabin and shot himself.

Repairs this time meant new electric motors. U-505 left Lorient again at Christmas with another new Captain, the inexperienced Oberleutnant Harald Lange, whose first task was to improve the now rock-bottom morale of the crew.

On their way through Biscay they rescued thirty-six survivors from German destroyers sunk in a battle with British ships, and took them into Brest. In April 1944 they began a completely barren four weeks patrolling the Gold Coast, then turned for home, hoping to catch something on the way back.

Lange tried throughout the night of May 29th-30th to surface and recharge the batteries, but every time he came up his Naxos radar detector receiver[1] screeched a warning of aircraft and he had to go down again. Finally he decided to turn east towards the African coast away from what he thought were the planes of an Allied carrier group but which were in fact transport aircraft on the South Atlantic run and bombers being ferried from South America to West Africa. Still the Naxos and the older Wanz receiver, which Lange had insisted in retaining, gave urgent warning of planes overhead and kept him down, but late on May 31st he managed to get a good charge into the batteries and turned north again.

By noon on June 1st Gallery had shortened the distance between him and his target but not by as much as he thought. He was expecting to get a contact that night but was still in fact 400 miles away, and did not entirely trust pilots' reports of propeller noises on sonobuoys and erratic blips on radar screens, being as wary of Aphrodite as Odysseus of the Sirens. When Lange surfaced that night, only to crash-dive again when Naxos crowed, the gap between U-505 and *Guadalcanal* was closing but was still 280 miles.

On the night of June 2nd-3rd the carrier ran over the submarine's reported position. About 1 a.m. a loud-mouthed sonobuoy dropped over the position of a radar blip began to sound off and Gallery thought he had a U-boat. Lange heard the T.B.M.s depth-charging sixty miles away from him, and when Gallery reached the sonobuoy there was no sign of a submarine.

Then a sombre-faced Commander Earl Trosino, Chief Engineer, came up to the bridge.

'Captain, we've got to quit fooling around here and get into Casablanca. I'm getting down near the safety limit of my fuel.'

Reluctantly Gallery resumed his north-easterly course. 'Earl, I *know* that was him last night. We drove him down before he'd finished charging his batteries. One more night on the spot might find him.' Trosino shook his head slowly.

That afternoon Lange took a chance and surfaced, as his batteries were almost flat and the air in the boat was so foul that the men were getting comatose. For two hours in broad daylight U-505 and *Guadalcanal* steamed just across the horizon from each other, sixty miles apart and converging. Gallery, assuming that a U-boat would not dare surface during the day, had kept only two fighters in the air. He browbeat Trosino, and finally the Chief said, 'Well, maybe we have enough oil for just one more day's operations, if you don't mind crawling into Casablanca with dry tanks.' They turned south at sunset and all serviceable planes were scrambled to work over the search area.

They were now actually steaming away from the U-boat, though twice VC8's planes narrowly missed her. She came up after dark to recharge, and a T.B.M. flew within six miles of her without its A.S.V. picking her up, or the sub's unreliable Naxos giving warning. Minutes after she had submerged another T.B.M. flew right over her. Unknowing, she settled down for a quiet Sunday, June 4th, on her way home.

At sunrise the *Guadalcanal* group had drawn a complete blank, and turned north for Casablanca. Earl Trosino came up to make his fuel report. 'You'd better pray hard at Mass this morning, Captain, you used more fuel than I figured last night.'

After prayers on the hangar deck, Gallery sat in his chair on the bridge overlooking the flight deck, his thin wiry body hunched. It was a beautiful, clear day, with blue skies, a light breeze and a gentle motion on the sea, but he could not enjoy it.

As he thought his only possible target was now out of

range astern, there were only two fighters aloft. Abruptly, at 11.10, the loudspeaker on the bridge blared raucously.

'Frenchy to Bluejay! I have a possible sound contact!'

'Frenchy' was the D.E. *Chatelain*. What had Dudley Knox found? Another whale? A cold water layer?

'Left full rudder,' ordered Gallery, 'Engines ahead, full speed.' He grabbed the microphone of the T.B.S. radio. 'Bluejay to Dagwood. Take two DEs and assist Frenchy. I'll manoeuvre to keep clear.' Freddie Hall in *Pillsbury* was now in tactical command.

In U-505 Lange had just had the hands piped to dinner when the hydrophone operator reported propeller noises, which seemed far off. As Lange took the boat up to periscope depth to have a look, *Guadalcanal* turned away to the west to give the DEs sea room, scrambling aircraft to assist, Gallery warning the pilots 'Don't use any big stuff if the sub surfaces – just chase the crews overboard with fifty-calibre fire!'

Lange looked into his periscope and saw three ships bearing down on him, one very close, aircraft diving, and a carrier and two more escorts in the distance.

'Take her down!'

He held the boat at shallow depth to give them a better chance of surfacing if the inevitable depth-charge damaged the hull. If they survived the first attack they would go deep. He jinked the boat to confuse sonar. Then they heard the frightening rumble of engines passing over them. They braced themselves and prayed.

Chatelain had picked up her contact at such short range that she steamed right over it before Knox could make up his mind what it was. As his sonar sang loud and clear he broadcast, 'Contact evaluated as sub. Am starting attack.'

In U-505 the expected clangour of depth-charges did not come, but they heard the sounds of fifty-calibre bullets rasping over the hull. With a vague hope of hitting something, Lange fired one acoustic torpedo.

Chatelain wheeled round under full rudder into the firing position and tossed a salvo of twenty Hedgehogs high into the air ahead. Knox counted ten seconds. When no explosions came he started to doubt whether the contact was a submarine at all. Within hailing distance *Pillsbury* and *Jenks* steamed, ready and willing to take over if he missed again.

Lieutenant Bill Roberts and Ensign Jack Cadle circled overhead in two Wildcats. Suddenly they dived and raked the water about a hundred yards from where the Hedgehogs had splashed with fifty-calibre fire.

Cadle yelled over the radio, 'Sighted sub! Destroyers head for the spot where we're shooting!'

Chatelain heeled over again and steered for the bullet splashes where the two pilots could see the dim shape of the U-boat. She fired a spread of twelve 600lb. D.C.s, set shallow. The charges splashed and sank.

Seconds later those above felt the sea quake, those below in the submarine thought the whole ocean was exploding round them in the most shattering, ear-splitting shock any of them had ever experienced. Lights went out as the boat rolled over on her beam ends. Mess tables, messtraps, crockery and food struck the men as they were hurled against the bulkheads. There was a shout of 'Water is coming in!' from the after torpedo room. The rudder could not be moved.

'Blow all tanks. Abandon and scuttle!' Lange shouted.

In all the ships gathered above, the loudspeakers broadcast Ensign Jack Cadle's voice.

'You've struck oil, Frenchy. Sub is surfacing!'

At 11.21 a.m. 150 miles west of Cape Blanco, French West Africa, U-505 broke surface, white water cascading off her rusty-grey conning tower.

Gallery could not be sure if the enemy had come up to abandon ship or to fire a final spread and try to take at least one of her attackers with her. Then he saw men leaping out of the conning tower and forward hatches. They met heavy fire from Oerlikons and machine-guns. Lange was first out and was knocked out by a forty-millimetre shell, with severe wounds on face and legs. Two men picked him up and dragged him overboard. The rest jumped off as U-505 with her jammed rudder circled to starboard, settling by the stern. As her bows swung head-on to *Chatelain* Knox thought she was going to torpedo him and got a torpedo off first, which missed.

Gallery broadcast to all ships, 'I want to capture that bastard if possible!' After some fifty men had left the U-boat Commander Hall in *Pillsbury* ordered 'Cease firing!' then, 'Away all boarding parties.'

With their advanced warning, his own boarding party, led by Lieutenant (jg) Albert L. David, was already in the motor whaleboat, on their way to the water. Crewmen knocked the pins out and the boat splashed in, helm already angled to take them towards the circling U-boat. Cutting inside her turning circle, the whaleboat drew alongside.

The first man of the boarding party leaped from the boat on to the slippery casing of the submarine. He had a coil of rope in his hand, and Gallery, watching through binoculars from *Guadalcanal,* yelled into the T.B.S.,

'Bluejay to Dagwood. Ride 'em, cowboy!'

Not knowing if they would be shot by men waiting below, or if the sub was about to sink or blow up, David scrambled down the conning tower ladder, followed closely by Petty Officers Arthur K. Knispel and Stanley E. Wdowiak. Running down the narrow passageway they found the radio room, smashed open lockers and found the ship's code books. Behind them Petty Officer Zenon B. 'Luke' Lukosius found an open sea cock gushing water, saw the cover lying close by, and sealed it off again. Water was now coming in down the open conning tower hatchway, and David ordered it closed above them.

Up above, a whaleboat was bringing Earl Trosino and more engineers from the carrier. A swell caught the boat and dumped it down on the sub's deck, breaking its back and spilling the men out on the casing. Trosino could not open the conning tower hatch because of the partial vacuum inside the boat. He hauled a German sailor out of the water, who showed him the small valve which let air into the hull.

182

'Thanks, bud,' said Earl, and shoved him back overboard. Then he went below and took over from David.

He had never been in a submarine, having spent most of his career in tankers, but he knew machinery. He soon found out which valves to open and which to close, while Gunner Barr rushed through the boat looking for the fourteen T.N.T. charges which he knew were normally set off to sink an abandoned sub, to find with relief that none of them had been activated.

Hall took *Pillsbury* alongside the U-boat to take her in tow but tore a bad gash in the DE's hull on one of the submarine's forward hydroplanes and had a struggle to keep afloat. *Guadalcanal* herself came forward to take over. U-505's stern came up as she gathered speed, and Trosino was able to open the conning tower hatch. Someone mounted a Stars and Stripes over a swastika flag on a boathook and stuck it in a voicepipe on the U-505's bridge.

From then on it was a battle of engineering skill and seamanship to bring the unwieldy, stern-heavy submarine into port at Bermuda. At midnight the towline parted and another hawser had to be attached. With her rudder jammed, the sub kept yawing off to starboard. To get control of the rudder Trosino had to get through the after torpedo room and set up the emergency hand-steering gear. Not only was the torpedo room possibly flooded, but the access door looked as if it might have been booby-trapped. Gallery himself boarded his prize and found by a rather tense piece of trial and error that the 'booby trap' was only a broken fuse box, and the compartment was dry. To raise electrical power to blow the after ballast tanks and lift the U-boat's stern, Trosino had Gallery increase the speed of tow. With the thick wire dangerously taut, *Can DO* and the submarine, now christened *Can DO Junior,* went up to twelve knots. The sub's propellers windmilled, turning the main shafts and the electric armatures, which acted as generators and recharged the batteries.

On June 6th, about the time the Allies were landing in Normandy, the oiler *Kennebeck* met them and topped up

183

the almost dry tanks of the task group. By this time Trosino
had brought the U-505 up to full surface trim. On June 9th
the tug *Abnaki* joined them and took over the tow. Ten
days later *Guadalcanal* escorted the victorious procession
into Bermuda, the traditional broom hoisted at her main
truck. It was the first time the U.S. Navy had boarded and
captured a foreign enemy man-of-war in battle on the high
seas since the U.S.S. *Peacock* had captured H.M.S. *Nautilus* in 1815. The Royal Navy had captured a U-boat earlier
in this war and sent her back to sea under the White
Ensign[1], but this was the first of such prizes taken by the
United States Forces. *Can DO* had done it.

With the U-boat came fifty-nine prisoners, including
Lange. Of far greater importance were the current code
books, the cypher machine, the hundreds of decoded
despatches, and the acoustic torpedoes taken. All U.S.
Navy crews involved were ordered to reveal nothing of the
capture of U-505. It was asking a lot, but Dönitz did not
discover the reason for the loss of U-505 until after the war.
Guadalcanal got her Presidential Citation, though she could
not fly the pennant until hostilities had ended. The captured
codes enabled the Allies to translate much of the signal
traffic between U-boats and their headquarters throughout
the remainder of the war.

Air power at sea had defeated Lange. In all the Atlantic
refuelling areas and wherever U-boats tried to concentrate,
the squawks of Naxos were heard like frightened game birds
in the shooting season. Whenever a U-boat came up to
replenish air and electricity there was a plane overhead.
The logical German mind invented a breathing tube, called
the *schnorkel*, through which the submerged submarine
could take in enough air from the surface to ventilate the
boat and run the Diesel engines at slow speeds. No longer
did a U-boat have to surface to re-charge batteries.

A patrol of five *schnorkel* boats was set up in mid-
Atlantic between Newfoundland and the Azores, each boat
with a meteorologist on board to give the Luftwaffe accurate weather forecasts and to watch the movements and

build-up of shipping for some forewarning of the date of the invasion of Europe.

Captain Vest's U.S.S. *Croatan*, with the F.M.2s and T.B.F.1cs of VC95, was sent to the old Azorean hunting grounds to raise a storm for the met men. On her way on June 11th she intercepted the 1,600-ton milch cow U-450, outward bound with sustenance for the Indian Ocean U-boats. A dawn attack with D.C.s brought no signs of a hit, and there was nothing on sonar, but screen commander Giambattista was an old Atlantic hand and could match veteran Oberleutnant Wilhelm Gerlach's cunning. Taking his three DEs off at high speed, he gradually slowed down, then turned and crept slowly back, allowing time for the U-boat's batteries to run out of juice, the air to turn foul.

He had guessed right. Gerlach had dived beyond sonar range and sat it out. But he had no *schnorkel*. When the air was unbreathable, the batteries almost dead and the crew on the verge of mutiny, he rose to periscope depth. The sea seemed clear, and he surfaced. Four miles away DEs *Frost* and *Snowden* were waiting for him.

He saw them too late. Just as they opened fire his signal lamp flickered in panic. 'SOS. Please save us.' From *Croatan* to Battista flashed the signal 'Don't take any of that guff. Illuminate and let him have it!' A hail of shells fell on and around U-490, Gerlach ordered the sea cocks opened, and just before 11 p.m. she sank stern-first. With some difficulty in the pitch-darkness the Americans rescued her whole crew of sixty.

For the U-boats the big battles were over. *Schnorkel* could not win the undersea war on its own. Using its breathing tube a U-boat could stay below and avoid aircraft. But down below it could only move at slow speed and could not develop a convoy attack, which depended on high speed manoeuvering on the surface. One shot was all it could hope for, and that would immediately draw down upon it more escorts than the old wolf packs had ever faced, with D.C.s, Hedgehog and the new, many times more deadly Squid weapon. Dönitz concentrated his *schnorkel* boats in inshore waters round the British Isles and against the constant invasion traffic. Royal Navy escorts, more used to deep water anti-submarine warfare, had another battle on its hands, but with the U-boats more closely concentrated they in turn could concentrate their countermeasures, and when in August the Allied invasion forces regained the Biscay ports the *schnorkel* boats had to make a long passage underwater from bases in Norway to the South-Western Approaches, which seriously reduced numbers in the attacking areas.

U.S. Navy C.V.E.s were concentrated within American areas of responsibility mainly against Axis submarines on passage to and from the South Atlantic, Indian Ocean and Far East.

On June 15th the old and bold Compo 9, pioneer *Bogue's* first squadron, was heard from again. With six T.B.M.1s, six T.B.F.1s and nine Wildcat F.M.2s, this veteran unit, still under Howard Avery, joined the new Kaiser-built *Solomons,* Captain Marion E. Crist U.S.N., which joined the ships of the Fourth Fleet in the South Atlantic, the first carrier to work with them since *Santee,* now in the Pacific, in March 1943.

For two months they had swept the Atlantic Narrows between Brazil and West Africa without so much as a sighting, then on June 15th Huff-Duff gave them a U-boat 575 miles due south of St Helena. Ensign George Edwards found the 1,200-ton U-860 at the end of the trail, impatiently attacked at once on his own, and was shot down before he could report his position to the carrier. Just before sunset Avery found the U-boat again and strafed it at long range until three more Avengers arrived. They attacked, one with rockets, through a fierce barrage from the aggressive enemy. It was getting dark when Bill Chamberlain, veteran of so many of *Bogue's* early battles with submarines, made his run. In the bad light he came in very low. His D.C.s exploded on the U-boat's deck, his T.B.M., engulfed in smoke and flame, crashed in the sea, and Chamberlain, his radioman Jim Finch from Leesburg, Florida, and turret

186

gunner Dick Hennick of Cincinnati, were all lost. U-860 sank, leaving twenty survivors.

On the day of this sad victory by her old squadron, *Bogue* herself, with Jesse Taylor's VC69, left her convoy to hunt down an H.F./D.F. position 850 miles west of the Cape Verdes. They had no luck until June 23rd when a blip appeared on a patrolling Avenger's A.S.V. Another Avenger picked up the contact, which was the right size for a sub, at dusk, dropped a flare, saw the silhouette of a strange submarine, attacked it and drove it down, then circled a sonobuoy listening to propeller noises while other planes headed for the scene. Just before 1 a.m. another Avenger followed the voice of the sonobuoy, dropped D.C.s, and heard the regular churning of props change to the awesome noises of a submarine breaking up. Next morning dismembered bodies, sixty-five bales of crude rubber and a sandal made in Tokyo were all that was left of the Japanese submarine I.52, bound for Bordeaux with her German pilot already on board.

Mopping up in the Atlantic, C.V.E.s reported isolated successes through the summer and fall of the year. On June 30th the *Croatan* group sank U-154 north-west of Madeira. On July 2nd young Ensign Freddy Moore's T.B.M. from *Wake Island*'s VC58, commanded by former *Guadalcanal* group commander Dick Gould, sighted homeward-bound U-543 200 miles south-west of Ferro, and sank her in spite of a heavy A.A. barrage. The same carrier was in Casablanca on July 24th when she was sent north to hunt three of the *schnorkel* weather boats still transmitting. Her encounter with U-804 some 500 miles north of Flores in the Azores on August 2nd proved that the U-boats were still fighting back. Turning on her attackers, the sub fired three torpedoes, sank the DE *Fisk*, and got away.

Bogue was sent to help track down the weather reporters, but after U-804's encounter with the *Wake Island* group they sailed north-east out of reach. In intercepting U-802, which was heading for Cabot Strait and the Gulf of St Lawrence on August 15th, the Avenger of Lieutenant (jg)

Wayne Dixon was lost, with him and his crew G. Scimio and
C.G. Melton, and the U-boat reached its objective, though
failing to do any damage there. Then on the morning of
August 20th Lieutenant (jg) A.X. Brokas in a T.B.M.
sighted *schnorkel* boat U-1229 about 300 miles south-by-
east of Cape Race, Newfoundland. His attack badly damaged the submarine's batteries and she submerged to
schnorkel depth to try to vent the choking, poisonous
chlorine gas which filled the boat. This was not successful,
and she was trapped, unable to dive or to re-charge her
damaged batteries. The only way was up, to face the bombs
and rockets of five T.B.M.s, which sank her just after 1
p.m.

Captain Thayer T. Tucker's *Tripoli* was in Recife, Brazil,
on September 18th, with all hands resting after a tiring and
unrewarding three weeks in the South Atlantic, when an
H.F./D.F. report of an impending rendezvous of two
U-boats off the Cape Verdes sent her to sea again in a
hurry.

The 1,080-ton cargo submarine U-1062, en route from
Penang with rubber for Germany, had been ordered to
refuel the outward-bound U-219 at a point six hundred
miles west-sou'-west of Fogo.

On September 28th Captain John R. Ruhsenberger's
Mission Bay group joined *Tripoli,* and the two Kaisers
alternated in maintaining continuous air patrols. Shortly
after the two groupshad merged, Lieutenant W.R. Gillespie
in a T.B.M. of *Tripoli's* VC6 radioed, 'I've got him. He's
shooting at me! I'm going in to make a run.' Those in
Tripoli could see the T.B.M. and one Wildcat attacking the
U-boat. Gillespie had his microphone keyed open. Aboard
the carrier they heard him cry out.

It was the last anyone ever heard from him or his crew,
radioman Ray Truss and Bob Hess, a reserve turret gunner,
and a relief for the regular crewman, who was sick. Hess,
who was thirty-six and had grey hair, was called 'The Old
Man' by the aircrews.

U-219, still looking for the milch cow, had shot down

Gillespie's aircraft, but the refueller herself, not far from the rendezvous, was picked up by an aircraft sonobuoy on the 30th and destroyed by Hedgehogs and D.C.s from *Mission Bay*'s screen. U-219 reached Batavia on December 12th.

A small rescue miracle was performed in this area one dark night when Francis 'Fearless' Daugherty of *Tripoli*'s post-flight check crew leaped from the path of a crashing T.B.M., missed the catwalk, went overboard into the wide South Atlantic, and with incredible luck was immediately spotlighted by the searchlight switched on against standing orders by the destroyer plane guard. When 'Fearless', a non-swimmer, was hauled out of the ocean his only injuries were facial bruises caused by flying fish attracted to the searchlight beam. There were constant dangers on the flight deck, one of the most common being from spinning air-screws, which killed instantly the member of *Tripoli*'s fire crew who jumped up out of the catwalk straight into the whirling blades of an F.M. which had crashed into the main barrier.

Among the forty-two survivors from U-1229, destroyed by *Bogue*'s aircraft on August 20th, was a man named Oskar Mantel. Mantel had been a bartender in Yorkville, New York. With him he carried 2,000 dollars, with which he was to have set up as a spy, having been put ashore by the U-boat at Winter Harbor, Maine. This capture reinforced rumours picked up by Allied Intelligence of an impending attack on U.S. East Coast cities by U-boats armed with the V2 rocket bombs which were falling on London. Special vessels were commissioned 'to search for, discover, attack and destroy enemy seaborne platforms for launching robot bombs.'

The six *schnorkel* boats of the *Seewolf* Group sailed from Norway in late March 1945 for the eastern seaboard of the U.S.A., but Admiral Ingersoll discovered their presence at sea in time to organise two Barrier Forces to stop them.

The First Barrier Force put to sea at the end of March. One line of destroyers took station along the parallel of St

Johns, Newfoundland, with the C.V.E. Mission Bay cruising some forty miles behind them in support. Another picket line composed of twenty destroyer-escorts steamed up and down a 120-mile stretch of the 30th meridian, passing between Fayal and Flores, with *Croatan* and her screen of four escorts backing them up in rear. The weather was very bad, with mountainous seas, and over a hundred men were injured in *Croatan* alone by crashing mess tables, benches and crockery, and accidents on deck. All ships were in position on the morning of April 11th, but when on the following day news came in of the death of President Roosevelt, the ferocity of the elements together with the urgency of the mission made it impossible to hold a memorial service for the Chief Executive who had always valued the Service so highly and supported it so well.

The seas were so rough that planes could not fly and the sea wolves battling their way across the grim Atlantic could not use their *schnorkels*. Then fog formed on the sea, adding to the burden of lookouts already red-eyed with trying to find periscopes in the seething turmoil of the wild ocean. *Croatan* managed the difficult and dangerous job of refuelling her escorts on April 15th. Operating aircraft was very hazardous and it was hard enough for the DEs to hold their course and keep station, but at half-past nine on the evening of the 15th *Stanton*'s radar picked up an echo under two miles away in the fog. She closed to half a mile and her sweeping searchlight settled on the wallowing shape of a submarine. U-1235, her *schnorkel* useless in the heavy seas, had come up to ventilate and re-charge. Screen commander Frank Giambattista sent Lieutenant-Commander Ritchie in *Frost* to assist John Kiley in *Stanton* in an attack with Hedgehogs which produced a series of explosions, the last of which smashed the remaining crockery in *Croatan*, twelve miles away, and threw men in the D.E.s off their feet. Frank Giambattista broadcast, 'That is the end of the attack. I think that is the end of the sub.' The same two ships sank U-880 next day 500 miles north of Flores after another searchlight hunt through thick fog. Another very

190

violent explosion gave weight to the theory that the *Seewolf* boats were carrying V2s. The sinking of U-518 by the D.E. *Carter* on April 21st was the writing on the sea for Dönitz. He disbanded the group on April 23rd and sent the individual boats to patrol off the East Coast. They did not carry V2s, and in fact no U-boats were ever fitted with them.

Bogue brought her VC19 and ten DEs from Quonset, *Core* twelve more escorts up from Bermuda, and the two forces met in mid-ocean to take over from the weary First Barrier ships. Fourteen DEs under Commander Fred Hall formed a picket line at five mile intervals along the 45th parallel, with *Core* forty miles north of the left flank and *Bogue* forty miles south of the right flank. After dusk on April 20th the whole line headed west, with the carriers pushing out round-the-clock air patrols. Early in the afternoon of the 23rd Bill South, C.O. of VC19, sighted U-546 surfacing near the centre of the DE line, seventy-four miles from *Bogue*. South attacked and the carrier's screen joined in, but this very tough enemy gave a good account of herself, sinking the *Frederick C. Davis* with a torpedo and coming up badly damaged with guns firing to fight to the finish, which came at 6.45 that evening. The two surviving boats of the *Seewolf* pack escaped attack, but the relief boat U-881 was sunk at dawn on May 6th by the D.E. *Farquhar* of *Mission Bay*'s screen.

These were the last actions of U.S. C.V.E.s in the Atlantic. It was fitting that the veteran *Bogue,* which had been the first, was there at the end, to help sweep the last wolves from the fold.

[1] Naxos, designed to pick up aircraft radar search transmissions on the 8-12 centimetre band, was introduced when the Kriegsmarine became convinced (erroneously, as it was discovered after the war) that the Wanz receiver, operating on the 120-180 band, gave out too much detectable radiation. Naxos was less easily detected but was delicate, unreliable and erratic, and could not register a specific range. It had to be set up on deck where it was highly susceptible to damage by salt spray. It was not pressure-proof, and having given its nerve-wrenching warning through its connected loudspeaker, vital seconds of a crash-dive were used up while its handler gathered up its aerial and trailing wire and bundled it below again.

[2] U-570, Later H.M.S. *Graph.*

11. 'Drive Carefully – Submarine Crossing'

After the German surrender an American crew took the captured U-505, cruising under her own power, on a war bond tour of the Atlantic and Gulf coasts of the U.S.A. At the end of the war with Japan the submarine was berthed in the Navy Yard at Portsmouth, New Hampshire. Her last crew removed any souvenirs which could be unscrewed, and she was left there to rust.

When two years had elapsed from the end of hostilities she would have been either scrapped or towed out to sea and sunk, following the terms of the Four Power Agreement covering U-boats, but Dan Gallery, by then a Rear-Admiral, raised objections, arguing that the ruling applied only to U-boats surrendered after the war. U-505 had been captured in action by a U.S. warship. She was therefore United States property, and should be preserved as some form of memorial.

It was Gallery's brother, Father John Ireland Gallery, who came up with the most practical suggestion. As a former Navy Reserve chaplain with Patrol Wing 7, which had hunted U-boats in the Bay of Biscay, he thought that U-505 would make an ideal exhibit at the Museum of Science and Industry in Chicago, near his parish, as a memorial to all U.S. seamen who lost their lives in two Battles of the Atlantic.

When he submitted the idea to Major Lenox Lohr of the museum he got an unexpectedly enthusiastic reception. When Julius Rosenwald founded the museum in 1926 he had wanted to include among the exhibits a full-scale coal mine and a submarine, following the example of the Deutsche Museum in Munich, which had both. Chicago had the coal mine, but requests over twenty-four years by the museum to the Navy Department for an obsolete submarine to put on display had produced nothing. U-505, with the story behind it, would be more of a prize than they could ever have hoped for. Of course, there were any number of obstacles to be surmounted. But Dan Gallery reasoned that with the sort of determination that had captured U-505 in the first place, her second capture, from the Navy Department, could be brought off.

Even with Gallery's energetic lobbying and some influential backing, including that of Colonel McCormick's *Chicago Tribune,* it was a hard struggle. Destruction of the U-boat was stopped, but it took two years for a bill to pass through Congress allowing the Navy to hand it over to the museum. This had to be done at no expense to the Government, and delivery taken at the dockside where the boat lay. Gallery was officially reprimanded for suggesting that it would be good training for the Navy to take over the towing of the submarine from Portsmouth to Chicago.

Early in 1953 Mayor Kennelly of Chicago appointed a committee to take charge of the project and raise the funds necessary to bring U-505 to the city. Estimates ranged from 50,000 dollars to 2,000,000 dollars, and eventually a target of 250,000 dollars was set. In eighteen months the fund-raising campaign, helped by coverage in the press, on radio and T.V., collected 125,000 dollars in cash and the equivalent in free services promised by civic corporations and various professional bodies. The Great Lakes Dredging and Dock Corporation, for example, after Dan Gallery had personally sold the idea to President William P. Feeley, pledged the use of its floating dock.

On May 14th 1954 U-505 started her journey to Chicago from New Hampshire via the St Lawrence River, the Welland Canal and Lakes Ontario, Erie, Huron and Michigan, towed by the tug *Pauline L. Moran*, with Gallery and Captain Earl Trosino, now back with the Sun Oil Company, aboard for the latter part of the trip.

The U-boat arrived off the Chicago waterfront in June to a big civic welcome. She was saluted by the hoses of fireboats, met by hundreds of yachts and pleasure boats, and received at the Michigan Avenue bridge by the Mayor. There followed six weeks at Calumet Harbor in preparation for beaching. First the submarine was placed in the American Shipbuilding Corporation's 800-foot graving dock for the removal of ninety-six tons of pig iron ballast from the keel, and 30,000 gallons of fuel oil left in her tanks, then she was moved to Great Lakes Dredging's floating dock. The 850-ton submarine normally drew nine feet of water, but in order to beach her near her museum site she had to be raised four feet above the level of the Lake. A special cradle of steel, timber and cement was constructed, hydraulic jacks boosted it under the hull of the submarine, then lifted the whole parcel high enough to insert several hundred two-inch steel rollers between the cradle and railway tracks laid along the bottom of the dock. On the other side of the Lake a special pier, strong enough to bear 1,000 tons and with four rail tracks on heavy timber along the top, was built fifty feet out into the Lake from the shore line near the museum, which was conveniently close to the water.

Meteorological forecasts for Lake Michigan were of great importance. A feature of the Lake's weather was the seiche, a sudden heavy surge of water raised by violent thunderstorms. There was a seiche on the day U-505 arrived at Chicago which drowned seven men fishing from a pier in Lincoln Park. If a bad seiche hit the U-505 tow on the Lake it could be disastrous. The trip would take four hours, and a forecast of twelve hours of clear weather would be needed for safety.

On Friday, August 13th, two tugs hauled the floating dock containing the submarine from Calumet City, nudged it up the dredged channel and against the pier. A small seiche caught the dock, lifting it out of position, but subsided again, and U-505 was finally beached soon after dark. The submarine was then raised on forty-two mechanical jacks to lift her the four feet, four inches necessary before she could cross the Outer Drive, Chicago's busiest highway.

194

On the night of September 3rd the Outer Drive was closed to traffic at 7 p.m., rails were laid across the road, and the U-boat dragged across the Drive at the rate of eight inches per minute. The unique notice DRIVE CAREFUL-LY – SUBMARINE CROSSING was put up to leave no doubts in the minds of the 15,000 people who stayed up until 4 a.m. to watch the U-boat's progress. The Drive was open again in time for the morning rush. Three hundred yards more and a 67° turn, and U-505 reached her final berth on a foundation of three concrete cradles outside the museum.

The submarine was anchored to the midships cradle but sat in the bow and stern cradles on twenty pairs of eight-inch steel rollers to allow for temperature variations between winter and summer, which caused the length of the boat to vary by as much as three inches, and would have cracked the concrete foundations if she had been rigidly secured from stem to stern.

On September 25th 1954 this German submarine was dedicated as a memorial to 55,000 American sailors who had lost their lives at sea in two world wars. The principal address was given by Fleet Admiral William Halsey, whose words of warning in 1940 had started the process resulting in the creation of the 116 U.S.-built C.V.E.s of which U-505's conqueror had been one. It seemed a pity that the *Can DO* herself, or the brave *Bogue* or *Card* or *Core* or *Santee* were too large to have been set down beside her.

Bishop Weldon, formerly of the U.S.S. *Guadalcanal*, now of Springfield, Massachusetts, gave the invocation, and some hundred men from the old Task Group 22.3 were present, including Captain Earl Trosino and nine former members of *Pillsbury*'s original boarding party. A crowd of 40,000 gathered under the trees in Jackson Park for the ceremony. 'The U-505,' said Bill Halsey, 'will always serve as a reminder of a Godless way of life that puts might over right and makes its citizens slaves of the state . . . it will always remind the world that Americans pray for peace and hate to fight, but we believe in our way of life and are willing and capable of defending ourselves against any aggressors.'

Holes were cut in the port side of the U-boat's hull, and covered passageways erected between these and the museum. Visitors entered the submarine aft, progressed forward through the boat and re-entered the museum through the forward passageway. During the first year of the acquisition of U-505 attendance increased by twenty percent. Two million and four hundred thousand people visited the museum, of whom 569,349 passed through the submarine. The latter figure could have been much higher but Lenox Lohr was insistent that the public should be given plenty of time inside *Can DO Junior*. Museum experts carried out a perfect job of restoration on the submarine. Every week some piece of equipment was refurbished and replaced until U-505 was in fact almost as seaworthy as on the day she had first put to sea to attack the Atlantic convoys. Lohr even fired up her diesels and ran them nostalgically for a short period.